D0284993

PRODIGAL PRESS

TURNING POINT Christian Worldview Series
Marvin Olasky, General Editor

Turning Point: A Christian Worldview Declaration
by Herbert Schlossberg and Marvin Olasky

Prodigal Press: The Anti-Christian Bias of the American News Media
by Marvin Olasky

Freedom, Justice and Hope:
Toward a Strategy for the Poor and the Oppressed
by Marvin Olasky, Herbert Schlossberg,
Pierre Berthoud, and Clark H. Pinnock

PRODIGAL PRESS

The Anti-Christian Bias of the American News Media

Marvin Olasky

CROSSWAY BOOKS • WESTCHESTER, ILLINOIS
A DIVISION OF GOOD NEWS PUBLISHERS

Prodigal Press.

Published by Crossway Books, a division of
Good News Publishers, Westchester, Illinois 60153.

Published in association with the
Fieldstead Institute,
P.O. Box 19061,
Irvine, California 92713.

Cover illustration by Sandra Filippuci/The Image Bank.

First printing, 1988

Printed in the United States of America

Library of Congress Catalog Card Number 87-72951

ISBN 0-89107-476-7

For Peter, David, and Daniel

TABLE OF

CONTENTS

ACKNOWLEDGMENTS ix
INTRODUCTION xi

PART ONE: DEPARTURE

1 The Decline of American Journalism 17
2 Spiking the Spiritual 31
3 Not Without Personal Cost 45
4 Man's Subjectivity *vs.* God's Plumb Line 59

PART TWO: EXILE

5 Ethics Without Christ? 75
6 Libel: Utilitarian Justice *vs.* Biblical Truth-telling 87
7 Press *vs.* Public 103
8 Perceptive Media Watching 119

PART THREE: RETURN?

9 Network News and Local Newspapers: The Coming Economic Judgment? 133
10 Coverage of Sensation and Disaster: The Gaining and Keeping of Audiences 145
11 Crusading on Social and Political Issues: Personalization and Persistence 157
12 A Christian Journalism Revival? 171

APPENDIX: Public Relations, Theology and Practice 183
NOTES 203
SCRIPTURE INDEX 239
INDEX 241

ACKNOWLEDGMENTS

My wife Susan listened to the ideas of this book during long walks; her intellect and insight improved every chapter. Our sons Peter, David, and Daniel love books and love God; the dedication to them is propelled both by fatherly pride and by the hope that they will help to revive journalism or other areas of American life during the twenty-first century. *Prodigal Press* owes its existence to the vision of Christian worldview publishing shared by Howard and Roberta Ahmanson at Fieldstead, and by Lane and Jan Dennis at Crossway Books. The book was helped in various ways by Rob Martin and Tom Thompson at Fieldstead, Rev. Gerald Taylor and Christine Morgan at my church in Austin, colleagues and students at the University of Texas and CBN University, and Ted Griffin at Crossway. Special thanks go to Herbert Schlossberg.

INTRODUCTION

One of Jesus' best-known parables is of the prodigal son who squandered his inheritance. Ridiculed and abused, the son saw the misery of his life and decided to return to his father, who greeted him warmly. The prodigal's brother, however, was angry, because a great banquet was served in honor of the returnee, but the brother who had led an upright life all along was not receiving attention.

The father told the jealous son: "You've done well, but he was lost and now is found, so let us rejoice." We do not know how the son responded to that good advice. For a long time the jealous son probably had been angry at his prodigal brother for abandoning the homestead, leaving him without company and assistance. It was probably hard for him to break out of an established pattern of thought.

Imagine, though, what the jealous son's feelings would have been had the prodigal not only taken the money and run, but boasted of the offense daily? What if the jealous son had received daily sneering letters from the prodigal? What if the prodigal son had constantly lied about his industrious brother, libeling and ridiculing him? How much greater the anger! And how much greater the need to pray for the prodigal's return, and to remind him constantly that he, despite sins, is still a member of the family.

American journalism is one of Christianity's prodigal sons. Until the mid-nineteenth century American journalism *was* Christian. But as the first part of this book will show, journalists influenced by anti-Christian humanism and pantheism abandoned their Christian heritage and ended up wallowing among the pigs. The situation is not completely analogous because the Biblical prodigal son soon was starving, while prodigal reporters of the present are well-fed. But in spirit, the living death is parallel.

The flight of the prodigal press has been hard on American

Christians precisely because journalism has departed in spirit but not in physical presence: The prodigal frequently files reports full of hatred for Christianity. Many Christians have responded angrily. Just as church-bashing is a favorite sport among some reporters, so media-bashing is the pastime of many Christians. This book, however, shows that there *are* ways for Christians to reclaim American journalism. We need to examine not just the abuses but the uses of sensationalism and crusading. We need to contribute our time and money. Most important, we need to pray for journalism and journalists.

Christians in the late 1980s and the 1990s should work hard on the reclamation project, because every year shows more clearly how journalism can have a positive as well as a negative impact on American society. Consider, for a moment, two sensational stories of 1987, those involving Gary Hart and the Bakkers.

Some Christians criticized the Miami *Herald* and other newspapers for breaking and then pushing the story of the Presidential candidate who could not keep his pants on. The story was more than titillation, though: It provided essential voting information for Christians, and for some non-Christians. Biblically, we should not vote for adulterers (unless the incident happened long ago and has been repented). Adultery is a grievous sin against God as well as spouse.[1] It shows not only a lack of judgment but a lack of trustworthiness.[2] The adulterer cannot meet the qualifications for office set forth in the Apostle Paul's writings to both Titus and Timothy.[3]

Many Christians know all of this. But the key question is: How do we apply these general principles to choosing leaders unless we learn about leaders' behavior? And how will we learn without journalism? Many Christians are queasy about looking at the underside of life. Biblically, however, truth must come out, even when it hurts. If Christians are to reclaim American journalism, we need to be hard-hitting, within Biblical principles. This book will discuss exactly how to do that.

The Bakker scandal also showed the importance of journalism, in a different way. Just as Presidential candidates used to be chosen by those who knew their personal habits and character traits, so congregant members could see their ministers up close and personal each Sunday. They would know if he was spending money unwisely or getting too close to an attractive member of the flock.

The political equation changed with the advent of mass primaries. Voters, making choices directly, became dependent on information provided by reporters covering campaigns. Religious relationships also changed as televangelism emerged. Contributors who wanted to know how their money was spent had to depend on public relations reports rather than firsthand observation. Christians capable of doing investigative reporting backed off, not wanting to help atheistic antagonists of the ministries. The result was that contributors did not receive information needed to make informed choices.

Many Christians learned from coverage of the Bakker scandal the importance of looking before we pledge. Many saw the difference between invading privacy and puncturing hypocrisy. Those are positives. But the Bakker coverage had many negatives also.

First, it's important to remember what was happening when the scandal broke. Federal District Court Judge Brevard Hand had just ruled that some Alabama school textbooks were promoting a religion by advocating secular humanism, the belief that universal moral standards have no relevance to our lives. His was a serious decision on a serious subject. It was becoming harder for anti-Christian journalists to ridicule all Christian thought. Many tried. For example, the editor of my hometown newspaper, the Austin *American-Statesman*, yelped about "book burning" and sneered at "the judge who made up a religion." But his sneers were not very convincing.

Coverage of the Bakker scandal allowed journalists to return to familiar ground—Elmer Gantry revisited—at just the time when it looked as if they finally might have to deal with basic presuppositions.

Second, we might also look at what was not being covered. While Jim and Tammy were on the front page of *USA Today* every day, Christians in the Soviet Union continued their grim twilight struggle. As one Soviet Christian, Alexandr Ogordinokov, wrote after eight years in the Gulag, "Concentration camps are scattered over the vast expanse of Russia, behind tall fences of barbed wire and high-voltage cables . . . you are buried in the tomb-like twilight of solitary punishment cells; the oppressive silence of faceless days turns time itself into an instrument of torture. Your tongue cleaves to the roof of your mouth in a senseless babble of misery. Hunger gnaws your belly, the cold numbs your flesh and desperation courses through your blood."

That reality of Christians suffering was not presented in major American media. Furs and air-conditioned doghouses were. The Bakker scandal showed Christians that activities of the church needed close coverage, but the front-paging of the story for months and months also showed bias. Which events receive coverage?

Which do not, and why? Christians have been asking these questions more insistently over the past year.

In this book I examine the influence of worldviews on reporting. I analyze the meanings of objectivity, sensationalism, crusading, and the impact of legal, ethical and technological changes. I explain how to read a newspaper with discernment and how to look at the lives of journalists with sorrow and sometimes pity.

What I refrain from is indiscriminate media-bashing, because the prodigal son deserves compassion, not condemnation. I used to be a reporter. I still love newspapers. I like many reporters, most of the time. The object of this book is not to wail, but to suggest how we can be God's servants in helping to bring that prodigal press home.

PART ONE

DEPARTURE

All the devils in hell and tempters on earth could do us no injury if there were no corruption in our own natures.
(C. H. Spurgeon)

O N E

THE DECLINE OF AMERICAN JOURNALISM

A recent study by New York University Professor Paul Vitz found that the vast majority of elementary and high school textbooks go to great lengths to avoid reference to religion. Vitz found American history textbooks defining pilgrims as "people who make long trips" and fundamentalists as rural people who "follow the values or traditions of an earlier period." One textbook listed three hundred important events in American history, but only three of the three hundred had anything to do with religion. A world history textbook left out any mention of the Protestant Reformation. A literature textbook changed a sentence by Nobel Prize laureate Isaac Bashevis Singer from "Thank God" to "Thank goodness."[1]

Standard journalism history textbooks provide similar distortions in their accounts of early nineteenth-century newspapers. Two chapters in the most-used textbook, Emery and Emery's *The Press and America,* deal with the 1800-1833 era of American journalism without once mentioning the Christian worldview that then characterized many major American newspapers and magazines.[2] The textbook does not even mention the New York *Christian Advocate,* in 1830 the weekly with the largest circulation in the country, or the Boston *Recorder,* which had the second largest circulation in that city.[3]

Other twentieth-century textbooks have similar blinders.[4] They ignore comments by early nineteenth-century press-watchers who noted, "Of all the reading of the people three-fourths is religious . . . of all the issues of the press three-fourths are theological, ethical and devotional." They do not mention that New York City alone boasted fifty-two magazines and newspapers that called themselves Christian, or that from 1825 to 1845 over one hundred cities and towns had explicitly Christian newspapers.[5] The facts, though, are irrefutable, once they are dug up: In the early nineteenth century, American journalism often was Christian journalism.

In those days, many Christian newspapers covered everything from neighborhood disputes to foreign affairs. They did not restrict themselves to church activities. The Boston *Recorder*, for example, included news of everyday accidents, crimes, and political campaigns. Its circulation success allowed one editor to conclude that the *Recorder* had gained "the attention of the public" and "stirred up the minds of Christians to duty."[6]

Recorder cofounder Nathaniel Willis was an experienced journalist. Born in 1780, he edited the *Eastern Argus*, a partisan newspaper in Maine, during the early years of the new century. In 1807, though, Willis' life changed. He went to hear what he thought would be a political speech by a minister, but the minister went back to Biblical basics. Willis, in his own words, "was much interested, and became a constant hearer. The Holy Spirit led me to see . . . that the Bible is the Word of God—that Christ is the only Saviour, and that it is by grace we are saved, through faith."[7]

The new vision changed Willis' life. First he "began to moderate the severity of party spirit in the *Argus*, and extracted from other papers short articles on religious subjects." He wanted to make the *Argus* an explicitly Christian newspaper, but local politicians who had backed the newspaper were opposed. Willis gave up the *Argus* and moved to Boston. He opened up a print shop there and investigated the journalistic marketplace.

Some newspapers, Willis found, were largely political and commercial, others largely church public-relations organs specializing in ecclesiastical news. Willis closely analyzed three religious weeklies in particular and would not even count them as newspapers, for "A proper newspaper . . . contains secular news, foreign and domestic, and advertisements." With coeditor Sidney Morse, Willis then produced the first issue of the Boston *Recorder* on January 3, 1816. According to the Prospectus published that day, the *Recorder* was to be a *news*paper with "the earliest information of all such events as mankind usually deem important," rather than a set of abstract sermonettes.[8]

Willis stuck to his plan, and did not consider it lacking in piety. He knew that news stories could be written in a way showing the consequences of sin and the need for Christ. For example, an article in 1819 headlined "Shocking Homicide" reported that a man had killed his own son after being "for a long time troubled with irreligious fears, and a belief that his sins were too numerous to be pardoned."[9] An 1820 article criticized Admiral Stephen Decatur for fighting a duel for fear of being declared a coward: He forgot "that there is no honor, which is valuable and durable, save that which comes from God."[10]

For Willis, in his own words, all kinds of stories provided "occasion to record many signal triumphs of divine grace over the obduracy of the human heart, and over the prejudices of the unenlightened mind." The *Recorder,* he wrote, was a record of "these quickening influences of the Holy Spirit."[11]

Christian-run newspapers in other cities had similar formats and success. The Baltimore *Chronicle,* in its international coverage, described the troubles of one king: "A bloody cloud now swims before his vision, distilling blood instead of rain; the agitated monarch sees nothing but mangled limbs and bleeding bodies. . . . If Divine Providence had intended to have produced a living instance of the worthlessness of human grandeur, could a more awful example have been afforded?" The Portland *Gazette,* for its local coverage, described how two persons were killed by lightning within a house, for want of a lightning rod. It then concluded, "By such events, as well as by a multitude of electrical experiments, Providence is teaching us."[12]

Christian newspapers through the mid-nineteenth century attempted to provide a Biblical worldview on all aspects of life. One Ohio newspaper declared in 1858 that the Christian newspaper should be a provider of not "merely religious intelligence, but a *news* paper, complete in every department of general news, yet upon a religious, instead of a political or literary basis." Another, the *Northwestern Christian Advocate,* proclaimed in 1860, "Let theology, law, medicine, politics, literature, art, science, commerce, trade, architecture, agriculture—in fine, all questions which concern and secure the welfare of a people—be freely discussed and treated, and this, too, for God, for Jesus Christ, and the advancement of the Redeemer's kingdom among men."[13]

Overall, many early Christian journalists showed an awareness of how the Bible uses bad news to show us the wages of sin and to prepare us for understanding the necessity of the Good News. The journalists knew that general statements about man's corruption were far less gripping than coverage with specific detail of the results of sin and misery.

A GREAT CHRISTIAN NEWSPAPER: THE NEW YORK TIMES

Harvard, Yale and other universities founded by Christians now preach an atheistic gospel. A similar story could be told of some of the great newspapers of the land, including the New York *Times*, established in 1851 by Henry Raymond, a Bible-believing Presbyterian.[14] The *Times* became known for its accurate news coverage and for its exposure in 1871 of both political corruption (the "Tweed Ring") and abortion practices. Tales of the *Times*' political exposés may be found in journalism history textbooks.[15] The abortion story is ignored, but it had a far greater long-range impact, one that shows how significant Christian journalism could be.[16]

Abortion was officially illegal but nevertheless rampant in New York City from the 1840s through the 1860s. *Times* editorials complained that the "perpetration of infant murder . . . is rank and smells to heaven."[17] But little was being done about it until the *Times* sent one of its reporters, Augustus St. Clair, to carry on an undercover investigation of Manhattan's abortion businesses. For several weeks St. Clair and "a lady friend" visited the most-advertised abortionists in New York, posing as a couple in need of professional services. The result was an August 23, 1871, story headlined "The Evil of the Age."[18]

The story began on a solemn note: "Thousands of human beings are murdered before they have seen the light of this world, and thousands upon thousands more adults are irremediably robbed in constitution, health, and happiness." St. Clair then skillfully contrasted powerlessness and power. He described the back of one abortionist's office: "Human flesh, supposed to have been the remains of infants, was found in barrels of lime and acids, undergoing decomposition." He described the affluence of a typical abortionist: "The parlors are spacious, and contain all the decorations, upholstery, cabinetware, piano, book case, etc., that is found in a respectable home."[19]

St. Clair also listed leading abortionists by name and noted their political connections: "You have no idea of the class of people that come to us," one abortionist said. "We have had Senators, Congressmen and all sorts of politicians, bring some of the first women in the land here." St. Clair concluded with a call for change: "The facts herein set forth are but a fraction of a greater mass that cannot be published with propriety. Certainly enough is here given to arouse the general public sentiment to the necessity of taking some decided and effectual action."[20]

When the *Times* laid out the basic facts public interest evidently was aroused, but a specific incident still was needed to galvanize readers. Tragically for a young woman, providentially for the anti-abortion effort, an ideal story of horror arrived within the week. St. Clair published his exposé on August 23; on August 27 a *Times* headline at the top of page 1 read: "A Terrible Mystery."

General facts of the story were miserable enough: The nude body of a young woman was found inside a trunk in a railway station baggage room. An autopsy showed her death had been caused by an abortion. The *Times,* though, provided evocative specific detail: "This woman, full five feet in height, had been crammed into a trunk two feet six inches long. . . . Seen even in this position and rigid in death, the young girl, for she could not have been more than eighteen, had a face of singular loveliness. But her chief beauty was her great profusion of golden hair, that hung in heavy folds over her shoulders, partly shrouding the face. . . . There was some discoloration and decomposition about the pelvic region. It was apparent that here was a new victim of man's lust, and the life-destroying arts of those abortionists."[21]

Details of the exciting "trunk murder" detective story were played out in the *Times* during the next several days, as police searched for the perpetrator. Meanwhile, the *Times* reminded readers every day that this particular incident showed what went on "in one of the many abortion dens that disgrace New York, and which the TIMES had just exposed as 'The Evil of the Age.' "[22] The police arrested one of the abortionists whose advertisements had been quoted in St. Clair's story, and the *Times* followed with an editorial, "Advertising Facilities for Murder." An editorial quoted St. Clair's article, discussed the death of the "golden-haired unfortunate," and asked whether "the lives of babes are of less account than a few ounces of precious metal, or a roll of greenbacks?"[23]

The *Times* also printed a superbly-written follow-up by St. Clair. "A Terrible Story from Our Reporter's Note-Book" revealed how St. Clair, in his undercover research for the exposé, had visited several weeks earlier the accused abortionist's Fifth Avenue office, with its "fine tapestry carpet" and "elegant mahogany desk." St. Clair described one of the patients he had seen: "She seemed to be about twenty years of age, a little more than five feet in height, of slender build, having blue eyes, and a clear, alabaster complexion. Long blonde curls, tinted with gold, drooped upon her shoulders, and her face wore an expression of embarrassment at the presence of strangers."[24]

St. Clair then quoted the abortionist's reply when St. Clair asked what would happen to the aborted infant: "Don't worry about that, my dear Sir. I will take care of the *result*. A newspaper bundle, a basket, a pail, a resort to the sewer, or the river at night? Who is the wiser?" On his way out, St. Clair glimpsed once again the beautiful young woman he had seen on his way in. This time, as a fitting conclusion to his story, he drove the point home: "She was standing on the stairs, and *it was the same face I saw afterward at the Morgue*."[25]

The abortionist was convicted and sentenced to seven years in prison. The *Times* insisted, though, that legal action by itself was not enough; only a change of heart among New Yorkers would bury the abortion business for several generations. Providentially, New Yorkers had been "grievously shocked by the terrible deeds of the abortionists," the *Times* could report, and it was clear that abortion would no longer receive approval.[26] Abortion continued to be considered disgraceful until the 1960s, when a much-changed New York *Times* and other newspapers began pushing pro-abortion positions.

A reading of the New York *Times* through the mid-1870s shows that editors and reporters wanted to glorify God by making a difference in this world. They did not believe it inevitable that sin should dominate New York City or any other city. They were willing to be controversial. One *Times* anti-abortion editorial stated, "It is useless to talk of such matters with bated breath, or to seek to cover such terrible realities with the veil of a false delicacy. . . . From a lethargy like this it is time to rouse ourselves. The evil that is tolerated is aggressive."

The editorial concluded that "the good . . . must be aggressive too."[27]

SUNSET FOR CHRISTIAN JOURNALISM

Aggressive journalism by Christians disappeared soon after one of its major successes, for four particular reasons and two underlying causes.

First, looking at the New York *Times* specifically, one generation died or departed. Owners and editors who knew not Joseph emerged. The newspaper's slogans became "It Does Not Soil the Breakfast Cloth" and "All the News That's Fit to Print." Evil unfit for breakfast table discussion or considered unfit to print was ignored and thereby tolerated. Several generations later, it was embraced.[28]

Second, many Christian publications began to prefer "happy

talk" journalism. They ran stories about individuals who seemed overwhelmingly decent, cooperative, responsible, and benevolent. Such coverage hardly left the impression that man is a fallen creature desperately in need of Christ. The refusal to cover evil also led to a certain dullness of copy, because without real villains there is little real drama. The *Central Christian Herald* once ran the following news report: "There is literally nothing stirring."[29]

Third, many Christian publications refused to meet the communication demands of an increasingly fast-paced marketplace. There is a place for both popular and elite publications, and there is always a need for careful scholarship, even when short attention spans become typical. Some Christian magazines, though, seemed to pride themselves on unnecessary verbiage. The classic statement of literary arrogance was offered by the editor of one very dull magazine, *Spirit of the Pilgrims*, when he announced that "extended and labored articles" were the best kind. Readers who "are uninterested in communications of this nature," the editor wrote, "may as well give up their subscription and proceed no farther with us." *Spirit of the Pilgrims* soon went out of business.[30]

Fourth, denominational infighting was on the rise. Some newspapers spent much of their space attacking their brethren. Other newspapers, noting that splits had resulted from differences on key issues such as slavery, thought that divisions could be resolved if Christian newspapers steered away from controversial issues.

Overall, however, the problem was not particular villains, but two underlying theological trends. One was anti-Christian, one operated within Christendom; but they worked together to provoke journalistic retreat.

The outside trend is obvious: During the last two-thirds of the nineteenth century, American society generally was casting aside the Christian principles on which it had been founded. Every area of American life was affected by this shift.

The Boston *Recorder*, located in the New England cockpit of theological liberalism, was hit very early by the great slide. It held its own against Unitarianism, which had captured Harvard College. *Recorder* editorials frequently explained the fallacy of believing in man's natural goodness, and complemented those editorials with stories showing the outworkings of original sin.[31] But in the mid-1830s, a new attack emerged from a peculiar merger of materialism and pantheism.

The threat had been building for a long time. Rousseau, Kant and other purveyors of intellectual romanticism—the idea that man's reason did not have to operate within God's revelation, but could actually *create* truth out of its own resources—had long been read at Harvard and absorbed by Unitarian ministers. But Harvard's alternative to Christianity seemed cold until 1836. In that year Ralph Waldo Emerson's essay "Nature" appeared, and the Transcendental Club, composed of young Unitarian preachers, began meeting at the parsonage of George Ripley, who later became an editor of the New York *Tribune*.

Emerson laid out the Transcendentalist challenge in "Nature," and more precisely in his 1838 speech at the Harvard Divinity School. Christianity, he said, speaks "with noxious exaggeration about the person of Jesus," instead of emphasizing "the moral nature of man, where the sublime is." Humanity, Emerson proclaimed, "is drinking forever the soul of God" and becoming Godlike itself. Speak no further of man's sin and his responsibility before God, Emerson suggested: Man is God, or at least part of God, because a little bit of godstuff is sprinkled everywhere.[32]

If God is everywhere, though, God is nowhere. Theoretical pantheism could merge nicely with practical materialism. Transcendental thinking was spread in magazines such as *The Dial* and then popularized through non-Christian newspapers and the new public school systems set up by Unitarian Horace Mann and his disciples. There was no need to report on "God's providence" if news events arose from a combination of natural chance and man's godlike skill. The movement away from Christianity was heightened after midcentury when Charles Darwin provided a convenient way to satisfy the long-felt desire of haughty hearts.[33]

Following the traumatic Civil War, even editors of some Christian publications succumbed to intellectual trendiness. For example, editor Lyman Abbott of the *Christian Union*, a large-circulation weekly newspaper of the 1870s, decided that the Bible was fable rather than fact. He became known for attacking God's sovereignty in the name of Darwin. With the support of others who were similarly swayed, Abbott eventually took Christianity out of the magazine's title as well as its pages, with the name becoming *Outlook* in 1893. By that time, other anti-Christian doctrines—Marxism, Freudianism, and a general emphasis on "science" as mankind's savior—had kicked in also, or soon would.[34]

And yet, just as those trends were gaining power, a counterinfluence was developing. The period of great advances for anti-Christian thought also was a great era of revivals. During the last two-thirds of the nineteenth century God used great evangelists such as Charles Finney and Dwight Moody to expound the gospel of grace to millions. Many were saved through their preaching. Many also learned, as Proverbs 1:7 notes, that "the fear of the Lord is the beginning of knowledge" and wisdom. They thus were kept from believing in evolutionary or Marxist scriptures.[35]

Revivalism, though, did not particularly help those Christian newspapers that were endeavoring to cover every aspect of God's creation and perhaps "stir up the mind of Christians to duty." The great revivalists' focus on evangelism tended to be specifically individualistic: Worldview was not stressed. Furthermore, many Christians began to believe that the general culture inevitably would become worse and worse. They thought that little could be done to stay the downward drift. Christian publications should cover church news, they thought, and ignore the rest of the world.[36]

The anti-Christian trend and separatistic Christian reaction combined to end the Christian presence in newsrooms. As journalists who had embraced materialism and/or pantheism advanced in newspaper and magazine work, Christians who embraced separatistic revivalism retreated. Some Christian newspapers may have died after being overrun, but many evacuated the social realm without ever engaging the invading forces.

The general result of the two underlying movements was that the Reformational idea of Christ as Lord of all of life was neglected. Relations of ministry and laity, and of sabbatical and general church activities, also were affected. Calvin and other leaders of the Protestant Reformation had argued that good work outside the pulpit glorified God as much as the activities of the ministry proper.[37] But as views of inevitable cultural decay began to grip nineteenth-century American Protestantism, some editors began to consider journalism inferior to preaching. The editor of one Ohio newspaper said that "the work of a Christian minister" was far more important than the work of an editor.[38]

As Christian publications became less significant, selection of editors became more haphazard. Often those who could, preached, while those who could not, edited—and the latter knew that they were considered second-class Christians. One minister thrown into an editor's chair in Cincinnati wrote: "I had never seen a newspaper made up. . . . I was stunned by the cry of 'copy!' 'copy!' " That newspaper ceased publication when a follow-up editor took a vacation and never came back. The editor of the *Southern Christian Advocate* proclaimed that it was better to "wander through the earth on foot, preaching Christianity, than to be the editor of a religious newspaper."[39]

Sometimes it even seemed that a sense of "Whew! Glad I'm

saved!" had replaced a strong sense of God's sovereignty over all areas of human life. The theological vision of social defeatism and separatism had some immediate practical consequences. With many Christian journalists hiding their light under a bushel, the newspaper field was wide open for the triumph of "yellow journalism" at the end of the nineteenth century, and the expulsion of God from the front page early in the twentieth.[40] By 1925, Christians often were voiceless, except in publications that largely preached to the choir.

The almost total dominance of major newspapers by non-Christians showed up in the way that news stories generally, and major news stories with obvious theological dimensions in particular, were covered. There were many examples of biased coverage, but one of the most striking involved coverage of a 1925 trial that divided believers in the Biblical account of creation from those who had made their peace with materialism or pantheism or some combination of the two.[41]

JOURNALISTIC MONKEYS

Two faiths were in conflict at that Dayton, Tennessee, "monkey trial." The New York *Times*, greatly changed from the 1870s, editorialized for "faith, even of a grain of mustard seed, in the evolution of life. . . ." Realizing that there were only two ways upward from sin and misery—God's grace or man's evolution—a *Times* editorial stated that evolution offered the most hope: "If man has evolved, it is inconceivable that the process should stop and leave him in his present imperfect state. Specific creation has no such promise for man."[42]

That faith ran up against Christian faith in God's sovereignty and the hope offered by Christ's sacrifice. Tennessee legislators passed a law forbidding the teaching of evolution as scientific truth. The battle was joined when one young Dayton teacher, John T. Scopes, responded to an American Civil Liberties Union plea for someone to agree to be the defendant in a test case, with the ACLU paying all legal expenses. Clarence Darrow, the most famous lawyer of the era, and an atheist, was hired to head the defense. William Jennings Bryan, thrice-defeated Democratic presidential candidate, former Secretary of State, and a fundamentalist Christian, became point man for the prosecution.

The issue and the superstars brought out the journalists. Over one hundred reporters were dispatched to the trial. They wired 165,000 words daily to their newspapers during the twelve days of extensive coverage in July 1925. In theory, trial coverage could have been an opportunity to illuminate the theological debate that lay behind the creation *vs.* evolution issue. But in practice, with few if any Christians among those reporters, the position established early on by columnist H. L. Mencken went apparently unchallenged: "On the one side was bigotry, ignorance, hatred, superstition, every sort of blackness that the human mind is capable of. On the other side was sense."[43]

Journalists from major city newspapers saw the story as one of evolutionist intelligence *vs.* creationist stupidity. Nunnally Johnson, who covered the trial for the Brooklyn *Eagle* and then became a noted Hollywood screenwriter, remembered years later, "For the newspapermen it was a lark on a monstrous scale. . . . Being admirably cultivated fellows, they were all of course evolutionists and looked down on the local fundamentalists." Such ridicule was not merely a function of geography or politics. Both liberal and conservative newspapers lambasted the creationists. Journalists constantly attacked the theology of the creationists, perhaps because it was something their cultures had only recently "outgrown."[44]

The New York *Times* even noted at one point "a certain unexpectedness in the behavior and talk of the Dayton people. The unexpectedness comes from the absence in these Dayton people of any notable dissimilarity from people elsewhere except in their belated clinging to a method of Scriptural interpretation that not long ago was more than common in both North and South." The *Times* writer in those two sentences understood that fundamentalist beliefs were far from bizarre. In fact, it was the newer method of Scriptural interpretation that had been regarded as bizarre in Times Square as well as Tennessee only a short time before.[45]

The Christian exile from mainline journalism—the absence of salt—led to poor reporting. The evolutionists, without anyone to check them, wrote that Christians were trying to make one pro-evolution book "a book of evil tidings, to be studied in secret."[46] This was nonsense: Hundreds of pro-evolution writings were on sale in Dayton. Even a drugstore had a stack of materials representing all positions. John Butler, the legislator who introduced the anti-evolution bill, had a copy of Darwin's *The Origin of the Species* for his teenage children to read. He told reporters, "I am not opposed to teaching of evolution, but I don't think it ought to be taught in state-supported schools."[47]

The key issue, clearly, was not free speech, but parental control over school curricula. Even in Tennessee, Christian parents were already beginning to sense that their beliefs were being excluded from schools they were funding. William Jennings Bryan spoke for them when he said he "never advocated teaching the Bible in public schools," but believed "There is no reason why school children should not hear of Bible characters as well as other characters. In other words, there is no reason why the reading of the Bible should be excluded while the reading of books about other characters in history, like Confucius, should be permitted."[48]

Tennessee legislators saw their anti-evolution bill not as a way of putting Christian religion into the schools, but of forbidding proselytization for what they saw as a trendy but unproved evolutionary faith. Tennessee Governor Peay opposed the uncritical acceptance of evolutionary material "that no science has established."[49] One anti-evolutionary organization called itself the Defenders of True Science versus Speculation, contending that evolution "is a theory not yet approved by science," particularly since species-transitional fossils ("missing links") had not been found. "Demonstrated truth," Bryan insisted, "has no terrors for Christianity."[50]

Journalists, instead of explaining that, wrote leads such as, "Tennessee today maintained its quarantine against learning." The battle was "rock-ribbed Tennessee" *vs.* "unfettered investigation by the human mind and the liberty of opinion of which the Constitution makers preached." Reporters regularly attacked Christian faith and "this superheated religious atmosphere, this pathetic search for the 'eternal truth.' "[51]

One journalist described Scopes, the teacher-defendant, as an imprisoned martyr, "the witch who is to be burned by Dayton." (Actually, Scopes did not spend a second in jail and was regularly invited to dinner by Dayton Christians.) If the creationists were to win, another wrote, "The dunce cap will be the crown of office, and the slopstick will be the sceptre of authority." Residents of Dayton were "the treewise monkeys" who "see no logic, speak no logic and hear no logic." When William Jennings Bryan Jr., an attorney, arrived for the trial, a columnist wrote, "Junior is bound to be a chip off the old blockhead. . . . Like father, like son, and we don't like either."[52]

Dayton jurors, who following the trial gave thoughtful accounts of the proceedings, were described in one New York headline: "Intelligence of Most of Lowest Grade." It seemed that "All twelve are Protestant churchgoers."[53]

There was not even accurate coverage of the debates between creationists and evolutionists. For instance, when Bryan debated

Darrow's associate Dudley Malone on July 16, the court transcript shows strong and intelligent orations by both sides. Bryan, within Christian presuppositions, made a sophisticated and coherent argument. He stressed the evolutionary theory's lack of scientific proof and emphasized its inability to answer questions about how life began, how man began, how one species actually changes into another, and so on. He pointed out the irreconcilability of Darwinian doctrines of extra-species evolution with the Biblical account of creation, original sin, and the reasons for Christ's coming.[54]

Malone stated the evolutionist position in a similarly cohesive way. Both sides apparently did well. But journalists wrote that Bryan's speech "was a grotesque performance and downright touching in its imbecility."[55] Bryan coverage by a variety of reporters was laden with sarcastic Biblical allusions: "Dayton began to read a new book of revelations today. The wrath of Bryan fell at last. With whips of scorn . . . he sought to drive science from the temples of God and failed."[56] According to the Chicago *Tribune*'s news coverage, the debate proved that "the truth as applied to man's origin was not locked in a book in the days of Moses."[57]

Overall, most major newspaper reporters produced so many unobservant stories that it often seemed as if they were closing their eyes and not even seeing the trial at all. The ultimate in this came when one New York scribe, under a headline "Scopes Is Seen as New Galileo at Inquisition," wrote that the "sultry courtroom in Dayton, during a pause in the argument, became hazy and there evolved from the mists of past ages a new scene. The Tennessee judge disappeared and I racked my brain to recognize the robed dignitary on the bench. Yes, it was the grand inquisitor, the head of the inquisition at Rome. . . . I saw the Tennessee Fundamentalist public become a medieval mob thirsty for heretical blood. . . . [It was] 1616. The great Galileo was on trial."[58]

It seemed that most reporters in Dayton, even when they tried to be fair—some had no such intention—could not help seeing the atheistic side as plausible and the Christian view as "nonsensical." The life and beliefs of one of the best of the Scopes trial reporters, Raymond Clapper, shows the pattern. In 1912, ready to enter college, he was leading Presbyterian church meetings in Kansas. But after four years at the University of Kansas, he chose "a more reasonable belief." By 1923 Clapper and his wife had "discarded the orthodox teachings of our youth. We could not believe the Old Testament prophets, whose teachings no doubt fitted well the savage age in which they lived but suited our world no better than the Greek oracles. The story of Christ we thought was moving and beautiful but we could not accept the virgin birth or the resurrection."[59]

Before Clapper arrived in Dayton to cover the trial, his mind already was made up: He believed that "the whole case of fundamentalism [was] ridiculous." It was no surprise, then, when Clapper's stories argued that "Fundamentalist justice has plugged up the ears of this Tennessee mountain jury." Olive Clapper, his wife, argued that "Unbelievable as the trial was to intelligent people, it did have value because the end result was greater enlightenment of people on the subject of evolution." Clapper had done his best to provide that enlightenment.[60]

The Clapper story could be repeated many times: Journalists who were or had become opposed to the Bible wanted to teach readers the anti-Christian "truth" as they saw it. There was no one to counterbalance their emphases, because Christians no longer had much of a presence in American journalism. Yes, there were denominational magazines and church newsletters, but coverage of major events such as the Scopes trial was in the hands of those who might be ever watching but never seeing.[61]

Mainline news coverage in the United States is still in those hands, as the next chapter will indicate.

TWO

SPIKING THE SPIRITUAL

American journalists and their critics have been engaged in a lively liberal *vs.* conservative debate over the past two decades. Many books and articles have been written about the tilt to the left at mainline media institutions.[1] But a far more crucial type of bias has been ignored almost entirely.

As noted in Chapter One, much of American journalism until the mid-nineteenth century emphasized God's sovereignty and man's responsibility. Kings who disobeyed God were exposed as sinful. Duelists were without honor because they thought esteem among men more important than following God's commands. Lightning storms taught spiritual lessons. Lack of repentance had murderous consequences. One minister said that he enjoyed opening up the newspaper to see what God had done that day.[2]

Non-Christian journalists who came to dominate newspapers following the departure of Christians tended to put out a very different kind of product. There is little evidence of editors explicitly banning God from the front page. Instead, they redefined "reality" to exclude the spiritual realm. For earlier editors, material and spiritual aspects of the world were both important. They knew that comprehensive news stories and news analysis requires reporting of the workings of Providence, as best we can understand them. But many editors of the past century have tried to publish God's obituary.

The Bible provides excellent examples of complete news coverage, coverage that takes into account both material and spiritual. News reports circulated immediately after the parting of the Red Sea (Exodus 15) or the defeat of the Canaanites (Judges 8) noted the interaction of spiritual and material forces. The Book of Job's report of a sensational disaster story—family wiped out, house smashed by tornado, herds stolen, and so on—is introduced by a dialogue in Heaven between God and Satan that is essential to an understanding of the drama below. One realm is no more "real" than the other. Both Heaven and earth are fact.

Earthly reporters, of course, cannot know exactly what is going on in Heaven; inspired Biblical reporting is greater than anything we can produce. But Christians do know that there is a spiritual realm as well as an earthly one, and that activities in the spiritual realm do influence the origin and outcome of news stories on earth. Christians know four spiritual facts that are essential to understanding earthly news events:

—God is sovereign, so events do not happen by chance. Obedience to God brings blessings; disobedience brings curses. The blessings and curses may not always be apparent immediately.

—Satan is active in the world, intent on doing evil. Since events on earth are subsets of a larger battle between God and Satan, we may not know why certain events occur.

—Because of the ravages of sin, man without God's grace is prone to do evil. Yet, the redemption brought about by Christ's sacrifice is real. It gives Christians not only eternal salvation, but the power to fight Satan's attempts to rule this world.

—God answers prayers. He does so not by making us feel better psychologically, but by actually transforming earthly situations, not always in the way we expect.

Few reporters now accept this spiritual reality as a necessary backdrop to stories, because fact has been defined to include only material. The result has been incomplete reporting. If, for example, we apply only the last of the spiritual facts listed above—God answers prayer—there emerges a different way of covering one of the major stories of 1986, the overthrow of Ferdinand Marcos in the Philippines.

The New York *Times*, ignoring its Christian origins once again, covered the material facts. But an article in the *Evangelical Beacon* by Robert Carey told a much deeper story: "Christians of all persuasions had been uniting in fervent prayer before, during and after the election. . . . Many churches held all-night prayer meetings. Others met for special times of prayer in homes or churches. . . . There is, I believe, no way to explain the events we have witnessed apart from answered prayer."[3]

There *was*, of course, another means of explanation, that used by the *Times*: Count the tanks and guns, and estimate popular support for each side. But Carey in his report asked a series of hard questions:

"What accounted for the fact that the military forces did not overrun the crowds? They had sufficient tear gas and water cannons to disperse the people.

"What kept hundreds of thousands of people from becoming a wild, uncontrolled mob? What held their emotions in check?

"What enabled President Marcos to exercise restraint and keep cool when his top military man called for action to attack and neutralize the rebel forces?

"What enabled the crowds to show kindness and offer food and drink to their 'enemies' in the government forces?"[4]

Carey concluded, "As I lay in bed listening to the radio through my headset during the wee hours of the morning, I heard an evangelical leader asking people to get up and wake their families and pray during a particularly crucial period. On two such occasions I woke [my wife] and we prayed together for God to control the situation. The same thing was taking place in thousands of households across Manila and throughout the Philippines. . . . And God answered prayer."

Carey's reporting was moving. That God did answer the prayers of Christians in the Philippines is clear. *How* exactly he answered them is not yet clear, and may not be for many years, if ever on this earth. We do not know what will happen in the Philippines—civil war may still occur. But the Bible does tell us that events happen not just because of individual or national sin or faith, but for God's glory. From observation, we know that those who spiked the spiritual by refusing to recognize the mystery of the Philippines crisis—the *fact* that something outside of what we perceive as the usual chain of events happened there—were missing a major story.[5]

Carey's story, then, was different from that of the New York *Times*: Different not only in *interpretation* of events but different in selection of details. A former *Times* editor, Lester Markel, described his newspaper's reporting and editing process by explaining that "The reporter, the most objective reporter, collects fifty facts. Out of the fifty facts he selects twelve to include in his story (there is such a thing as space limitation). Thus he discards thirty-eight. This is Judgment Number One.

"Then the reporter or editor decides which of the facts shall be the first paragraph of the story, thus emphasizing one fact above the other eleven. This is Judgment Number Two. Then the editor decides whether the story shall be placed on Page One or Page Twelve; on Page One it will command many times the attention it would on Page Twelve. This is Judgment Number Three. This so-called factual presentation is thus subjected to three judgments, all of them most humanly and most ungodly made."[6]

Markel's description of the "ungodly" process is generalizable: Reporters and editors, like all of us, are always making choices. New York *Times* reporters in the Philippines, if they were pounding the pavements or even listening to local radio, had to be aware of what Filipinos were calling "prayer power," but they evidently saw that set of activities as relatively insignificant. Robert Carey was clearly aware of the military and public opinion configurations, but he considered those facts to be of secondary importance.

Many major American journalists would prefer, for three reasons, the materialistic accounts of the *Times* to the spiritual/material accounts of Carey.

First, many would say that the *Times* is objective. But the Bible points out, and philosophers from many backgrounds have tended to agree, that all descriptions of human activities are based on certain convictions as to the nature of the universe. Readers of every news story are receiving information but are also being taught, subtly or explicitly, a particular worldview, whether it is theistic, pantheistic, materialistic, or whatever.

In philosophical terms, newspapers offer not only phenomena, but noumena; not only facts learned from study, but an infrastructure that gives meaning to the facts. When the Detroit *Free Press* offered its readers a typical newspaper report on urban crime, introductory facts and anecdotes were immediately followed by a list of "things that spur killings . . . stress, joblessness, poverty, guns and subcultures of violence." Sin was not mentioned.[7]

The key line of defense for most journalists would be the second: That the New York *Times*, in describing material, was describing fact. Anyone with sight, regardless of his theology, could see the tanks and guns, and those who could not see could touch. Therefore the tanks and guns were really there, while the spiritual world cannot be seen or touched by many people, so it might not be there.

And yet, without diving too deeply into the philosophical black hole of epistemology (how we know things), we could say that the tanks and guns were not dependent for their existence on the ability of reporters to see or touch them. If all reporters were blind and deprived of their other senses as well—in which case, obviously, they would be inadequate reporters—the tanks and guns would still have been there.

The Bible makes a similar point about spiritual things. Paul writes in Romans (1:20), "Since the creation of the world God's invisible qualities—his eternal power and divine nature—have been clearly seen, being understood from what had been made." That some do not see has no more to do with the factuality of the matter than the absence of sight or touch in some has to do with the factuality of tanks.

Psalm 19 discussed this crucial point more poetically: "The heavens declare the glory of God; the skies proclaim the work of his hands. Day after day they pour forth speech; night after night they display knowledge. There is no speech or language where their voice is not heard. Their voice goes out into all the earth, their words to the ends of the world." Many reporters do not acknowledge God's glory. They develop convoluted interpretations to avoid admitting that creation is His. But, as Romans 1:20 notes, they are without excuse.

Just because reporters do not see spiritual things, or admit to seeing spiritual things, does not mean that spirit is not fact. John Newton, a slave trader who became a Christian, wrote of differential sight two centuries ago: "Amazing grace, how sweet the sound, that saved a wretch like me. I once was lost, but now am found, was blind, but now I see."

Reporters might say that everyone with normal senses can experience tanks, but not everyone with normal senses can experience spirit—yet what makes us think our senses are normal? The Bible says they are abnormal apart from God's grace, since man's fall from the garden of Eden onwards has cut us off from natural perception of the spiritual. The Bible also tells us that man's decision to suppress the truth by ignoring the spiritual is a conscious, deliberate result of sin and guilt.

The third, fall-back defense of journalists who defend the reporting of material fact and the spiking of the spiritual is journalistic tradition, backed up by their own personal sense that the tradition is right. Reporters are right to assert that tradition is now on the anti-spiritual side. Let's look at a few examples of the ways in which materialist reporters have missed stories of man's sin and redemption, God's sovereignty, and Satan's activities.

IGNORING FACTS OF SIN AND REDEMPTION

Whittaker Chambers and Alger Hiss were the two major figures in a big story of the late 1940s.[8] Chambers was a former Communist Party member and spy who had become a Christian. He gave investigators solid evidence (unlike most of that produced by Joseph McCarthy during the 1950s) of Soviet espionage in the State

Department. Alger Hiss was a former State Department official with favorable recommendations in his file from Presidents, Supreme Court Justices, and dozens of other leaders. Chambers charged that Hiss had been a spy, and produced microfilm and other evidence to back up his accusations.[9]

Washington *Post* reporters, for two reasons, refused to believe Chambers' charges, even when the evidence became overwhelming. One reason apparently was economic: Chambers was casting doubts on not only the integrity of Hiss but the management of the federal bureaucracy generally. The growth of that bureaucracy, Washington's major industry, was crucial to the *Post*'s economic future; the *Post* regularly sprang to the defense of that industry just as newspapers in other cities tended to protect their own.

The second reason, judging from *Post* articles, was theological. Reporters evidently did not understand that the ravages of sin had turned Hiss into a traitor. Nor did they see that the grace of redemption propelled Chambers to leave a comfortable job to become a witness against communism.[10]

Chambers tried to teach the reporters. He told them of the true *evil* of communism (not just mistake, or misfortune, or trying too hard to make progressive changes, but satanic evil). He described the true grace of God (not just existing in some abstract form, but actively changing men's hearts and creating the opportunity for new lives). His first statement to the press, shortly before appearing at a Congressional hearing, was that he had left the Communist Party because "it was an evil." He continued to use such blunt words throughout his public agony.[11]

Chambers consistently stressed religious presuppositions. He criticized "the great alternative faith of mankind," the Communist vision of "Man without God . . . man's mind displacing God as the creative intelligence of the world." Chambers argued that many non-Communists also had the modern "vision of man, once more the central figure of the Creation, not because God made man in His image, but because man's mind makes him the most intelligent of the animals." Chambers testified that he had been consumed by that sinful vision also, until God had changed his heart through free grace. Sin and grace—Chambers' story was impossible to understand unless those concepts were taken seriously.[12]

Articles from both liberal and conservative newspapers, though, indicated that many journalists did not consider sin and grace to be facts of human life. It made no sense that officials with impressive resumés should become traitors—but it made perfect sense, given an awareness of original sin. (Biblically, scribes and

Pharisees often are traitors.) It made no sense that a liar such as Chambers should now be trusted—but it made perfect sense if there is a God who so transforms hearts that those who once loved lying now find false witness abhorrent.[13]

MINIMIZING THE SPIRITUAL DIMENSIONS

Newspaper coverage of two major stories of 1962—the public school prayer debate in June and the beginning of the modern abortion controversy in July—showed how unimportant spiritual dimensions had become to many journalists.

The U.S. Supreme Court's contention in June 1962 that prayer in public schools is unconstitutional was heatedly denounced by many Christians. Major newspapers downplayed the controversy, though. The New York *Times* complained about "far-fetched attacks" by opponents of the decision. The New York *Herald-Tribune* suggested that "we accept the ruling with respect, and calm." Other newspapers that waxed fervent even about small political issues editorialized that the prayer question was unimportant, or almost entirely ignored it.[14]

Another need for some spiritual discernment arose the following month (July 1962) when "Miss Sherri," star of the Phoenix version of "Romper Room" (a nationally syndicated kiddie program), decided to have an abortion. Sherri Finkbine was the "pretty mother of four healthy children" and the wife of a high school history teacher who also gave swimming lessons in the family pool behind the house. She was an attractive woman with high professional status who decided to have an abortion because the child she had been bearing for two months faced the possibility of birth with substantial birth defects.[15]

Concerned journalists could have covered the story in this way: "She has a pleasant home, adequate finances, and a supportive husband, but plans to kill her baby." Or this way: "Woman insists on abortion even though there is only a 20 percent chance of deformity in the child she carries." Newspapers could have run features on babies with birth defects who were nevertheless thriving. But with isolated exceptions—one Catholic newspaper editorialized, "Brush away the sentimental slush of a thousand sob-sisters and the cold fact remains that this woman wants to kill the child now living within her"—reporters rallied behind the visible and even changed typical vocabulary in order to ignore the hidden.[16]

Some examples: The Los Angeles *Times* defended Miss Sherri, a "tanned brunet wearing a sleeveless dress of white linen," and instead of using the word "abortion," headlined her desire for "Baby Surgery." A columnist wrote of Finkbine's desire to avoid the possibility of "mothering" a drug-deformed child. The New York *Journal-American* described an operation to "lose the baby," and the New York *Times* reported, "Couple May Go Abroad for Surgery to Prevent a Malformed Baby." Eventually, reporters dropped use of the word "baby" entirely, and substituted the medical term "fetus."[17]

There is no evidence that reporters were trying to be daring, or that they were thoughtfully attempting to transform editorial interpretation by changing abortion terminology that had been dominant for almost a century. Reporters were only doing what came naturally, telling a story about likable folks in trouble. But in doing so they ignored key questions.[18]

MISUNDERSTANDING BASIC QUESTIONS

By the 1970s, many reporters seemed unable to understand even basic Christian concepts. Ignorance of fundamental definitions of *sin* was evident on Easter Sunday, 1973, when embattled President Richard Nixon went to church in Key Biscayne, Florida. Minister John Huffman noted in his sermon, "I don't like to talk about sin. But let's face it. It's a fact of society and a fact of your and my life. We can sweep it under the rug and dismiss it . . . or you can walk out of here transformed individuals by the power of Jesus Christ."[19]

One member of the White House press corps, doing his job, asked Huffman after the service, "Was this aimed at the President?" Huffman said, "No." A reporter asked, "Was it a Watergate sermon?" Huffman said, "No, it was not a Watergate sermon." A reporter then asked, "Well, then, apparently you are saying that nothing in your sermon had any relation to the President?" Huffman replied, "Absolutely not. I wouldn't say that at all, because if I single out anyone in the congregation and say a sermon had nothing to do with them, that person might as well not come to church."

The press corps persisted. Another reporter asked, "Well, then, you're saying that you *were* preaching to the President." Huffman replied, "No, I did not say I was preaching to the President as far as singling anyone out." A reporter demanded, "Well, what are you saying?" Huffman responded, "I'm saying simply this: that I preach the gospel of Jesus Christ. I try to preach it as clearly as possible, as faithfully to the Scripture as possible, and I start with myself, and I am a sinner. I need to repent and every one of us in the room is under the same conditions and whatever the President wants to make of what was said this morning is between him and the Lord."

Many reporters evidently refused to accept this basic concept of original sin, and persisted in thinking of the sermon in terms of a particular sin. News stories the next morning were predictable: Huffman had warned Nixon he should quit pretending to be a Christian, Nixon should repent of his Watergate sins, Nixon had been chastised, and so on.[20]

In one sense, such stories were predictable. It was open season on Nixon, and he had brought that particular volley on himself. But the story behind those stories is threefold: Sometimes a lack of understanding of basic Christian concepts; sometimes a refusal to believe that intelligent people actually take those beliefs seriously; and, probably most often, deliberate suppression of truth about God and self. As sociologist Robert Bellah generalized about the attitude of journalists toward Christianity, most "think it's somehow slightly embarrassing, a holdover from the Dark Ages . . . something only ignorant and backward people really believe in."[21]

Many Washington correspondents, living in a politicized world, see error or plot in politics and economics, but will not accept its origin in the original sin within individuals. They consciously avoid admission of sin's power, for such admission would condemn themselves. Journalists, like all of us, have trouble answering Jesus' question: "Why do you look at the speck of sawdust in your brother's eye and pay no attention to the plank in your own eye?" (Luke 6:41).

REFUSAL TO ACKNOWLEDGE WARNINGS

Pharisees in New Testament times liked to believe that everyone on this earth received what they deserved—which meant that those who were healthy and materially prosperous could assume that their spiritual health also was good. But Jesus said, concerning Galileans who had been brutally treated by Pilate, "Do you think that these Galileans were worse sinners than all the other Galileans because they suffered this way? I tell you, no! But unless you repent, you too will all perish. Or those eighteen who died when the tower in Siloam fell on them—do you think they were more guilty than all the others living in Jerusalem? I tell you, no! But unless you repent, you too will all perish" (Luke 13:2-7).

The current AIDS plague has provided an opportunity for widespread repentance. Paul told the Romans that when men do not give thanks to God, their thinking becomes futile, and then

God lets them turn thought into action: Men abandon "natural relations with women," are "inflamed with lust for one another," and "commit indecent acts with other men." Finally, they receive "in themselves the due penalty for their perversion" (Romans 1:18-32). Recent news accounts have speculated about a variety of potential causes of AIDS, but materialist reporters could not take seriously the belief that AIDS is a God-sent warning to homosexuals and to adulterous heterosexuals and to anyone who scorns Him.[22]

In spiking the spiritual concerning AIDS, many mainline journalists did not merely choose one worldview over another. By ridiculing even the idea that the terror of AIDS was providing an opportunity for repentance, they were suggesting to all of us that the "liberated" lifestyle popularized in the 1960s could continue, with "safe sex" modifications. Homosexuals could continue their practices as long as they chose partners carefully and used condoms; heterosexuals could continue in adultery, as long as one-night stands tended to be on the second night rather than the first. Other subsets of the one real sin—disobedience to God—could continue.

Journalists who refused even to consider a spiritual/material interface further weakened their stories by not acknowledging what is right in front of their eyes. For example, a *Newsweek* article gave accounts of AIDS patients, all of whom (with one exception) were heterosexuals; this was an obvious attempt to give a false impression of reality. A more subtle newspaper article, "Gays Rally for Right and Respect," reported a homosexual march as if it were an Easter parade, with the emphasis on "diversity" and "family."[23]

Missing were accounts of groups such as Dykes on Bikes, the pederastic North American Man-Boy Love Association, or the Society of Venus (a group that promotes sadomasochism as safe sex). Those details might have made readers wonder if whips and chains make for "safe sex," so specific detail (which makes for strong reporting) was covered up.

The Bible uses specific detail to show the nature of sin. Amnon's rape of Tamar, Canaan looking on his father's nudity, Lot's sexual relations with his daughters—all make for vivid reading. The Bible is not shy about showing the ugly deeds of man; the Bible is not sanitized. But for ideological reasons, much of the news we read today is. By sanitizing homosexual marches, materialist journalists turn aside readers from the necessity of choosing between right and wrong (and avoid condemning themselves). Cover-up is no favor to readers, and no service to the cause of printing the truth, or even a vivid story.[24]

RIDICULING THOSE WITH SPIRITUAL VISION

Lack of understanding, along with outright anti-Christian prejudice, leads to journalistic amazement or horror at the supposed self-deception of those who do see a spiritual realm. Materialist reporters have been blind persons thinking that those with sight are obstinate for not employing the blind as guides. For example, the New York *Times* typically attacks theological conservatives as "inflexible" persons who want to "set a tone of anti-intellectualism" and "start exorcising the demon they call liberalism."[25]

The scorn particularly comes out, now as in the 1920s, when the topic of evolution *vs.* creation is debated. In 1986 Tennessee Christian parents asked their school district either to create alternative classes with alternative books for the children, or to pay for their private school tuition. They said there should be some choice in public education, not just the foisting on their children of anti-Christian books. They said that if public schools cannot provide choice, parents should not be penalized financially for finding alternatives.

The case, referred to as "Scopes II," brought up important questions. Are the public schools infringing on the right to free exercise of religion? Can we move toward a pluralistic public school system? But many newspapers missed the real issues once again, as they did during Scopes I. Instead, the lead on one story in the Austin *American-Statesman* was, "In the peaceful hills of Tennessee's Bible Belt, Dorothy and Toto and the Good Witch are on trial this week."[26] The reporter did not understand or did not want to deal with the real, serious issue of the case, so he chose the weasel strategy of six decades ago: Poke fun at Bible thumpers.

BEYOND THE LIBERAL-CONSERVATIVE DEBATE

Again and again over the past half-century, the same story emerges: Spike the spiritual. Seeing the consistent downgrading of the Biblical worldview of spiritual/material interface helps us to go beyond media debates of the past two decades. The liberal *vs.* conservative debate is an important one, but some conservative reporters are as materialistic in philosophy as their liberal counterparts. Non-Christians of both sides tend to give only half the facts.

Often this is not conscious. As John Corry of the New York

Times acknowledged, "There are fewer rules of pure journalism here than journalists pretend, even to themselves. Journalists, especially big-time journalists, deal in attitudes and ideas as much as events." Those attitudes and ideas lead to formation of journalistic plausibility structures, their senses of what makes sense and what does not. Busy reporters often do not have time to think things through. As one Washington hand noted, "If I got to think about a story at all, it was in the few steps running from a Senate hearing room to the phone booth." Journalists, under such pressure, tend to make snap choices of emphasis based on their basic ideas of what is important and what is not.[27]

Some would say that personal beliefs are unimportant because "professionalism" takes over, but a few journalists with good senses of self are also aware of the effect of "selective perception." William Rivers, a reporter turned professor, has written frequently about the effect of attitudes on the ability of even well-trained reporters to spot a story. In describing one story he wrote, Rivers noted that "My prejudices did the work and I was unaware of it until, much later, I read about the phenomenon known as 'selective perception.' " As *Time*'s former chairman of the board, Andrew Heiskell, observed, "All writers slant what they write no matter how hard they try."[28]

The slant is obvious at times. Washington *Post* foreign editor Karen de Young, in explaining her positive coverage of the Sandinistas during their seizure of power, noted that "Most journalists now, most Western journalists at least, are very eager to seek out guerrilla groups, leftist groups, because you assume they must be the good guys." Former ABC newsman Geraldo Rivera, reporting from Panama during the 1970s, had a problem: The U.S. Senate was about to vote on U.S. relinquishing of the Panama Canal, and violence engaged in by the Panamanian National Guard showed that the government of Panama was not exactly a trustworthy guardian of the Canal. Rivera admitted later, "We downplayed the whole incident. That was the day I decided that I had to be very careful about what was said, because I could defeat the very thing [passage of the Treaty] that I wanted to achieve."[29]

Most reporters want to display the world as they see it, with the goal of presenting how they think the world works. But instead of seeing pattern in events, journalists with materialist worldviews simply see the random effects of time plus chance. When readers and viewers complain about the patternlessness of it all, journalists in turn tend to complain about readers and viewers demanding more than they feel they can offer.

The end result of this spiking of the spiritual is what could be called Wheel of Fortune journalism. The name comes from television's most popular game show. The game takes some skill, but winners are generally those who avoid a bad spin of the wheel. Chance apparently rules, and the audience tunes in regularly.

"Wheel of Fortune's" success has the heads of television journalists spinning. When a local station puts "Wheel" on against news shows, the game show often gets higher ratings than Dan Rather, Tom Brokaw, or the local anchor. One network executive said, "You try to do everything right journalistically . . . and then the most successful game show in the history of the land comes along and cuts your head off." Another executive said, "It's dumb luck."

But is it dumb luck? Or does "Wheel's" success reveal something about the failure of typical news shows? News shows tend to have standard stories of people murdered, houses destroyed by fire, and so on. There is no explanation, and the game goes on: Some are winners, most are losers. That description of a news show sounds like "Wheel of Fortune." The main difference is that "Wheel of Fortune" has flashing lights and more glamour: Same product, better package. Why shouldn't viewers prefer it?

Typical newspaper stories also show the tendency to ascribe events to chance. A Houston *Post* article related that a twenty-year-old woman "was killed because her hand accidentally snagged on a purse that had been grabbed by a man" who demanded money and shot her when she seemed to be resisting.[30] The *Post's* cause of death, explicitly, was bad luck on the wheel of fortune. Yet, what about the sin of a murderer on drugs who had become so corrupt that he was willing to kill? What about the sin of cultural leaders who tolerate and even encourage drug use? What about the activity of the murder victim who was sitting in a park at 3:30 A.M. after an evening of drinking? (She was certainly not to blame for what happened, but foolish actions do have consequences.)

Instead of probing, typical materialist explanations trivialize. One Wednesday, a fourteen-year-old student received on his report card an "F" for French. The next day he went to school, attended his classes, and at about 1 P.M. went to his French class. He waited outside the door for the previous class to be dismissed. The bell rang. The teacher opened the door. The student calmly shot her dead and wounded three others.

In the irony of God's providence, the student had mistakenly killed a substitute teacher. An NBC reporter told the story, explaining that the student was "upset" over the "F." A mild word, "upset," to describe lack of self-control leading from anger to murder.

A bland word, "upset," to leave us shaking our heads over the wheel of fortune and saying, "How could a nice young man do such a thing?"

Deeper causes of the deaths of the twenty-year-old woman and the substitute French teacher—the war of Satan against God, and Satan's use of corrupting sin—are hidden from us. We do know, however, that every skirmish does have some significance in that war. Even without speculating about the heavenlies, a reporter looking for pattern in life and death, rather than assuming the operation of chance, can produce far richer stories than those developed by spiking the spiritual.

According to materialist reporters, though, life is a process of chance. Spin the wheel and see what number comes up. Most readers and viewers are so used to this method of presentation that it is difficult to imagine the news being done in any other way. Yet, what a weak and superficial journalism we have when materialism rules! What a profligate wasting of a proud heritage!

THREE

NOT WITHOUT PERSONAL COST

Chapter One discussed the decline of Christian journalism. Chapter Two argued that journalism without an awareness of the spiritual realm makes for incomplete journalism. This chapter will suggest that the lack of spiritual awareness also makes for incomplete journalists. Journalism history's pantheon is filled with statues of great crusaders, but crusades based on false ideology invariably come up short.

Some journalists were honest enough and smart enough to see their failure, with enormous personal repercussions later in life. The most innovative journalists, though, often were the most arrogant, slow to recognize that their leaps forward were taking them in circles. Yet, it is these journalists who are held up to journalism students as the giants of the field. The sin and misery of many of these great lives cannot be scientifically measured, nor can it be proven that writers without God fall into a pattern. But to get an impression of the personal costs involved in seeing self as God, we might briefly chronicle the lives of eight of the greats during the 1840-1940 period. That is recent enough so that their influence is still felt, long enough ago so that gossip has receded.[1]

GREELEY

First of the key journalists during our period (and famous for the phrase, "Go west, young man") was Horace Greeley, editor of the New York *Tribune* from 1841 to 1872. He was a hands-on manager who demanded strong local reporting: "Do not let a new church be organized, a mill set in motion, a store opened, nor anything of interest to a dozen families occur, without having the fact daily, though briefly, chronicled in your columns." He was a beloved leader of reporters, as "He steered the *Tribune* with relaxed, easy reins, and enjoyed giving his men their head." With a background as a printer, he had an excellent sense of typography.[2]

But Greeley's theology was Unitarian. He thought that man was naturally good and could "enoble" himself. Greeley did not understand original sin, so he thought that man's corruption came from outside, from corrupt institutions. Believing that all would be well if only major institutions were transformed, he began crusading for societal change.[3]

First, Greeley saw private property as the corrupting force, for economic competition made man evil. So Greeley backed, with profits gained from the *Tribune*'s competitive success, the founding of some forty communes during the 1840s. All of them failed. Then he moved on to other causes: Agrarianism, anti-rentism, "free love," always something new, always something that supposedly would lead to a man-made utopia just around the corner.[4]

When each idea failed, Greeley often would blame those he had previously backed for their inability to implement the impossible. He eventually inspired a poem by William Grayson in 1856: "There Greeley, grieving at a brother's woe,/ Spits with impartial spite on friend and foe . . ./To each fanatical delusion prone,/He damns all creeds and parties but his own;/And faction's fiercest rabble always find/A kindred nature in the Tribune's mind;/ Ready each furious impulse to obey,/He raves and ravens like a beast of prey."[5]

None of the causes panned out, but Greeley kept trying something new. So did his wife Mary Greeley. At one time she was violently opposed to the killing of animals for any reason. She met writer Margaret Fuller on the street one day, touched Fuller's kid gloves and began to scream, "Skin of a beast, skin of a beast." Mary was wearing silk, and Margaret Fuller had the presence of mind to begin yelling, "Entrails of a worm, entrails of a worm."[6]

Horace and Mary Greeley believed that children were without sin; the prime parental goal was to keep them from corruption. Their son Arthur (Pickie), born in 1844, spent most of his first five summers in various communes. At age five his hair had never been cut, lest that constrict his freedom, and he still wore baby clothes, to give him freedom of movement. He was to be a beautiful combination of intellect and nature, equipped with "choice" thoughts and language. But one day Pickie, age five, stood up before a commune meeting and started complaining that his mother was "so particular, particular, particular, particular." When she reminded him that he had been saved from corruption, he began shrieking at her, "Don't you dare shut me up in a room. . . . I want fun." The Greeleys did not change Pickie's regime, but he died shortly after during a cholera epidemic.[7]

Greeley's causes were no more successful than his utopian ideas of child-raising. When he tired of marriage and proposed "social enjoyment" and "individual sovereignty," he was attacked for proposing "only a brothel on a new plan."[8] When he ran for President in 1872, he was politically crushed. Following the election, he reflected on his life and saw it as a waste, a sacrifice to foolish crusades. In one of his last statements before death took him on November 29, 1872, Greeley wrote, "I stand naked before my God, the most utterly, hopelessly wretched and undone of all who ever lived. I have done more harm and wrong than any man who ever saw the light of day. And yet I take God to witness that I have never intended to injure or harm anyone. But this is no excuse."[9]

STOREY

Greeley was the father of modern journalistic crusading. Wilbur Storey of the Detroit *Free Press* and the Chicago *Times* could be called, similarly, the father of modern journalistic sensationalism. Storey, an innovative editor from 1855 through 1884, anticipated the racy details of New York "yellow journalism" by running headlines such as "How to Get Rid of a Faithless Wife," "Suicide by Swallowing a Red-Hot Poker," "Fountain of Blood in a Cavern," and "Saved by His Wife's Corpse."[10]

Storey became particularly known for decked headlines such as this one from 1871: "Spouse Roasting/The Massachusetts Husband Who Cooked His Wife in Kerosene/A Sample of New England Conjugal Bliss."[11] Storey believed strongly in material causes for all tragedies, with individuals often left helpless, as related in this headline: "The Arsenic Fiend. Full Confession of Lydia Sherman, the Connecticut Arch-Murderess/The Remorseless Murder of Three Husbands and Five Children/A Story of Arsenic, Arsenic, Arsenic/A Constant, Itching Temptation Which She Was Powerless to Resist." His political reporting of the Chicago city council also was grabbing: "Bastard 'City Fathers'/Chicago's Prize Rummers Hold Their Weekly Carnival at the City Hall/And, As Usual, Disgrace the City Over Which They Should Exercise All Care."[12]

Storey became the dictator of Chicago. In the words of his closest *Times* associate, Franc B. Wilkie, "Wilbur Storey was a

Bacchus, a Satyr, a Minotaur, all in one. . . . Possessed of no consideration for the feelings of others, he fancied himself infallible." Storey attacked with impunity anyone who crossed his path and did not bow; sued often for libel, he always managed to avoid heavy penalties. He made up stories which ruined reputations and said he did not care.[13]

Storey tended to hire editors and writers in his own image. Probably his most famous reporter, "Shang" Andrews, was a drug addict. Storey's city editor once called his staff "a great force. . . . Two of my men are ex-convicts, ten are divorced husbands, and not a single one of them is living with his own wife." *Times* reporters were almost invariably anti-church, producing bitter attacks on "The Preachers of the Period" and "The Peculiarities of Shepherds and Flocks."[14]

Storey's life, though, became evidence for the often-repeated maxim that those who do not believe in Christianity eventually find themselves ready to believe not nothing, but anything. The materialist Storey in his fifties became interested in the spiritual, but in his own way: He installed a permanent "spirit-rapping" medium in his home and turned the *Times* into the editorial organ of "Spirit Intercourse." In one article Storey renounced "forever" Christian communion and said he would pay attention to the "mystic and invisible communications" that came to him alone. Through frequent seances he searched for a spiritual realm he could control as he controlled Chicago.[15]

Then doctors found that Storey had contracted syphilis which had advanced to such a stage that his intellect was threatened. Storey moaned to his sister, "Why have I worked so hard, and accumulated money, and planned, and given all my years to building up a great business, when I know that at any moment I may become a helpless mass?" On doctor's advice he took a long tour of Europe in 1878, but seemed to notice nothing. His associate Wilkie wrote that Storey "seemed keenly and unfavorably impressed in a persistent environment of gloom."[16]

Storey lived for six more years, sinking deeper and deeper into what became a permanent depression, raging on in his newspaper's columns. His third wife hounded him, demanding changes in their prenuptial agreement that precluded her from receiving most of his estate. Nor did anyone else apparently have any fondness for Storey. With the reputation of a rattlesnake, he was seen as being not only critical—that his former friends could stand—but cruel. Storey died hated and alone in 1884 at age sixty-four.

HOWE

Greeley's crusading and Storey's sensationalism both included anti-Christian components. A third nineteenth-century editor, E. W. Howe, was the first to see his role as that of community educator in atheism. While writing an influential novel, then editing a Kansas daily and a national weekly from the 1870s into the 1930s, Howe "envisioned himself as a man whose mission was to pull the people of Atchison, and readers everywhere, out of the muck of ignorance."[17]

Calling himself a "lay preacher," Howe told newspaper readers that Christianity was "baseless from top to bottom," with "no foundation in history or probability." Howe said the story of Christ's birth and ascent were taken directly from Buddhism and that the Ten Commandments were stolen from the Egyptians. He also wrote that all intelligent folk knew the Biblical stories of creation, original sin, flood, and resurrection were lies, along with all miracles, all prophecies, and all commandments. He told any readers with doubts that they could check those "facts" in the American Cyclopedia, a truer book than the Bible.[18]

Howe had a credo which he put into effect in his own professional and personal life: Selfishness, not Christian belief, is the savior of mankind. He put it into practice in his own family, where an increasingly bitter marriage eventually resulted in a 1901 divorce. Two of Howe's five children died young, and the other three became estranged from their father. But Howe received honorary degrees and much praise, particularly for his "fearless" attacks on Christianity. Yet, when he died in 1937 at age eighty four, his burial service was conducted in a church, as he had requested.[19]

Following Howe's death his son Gene would write in the *Saturday Evening Post* a remembrance of his father entitled, "My Father Was the Most Wretchedly Unhappy Man I Ever Knew." Gene wrote that his father had been "a master of English, a pioneer in literary style, and he had a great wealth of fire and force and enthusiasm." But the son wrote sadly, "I know of no one endowed as he was who accomplished so little."[20]

PULITZER

Greeley crusaded for utopian schemes, Storey sensationalized for circulation and power, Howe proselytized for atheism out of his presuppositions. Joseph Pulitzer became the most famous editor-publisher in the United States during the last quarter of the nineteenth century by combining the three in both St. Louis (from the 1860s to the 1880s) and New York (from then to his death in 1911).

Pulitzer was undoubtedly a genius, with a penetrating intellect, wonderful memory, and superb journalistic instincts. His early years as reporter and editor were happy. But Pulitzer was always looking for love and salvation in all the wrong places. That fruitless search for permanent satisfaction apart from God turned Pulitzer's brilliant promise into one of the great tragedies of American journalism history. Pulitzer's desire to be a god unto himself turned him by 1885 into a man who "exudes the venom of a snake and wields the bludgeon of a bully."[21]

That was the verdict of a competitor. Even Pulitzer's friend and top editor, though, said that Pulitzer was the "best man in the world to have in a newspaper office for one hour in the morning. For the remainder of the day he was a damned nuisance." Wanting to be omnipresent, Pulitzer instructed his editors and reporters to spy on each other and send reports directly to him. He purposefully created overlapping authority so that he would have to be called in to break deadlocks. Pulitzer's system, according to one journalist, "produced in time a condition of suspicion, jealousy and hatred, a maelstrom of office politics that drove at least two editors to drink, one into suicide, a fourth into insanity."[22]

Everyone told Pulitzer to stop worrying, but he could not. One reporter wrote that "When anything went wrong, and things seemed to go wrong with him very often, there would come from his office . . . a stream of profanity and filth." Pulitzer's fellow newspaper editor Henry Watterson noted that "Absolute authority made Pulitzer a tyrant."[23]

Things became worse when Pulitzer gradually became blind during the 1890s. He called himself "the loneliest man in the world." Even his laudatory biographer, however, noted that "the loneliness, although real, was instead the terrible isolation of the helpless megalomaniac and egocentric, the perfectionist who loved to criticize." Pulitzer was separated from his wife and children for most of his last twenty years because he wanted around him only "compliant attendants." His wife often wanted to join him, writing that "You would be much happier my dear Joseph if you would only believe in the friendly intentions & good feeling of the people about you." But Pulitzer raged at her, then complained that he had to eat dinner with "nobody at my table except paid employees."[24]

Pulitzer could never feel loved. He employed hundreds of assistants over the years, always searching for a friend and confidant. Many admired him at first, but later or usually sooner he would turn on them, then write letters such as the following: "How much I would give if I could only deceive myself with the thought that my anxiety to attach you to me as my long lost and longed for friend is not entirely unappreciated." Pulitzer would swear at an assistant, swing a whip at him, and then plead with the assistant to "tell him why he [Pulitzer] was treated so cruelly."

It seems likely that Pulitzer truly wanted God's love but was too proud to acknowledge anyone above him. When Charles Evan Hughes, later to be the Supreme Court's Chief Justice, visited Pulitzer in 1903, he reported that "One would have supposed that Mr. Pulitzer was sitting as the judge of all the earth." For a time Pulitzer sent an atheistic employee to church every week to place a new $5 bill on the offering plate and then leave. Another of Pulitzer's assistants explained, "Mr. Pulitzer has then attended church."[25]

Pulitzer spent his last years sailing constantly in a yacht with seventy-five employees trained to cater to his whims. As one biographer put it, "The yacht represented the logical end toward which the eccentric despot, so concerned with democracy, had been working for decades. It gave him *complete control.* It was an absolute monarchy." But Pulitzer still had no peace of mind, and ended his life agitated by what he called his "constant and manifold failures." Having forsaken God, he was left merely to complain that he had been "forsaken and deserted and shamefully treated by fate." Now, on the days Pulitzer Prizes are handed out, Pulitzer is remembered, and perhaps even loved by the winners.[26]

SCRIPPS

The early professional life of E. W. Scripps—the man who developed a central institution of twentieth-century American journalism, the newspaper chain—also was filled with journalistic joy. Born in 1854, he became city editor of the Detroit *Evening News* at age twenty-one and established America's first effective chain during the 1880s and 1890s. Scripps also extended the Greeley-Pulitzer concept of newspapers as voices of the theological and political left. He called his editorials the "teaching department, the statesmanship department and the spiritual department," said he was not out to make a profit, and made enormous profits before dying aboard his yacht in 1926.[27]

Scripps acknowledged that the Christian ethic in which he had been raised gave him the discipline he needed to be successful: "I believe that . . . in 999 out of every 1,000 of my activities, physical and mental, I am prompted to action or thought, or restrained from action or thought, by what might be called Christian tradition." But Scripps made the typical fallacious distinction between "Christ's Christianity of love" and what the Bible actually said about God's justice and mercy. Scripps never wanted to study Biblical verses in context, because that would be putting God above his own understanding; eventually Scripps wrote straightforwardly, "I do not believe in God, or any being equal to or similar to the Christian's God."[28]

Politically, Scripps became a prominent advocate of socialism; economically, he was a successful capitalist; yet, Scripps was one more person who, looking back late in life, rued his actions. Scripps in 1914 saw "no hope" in socialism. He could see that "socialism is based really upon a spirit of conservatism, of nonproductiveness. The effect of socialism would be that society would not only be satisfied with the knowledge it at present possesses, but that there would be no increase by discovery of new fields of human activity."[29]

Scripps complained further that "The socialist would take possession of the world—material and social—as it exists today, and divide it up into shares, and thereafter have society continue to exist upon the product hitherto accumulated, taking no further step forward into the undiscovered and virgin fields of opportunity." Yet Scripps continued propagandizing for socialism, "despite my will and my reason," because he was "human and normal, and hence weak."[30]

Later he wondered if he had been right in "devoting my energies to denouncing wealth and inspiring the masses to jealousy and revolution." But Scripps also stayed consistent, writing in 1921 an essay, "Wanted—a Tryant," in which he argued that "as Lenin has striven and is still striving to seize and hold power of dictator in Russia, so may we have to depend on some coming strong man." (Edmund Burke's comment on the French revolutionaries comes to mind here: "In the groves of their academies, at the end of every vista, you see nothing but the gallows.") Scripps left to posterity the news service that became United Press International and a maxim for never-ending revolution: "Whatever is, is wrong."[31]

HEARST

William Randolph Hearst was the most powerful journalist of the early twentieth century. Born in 1863 and given the San Francisco *Examiner* by his father in 1887, Hearst moved to New York in

1895 and built a newspaper chain far greater than that of Scripps. By 1935 Hearst controlled 14 percent of daily newspaper circulation nationwide and 24 percent of Sunday circulation. What struck early observers of Hearst and his newspapers, though, was passion as well as money. Early on, Hearst so loved his newspapers that he would examine pages by standing over them and dancing out of sheer pleasure as he turned the pages with his toes.

Hearst, when young, also enjoyed leading his reporters to breaking new stories. The reporters would race to the scene on bicycles or cavalry horses, while Hearst could be seen "leaping wild-eyed and long-legged into a carriage, to be whisked like a field marshall to the scene of battle." Hearst and his editors put out the most exciting newspaper of the late nineteenth and early twentieth centuries, but they rarely moved beyond Wheel of Fortune journalism. Hearst's slogan became, "There Is No Substitute for Circulation," and his practice a mixture of demagogic politics and sensationalism: "Make a great and continuous noise to attract readers; denounce crooked wealth and promise better conditions for the poor to keep readers. INCREASE CIRCULATION."[32]

Hearst made an idol out of circulation, but he also tried making one out of himself. He began instructing his reporters and editors to praise him at every possibility. He began to pose as a benefactor of the poor, sending pale children on jaunts to the beach. A reporter sent to cover one expedition, though, later wrote that she was given only one container of ice cream to be dealt out on a Coney Island trip: "When at last I placed a dab on each saucer, a little fellow in ragged knickerbockers got up and declared that the *Journal* was a fake and I thought there was going to be a riot. I took away the ice-cream from a deaf and dumb kid who couldn't holler and gave it to the malcontent. Then I had to write my story beginning: 'Thousands of children, pale-faced but happy, danced merrily down Coney Island's beaches yesterday and were soon sporting in the sun-lit waves shouting, "God bless Mr. Hearst." ' "[33]

Hearst made sure that his good deeds were surrounded by trumpets for him personally and publicity for his newspaper. His instructions sometimes led to bizarre coverage. When all Hearst writers were ordered to mention "comic supplements" in their stories whenever possible, one reporter noted concerning a disaster scene, "I was the first to reach the injured and dying. 'God bless Mr. Hearst,' a little child cried as I stooped to lave her brow. Then she smiled and died. I spread one of our comic supplements over the pale, still face."

The goal of such efforts was not only to sell newspapers but to get Hearst elected President. When he could not get the Democratic nomination in 1904, he called Judge Alton Parker, the party's nominee, a "living, breathing cockroach from under the sink," and labeled the party's chairman "a plague spot in the community spreading vileness."[34] Hearst began using his New York *Journal* as a club against anyone who did not bow down to him. At one time the newspaper had two thousand names on its S-list (persons to be mentioned only with scorn).

At first Hearst used his growing newspaper chain as a whip to promote his own political and ideological interests, which included the bringing about of a big government-big business partnership; Hearst wrote, in a signed editorial, "Combination and organization are necessary steps in industrial progress. We are advancing toward a complete organization in which the government will stand at the head and be the trust of trusts. It is ridiculous to attempt to stop this development." But, frustrated when he actually saw his vision pushed along during the New Deal, Hearst turned on the man he had endorsed, Franklin Roosevelt, and gave up his dreams of government.[35]

Hearst spent his last decades estranged from wife and family. He lived with actress Marion Davies, who ate dinner with a special servant standing behind her throughout the meal to hold powder, rouge, and lipstick, and another servant to bring Miss Davies' dog "Gandhi" sliced ham or turkey on a silver platter. Hearst's house guests abided by a strict rule: "Never mention death in Mr. Hearst's presence." Orson Welles' movie *Citizen Kane* is too loosely founded on Hearst's life to satisfy an historian, but it nevertheless gives a good sense of the isolation of Hearst's later years as he removed himself from both man and God.[36]

STEFFENS

A seventh journalistic innovator, Lincoln Steffens, was the modern inventor of "muckraking." He exposed the corruption of a dozen municipal governments early in this century and recognized that the problem was not so much particular individuals as a general disposition to sin. Steffens read the Bible and almost seemed ready to bow his head. But he went to church for several years and decided he was superior to those around him. He *was* intellectually (but not spiritually).[37]

Steffens also was aware of the supercilious stares from friends that a Christian conversion would bring. He turned back toward materialism. The political form that materialism took could no longer be liberalism, since he had realized its limitations. He became, instead, a Marxist (of the kind who could be described as "talking revolution and blood—and sucking the guts out of a chocolate eclair impaled on an upright fork"). Steffens became an apologist for the Soviet Union, praising Stalin and others for carrying through "ruthlessly" a plan to change human nature.[38]

The hard-line Communists thought Steffens soft, a playful child of the despised bourgeoisie "wandering among the social battlefields." But Steffens proved himself by turning on a fellow Marxist and former friend, Max Eastman, who had been courageous enough to report accurately on suppression in the Soviet Union during the 1920s and early 1930s. Steffens won Party praise by joining in what Sidney Hook called "a campaign of brutal repressions, slander and character assassination."[39]

Steffens had come a long way. Previously an apostle of man's reason as the glory of existence, he was saying in 1932 that "there comes a time to close our open minds, shut up our talking, and go to it." Steffens praised Stalin's purges when they began in 1934, writing that Stalin had "put sixty or more men to death" because he had wisely realized "that the job was not yet done, that security was not yet secured." Steffens apparently realized his lies and contemplated suicide, but he stayed on the path he had chosen, writing in 1936 that "Poetry, romance—all roads in our day lead to Moscow."[40]

Steffens thought again of God and sin as he sickened, but he continued to maintain that "treason to Communism" would be a "sin," for "Russia is the land of conscious, willful hope." Eastman called Steffens "a pillar of the Stalinist church in America," and Steffens apparently died that way in August 1936. But he must have had some realization of the stakes, for on the last page of his autobiography he also noted, "I have been contending, with all my kind, always against God."[41]

DURANTY

Last of the great journalistic innovators during the 1840-1940 period was the first of the very influential foreign correspondents, Walter Duranty. Covering the Soviet Union for the New York *Times* during the 1920s and 1930s, Duranty was the father of all those who covered the rise to power of Mao in the 1940s, Castro in the 1950s, and the Sandinistas in the 1970s. Similarly, those who apologized for the Communist regime during Ethiopia's state-caused famine during the 1980s merely were following in Duranty's footsteps.[42]

Duranty received a Pulitzer Prize in 1932 for his work's "scholarship, profundity, impartiality and exceptional clarity, and an example of the best type of foreign correspondence." Historial hindsight is not so kind, nor were the few among Duranty's journalist colleagues who were not tied to the left. Duranty's clarity was actually false analogy, as when he acknowledged that the Russian people were anti-revolutionary only because they "are in the position of children at school, who personally might sooner be out at play and do not yet realize that they are being taught for their ulitmate good."[43]

Duranty equated Stalin's opponents with the Ku Klux Klan and wrote that "the peasants by and large at last have begun to realize the advantages offered by the new system, just as a plebe at West Point comes later to admire what at first he found so rigorous." Plebes, of course, are not killed, but neither were resisters to Stalin, according to Duranty. Rather, they could redeem themselves by working in Gulag lumber camps, those "communes" where "the labor demand exceeds the supply" and prisoners have the satisfaction of working "for the good of the community."

Duranty ascended in apologia once the Depression began and more Americans began praising Soviet "full employment." In 1930, discussing Stalin's Five Year Plan, Duranty wrote that there may be problems, but "what does count is that Russia is being speeded up and fermented—and disciplined—into jumping and making an effort." Stalin once again was portrayed as a harsh but kindly teacher, trying to "stir the people up, force new ideas into their heads and make them talk and think and learn despite themselves." Duranty equated the Five Year Plan with the Biblical exodus from Egyptian slavery: "Moses and Aaron can become Lenin and Trotsky, Joshua becomes Stalin."[44]

In 1932 and 1933, though, the Soviet countryside neared collapse in famine. About five million persons probably died in the manner later described by Victor Kravchenko: "Everywhere we found men and women lying prone, their faces and bellies bloated, their eyes utterly expressionless." In Fedor Belov's words, "The people were like beasts, ready to devour one another. And no matter what they did, they went on dying, dying, dying." Alexander Solzhenitsyn later wrote that "long lines of [peasants] dying of famine trudged toward the railroad stations in the hope of getting to the cities . . . but were refused tickets and were unable to leave—and lay dying beneath the station fences in a submissive heap of homespun coats and bark shoes."[45]

Horace Greeley had praised American collectives in the 1840s, but had not covered up small flaws; after a century of progress in journalism, Walter Duranty would praise Soviet collectivization in the 1930s and cover up such murder. Stalin needed Duranty's help, because Stalin was shipping grain to the West in order to get cash to buy machinery for the steel industry; coverage of the famine might have led to protests that could have stopped the big deals. Duranty did help. He not only wrote that "There is no actual starvation or deaths from starvation," but he wrote that those reporters who were trying to tell the truth were concocting a "big scare story." Such was the prestige of Duranty, and the ideological mood of the times, that the honest reporters often had trouble with their editors.[46]

Duranty knew what he was doing. Malcolm Muggeridge, then also a Moscow reporter, remembered Duranty acknowledging in conversation the famine but saying "you can't make omelettes without cracking eggs." Some say that Duranty was bribed or compromised by the Soviets, but it was just as likely that he had made an idol of the Soviet Revolution generally and Stalin specifically; Duranty's favorite expression was, "I put my money on Stalin."[47]

At the end of Duranty's tour of duty in Moscow, he wrote that it had really been a tour of love: "Looking backward over the fourteen years I have spent in Russia, I cannot escape the conclusion that this period has been a heroic chapter in the life of Humanity."[48] Duranty's Pulitzer Prize led to other honors, a well-fed retirement in Southern California during which he continued to worship capital H "Humanity" rather than capital G "God," and a well-attended funeral in the mid-1940s.

Four decades later, books such as James Crowl's *Angels in Stalin's Paradise* and a documentary shown on the PBS show "Firing Line" made Duranty famous once again: This time as an accomplice to mass murder.

CONCLUSION

Proverbs notes that "He who digs a pit falls into it." That often happens, but not always. Justice sometimes requires more than one life span to complete, and poetic justice in this life is sometimes found in poems but not outside.

Nothing can be proved by eight brief biographical sketches or eighty more, but certain lines of sight are suggested. Individuals often held up as among the most prescient of journalists suffered a limitation of vision. They did not become better journalists for stressing only the material, not did they hit upon real solutions. They went on one mistaken, idolatrous crusade after another. They lived and died by ideological myths.

FOUR

MAN'S SUBJECTIVITY *vs.* GOD'S PLUMB LINE

"Objectivity" has been a major goal of twentieth-century American journalism. New York *Times* editor Sydney Gruson demanded "purity of the news columns. Pure objectivity might not exist, but you have to strive for it anyway."[1] Associated Press General Manager Wes Gallagher argued that "all men and women must have a Holy Grail of some kind, something to strive for, something always just beyond our fingertips even with the best of efforts. To the journalists that Holy Grail should be objectivity."[2]

Textbooks and codes of ethics still insist upon "objectivity." Yet, the concept has been under attack since the 1960s, first by fringe groups of "new journalists," now by those thrusting microphones in power-laden corridors. Robert Bazell of NBC, interviewed in 1986, said flatly, "Objectivity is a fallacy. . . . There are different opinions, but you don't have to give them equal weight." Irving R. Levine of NBC noted, "The reporter has got to determine, ultimately, what is valid and what is not." Linda Ellerbee wrote that "There is no such thing as objectivity. Any reporter who tells you he's objective is lying to you."[3]

We will see in this chapter that Christians should side with neither the current objectivists nor the new subjectivists. First, though, we need to examine some basic dictionary definitions of "objective": "Existing independent of mind; emphasizing or expressing the nature of reality as it is apart from personal reflections or feelings." An objective report, clearly, would be one "stressing objective reality as distinguished from subjective experience or appearance." But what is reality?

Look at it this way: An atheist would argue that God, as a product of imagination, has no real place in an objective news report. A Christian would argue that God's existence and sovereignty are objective truth, regardless of an atheist's personal belief in God's nonexistence. Is an objective reporter supposed to treat God as matter of fact (in which case he is joining the theistic side) or matter of opinion (in which case he has assumed the truth of atheism)?

There is a similar debate over what is "fact" and what is not. The *Oxford English Dictionary* defines fact as "A thing done or performed . . . something that has actually occurred or is actually the case . . . truth attested by direct observation or authentic testimony; reality." Typical usage in 1794 was, "The evangelists wrote from fact, not from imagination." That definition goes against the common journalistic tendency today to say that anything dealing with religion is a matter of opinion, not fact. That definition may open our minds to understand the four different phases of objectivity within American journalism history.

PHASE ONE OBJECTIVITY: SPIRITUAL/MATERIAL INTERFACE

Many early American journalists assumed that God is objective reality, with an existence independent of our minds. The first American newspaper, *Publick Occurrences Both Foreign and Domestic,* was filled with statements in which God's "Merciful Providence" was noted as fact, not opinion. Editor Benjamin Harris reported on September 25, 1690, that Plymouth residents "have newly appointed a day of Thanksgiving to God for his Mercy in supplying their extreme and pinching Necessities under their late want of Corn, & for his giving them now a prospect of a very Comfortable Harvest."[4]

Although no one in early American journalism used the term "objective reporting," some editors obviously understood that factuality demanded taking into account the spiritual. The Boston *Recorder* reported that "on a Sabbath, when church members were partaking of the Lord's Supper," members of an "infidel club" went to a nearby creek: "One of them, with the approbation of the rest, administered the Sacrament to dogs."

The *Recorder* did not argue that vicious and unrepentant blasphemers normally die quick and horrible deaths; obviously, some escape physical punishment in this life. But in this case, "on the same evening, he who had done the impious deed was attacked with a violent inflammatory disease; his inflamed eye balls were protruding from their sockets; his tongue was swollen in his mouth;

and he died before morning, in great mental and bloody agony." The *Recorder* saw the horrible death as God's judgment.[5]

Recoveries from illness also were reported as acts of God. One *Recorder* story began with a note that when a ship sank "by the will of Providence" and a merchant lost all he had, his wife "was rendered altogether insane, and that to such a degree, that it was necessary to confine her in order to prevent her from doing herself and others harm."[6]

The wife's insanity continued until her father, who lived one hundred miles away, received a letter describing what had happened, and immediately "gathered together at his house many of the brethren of the Church for the purpose of pleading with God on her behalf. It was a solemn season of united and earnest supplication to the Lord." A few days afterwards the father received a letter saying his daughter had suddenly "sat up in bed . . . in an instant restored to her usual health."

The story concluded, "Here we cannot but notice, in grateful acknowledgement, the goodness and mercy, compassion and faithfulness of that God who has said, 'Call upon me in the day of trouble, I will deliver thee, and thou shalt glorify me'—for that evening and that hour of restoration, were the same evening and the same hour when many were gathered together, and prayer was made unto God for her."[7]

Just as *Recorder* editors knew that few blasphemers died immediately after notorious offenses with inflamed eyeballs protruding from sockets, so they knew that many individuals recover after prayer, but many others die. There is a problem when Christians want so much for God to "do justice" right away that they exaggerate reports of His intervention; God does not need public relations help. But when truly miraculous cures do occur, a *Recorder* editorial writer asked, "Can you rationally draw any other inference" than that of God's sovereignty?

Many early American journalists would have been amazed to hear that those who ignore the spiritual now consider themselves objective. Then, those who ignored the spiritual were considered subjective atheists, allowing their own feelings to overcome what really was there. The Book of Colossians had noted that Christ "is before all things, and in him all things hold together" (1:17). How then could a reporter, in describing reality, not refer to God, the Creator of reality?

Throughout phase one of American objectivity, mentions of God or Providence were not inserted into articles merely for ritualistic purposes. Journalists evidently saw that the world could not be understood apart from a Biblical context. Furthermore, early Christian journalists knew the Biblical view that all of man is fallen and needs regeneration, and that man unaided by God's grace cannot interpret correctly the facts of the universe.

PHASE TWO OBJECTIVITY: STRAIGHTFORWARD MATERIALISM

As Christian journalism was declining midway through the nineteenth century and materialism was becoming dominant, "fact" was redefined to mean only that which was scientifically measurable. Journalists were told to emphasize "Facts; facts; nothing but facts. So many peas at so much a peck; so much molasses at so much a quart." Materialists who wanted to pursue their own desires without thought of morality particularly relished their new "freedom" in journalism, literature and other spheres. Theodore Dreiser enjoyed the journalistic experience he had before gaining novelistic fame: "One can always talk to a newspaper man, I think, with the full confidence that one is talking to a man who is at least free of moralistic mush."[8]

Economic as well as presuppositional reasons backed the materialist trend. Beginning in the 1830s, the "penny press" began pushing for larger and more diversified circulation, which would bring with it the opportunity to raise advertising rates. On some newspapers, avoiding religious offense became critical. Mid-century brought with it development of the Associated Press and an increased push for a lowest common denominator view of news content: Describe who, what, when, and where, but often leave out the why and the how.

As the pressure for journalistic speed increased, reporters found that they could turn out more copy by ignoring deeper questions. Some editors resisted this movement toward superficiality, but others proudly proclaimed that their job was to put out a newspaper, not run a theological debating society. They did not understand that an editor inevitably has to do both.

The new definition of objectivity, as coverage of material alone, also required several assumptions about man and the world. Reporters had to be seen as capable of seeing things as they are. An innocent American Adam, before the fall, would name what had to be named. The world would have to be seen as a generally unmysterious place, with the visible equated with the real. Reporters could believe that what they saw naturally was a rational order, and that their own minds were the standard of authority. This represented a considerable departure from Biblical notions of fallen man and complicated world.

Soon after gaining ascendancy, though, the concept of reporter as camera began to fall apart theoretically and practically. Early in the twentieth century some journalists rebelled against the idea, not because of questions brought forward by Christians, but because of the impact of Marxism and Freudianism. Marx argued that much of what was called objectivity actually was class subjectivity, with one class-bound vision of the world up against another's, thesis *vs.* antithesis. Freud contended that much of what affected individuals was unknown, even to the individuals themselves, so it could not be assumed that judgments were unimpaired.

Economic society and individual psychology were both in flux, journalists came to believe. Christian objective reporting had depended on the understanding that the material/spiritual interface could be understood by man, with God's grace. Materialist objective reporting had grown up with the notion that a stable, easily understandable material world was there for the taking: What you see is what you get. In the twentieth century, it was being said that all was confusion. How could one reporter figure it out and get it down?

PHASE THREE OBJECTIVITY: BALANCING OF SUBJECTIVITIES

Walter Lippmann, probably the most influential newspaper columnist of the twentieth century, was a Marxist in his early years and an admirer of Freudian thought. He used those ideas to become in the 1920s a philosopher of journalism as well. Lippmann was sarcastic about reporters' claims to objectivity, arguing that "For the most part we do not see first, then define; we define first and then see. . . . We pick out what our culture has already defined for us." Lippmann viewed the typical reporter as akin to the traveler who liked trains but did not think it proper to tip station agents and ushers: "His Odyssey will be replete with . . . train escapades and voracious demands for money."[9]

Others during the 1920s had similar scorn for pure fact, whether material or spiritual. Ivy Lee, one of the founders of public relations, said that it was "humanly impossible" to state a fact: "All I can do is to give you *my interpretation of the facts*." Many others came to believe that the journalist could not be a camera, since no one viewpoint could possibly be accurate. Henry Luce, founder of

Time magazine, said, "Show me a man who thinks he's objective and I'll show you a man who's deceiving himself."[10]

"Objectivity" in journalism, therefore, went through its second reconstituting. First, it had been redefined to mean an ignoring of the spiritual; now it had to be redefined to mean an ignoring of part of the material that the reporter himself might observe—for that part might be gained through bias. Instead, the reporter would forego his own reporting in order to assemble as many reports from others as he could.

"Objectivity" could be reached only through a balancing of multiple subjectivities. The outcome might be neither truthful nor accurate, but who knew what accuracy, let alone truth, really was? The important thing is that different points of view would be reflected. The desire to reflect multiple subjectivities, in the eyes of its proponents, was not an invitation to nihilism, but a pluralistic recipe for compromise and harmony. Since a variety of views were strongly held, this belief suggested that probably none of them was right, but all of them might have some truth.

The triumph of theological liberalism in major Protestant denominations occurred at the same time as the development of phase three objectivity in newspapers. This was no coincidence, since the balancing-of-subjectivities mode often suggested that there is no right or wrong, just opinion. The idea of absolute truth existing outside of man could not be taken seriously within phase three objectivity, because that would suggest the existence of real objectivity.[11]

To summarize, phase three objectivity became not a reporting of both material and spiritual, nor a reporting of material only, but a reporting of what a variety of observers thought about material. Phase three objectivity became the journalist's theoretically even-handed reporting of subjective impressions or reactions of participants in an event. Journalists from the 1920s through the 1960s generally did not attempt to hold up the mirror to society. Instead, they urged others to hold up their own mirrors, so that reporters could then describe the funny shapes each mirror produced.

Such subjectivity-balancing objectivity was concretized in the Society of Professional Journalists, Sigma Delta Chi code of ethics. In it, journalists proclaimed that "Truth is our ultimate goal," but "Objectivity in reporting the news is another goal, which serves as the mark of an experienced professional." Such constructions were typical when Bible-based spiritual confidence was lost: Objectivity might become "another goal," but it could not be part of the goal of truth, since truth, while ultimate, was ever receding.[12]

As the number of cities with competitive newspapers declined from the 1920s onward, lowest-common-denominator pluralism and superficiality on the news pages was increasingly seen as essential both to profitability and to community service. It would be neither fair nor smart to upset the apple cart in order to search for better apples. Biblical beliefs generally were excluded from the lowest-common-denominator "consensus," but pietistic Christians tended not to complain.

JOURNALISTIC CRITICISM OF SUBJECTIVITY-BALANCING

Many journalists came to find phase three objectivity frequently boring, occasionally demeaning, and generally purposeless. Boredom tended to set in because the reporter, if he was not to tip his hand, was forced to tell much less than he knew. Specific detail might be damning to one side or the other; the reporter, typically, would have to quote a variety of positions while keeping the more interesting—but biased—story buried in his notebook.

Some reporters became ascerbic about objectivity. Former New York *Times* reporter David Halberstam complained that "objectivity was prized and if objectivity in no way conformed to reality, than all the worse for reality." Douglas Cater put it succinctly: The straight reporter is a "straight-jacket reporter."[13]

A few reporters escaped from the straightjacket by becoming known for "interpretive reporting" or "news analysis." Columnists such as James Reston could claim that they had "a wider vision of our duty," and were learning "to put the event of the day in its proper relationship to the history of yesterday and the dream of tomorrow." But only a favored few could indulge themselves in that way. Most journalists were demeaned, at least in their own eyes and often objectively, as they became delivery boys, used by politicians and others to carry their messages.[14]

Subjectivity-balancing became particularly obnoxious to many liberal reporters during the early 1950s, as Senator Joseph McCarthy gave speeches about 57, then 205, then some other number of Communists in the State Department. The "balancing of subjectivities" approach forced reporters to quote McCarthy, then quote some other "authority" in a sputtering refusal, with the result that fallacious accusations received wide publicity. One reporter concluded that he and others were manipulated "like Pavlov's dogs."

Subjectivity-balancing also tended to create or reinforce, as Edward Jay Epstein has written, the "impression that at the root of political controversy is an intelligent argument between evenly matched opponents—an impression fostered by the articulateness of the opponents." When opponents were not equally articulate, the balancing mode favored, particularly on television, the articulate over the inarticulate.[15]

This proved distasteful because journalists knew that most people do not communicate well in public, and that those who do so generally have considerable practice. Since the articulate often are interview professionals, hired to come across well regardless of the validity of their position, balancing stories often do not get at the truth at all. They only create a seller's market for glibness.

Some journalists did find uses for a subjectivity-balancing approach. Reporters as late as World War Two did not balance comments by Franklin Roosevelt with those of Hitler; American journalistic objectivity, like American political debate, extended only as far as the water's edge. In 1966, though, reporter Harrison Salisbury of the New York *Times* could journey to Hanoi to get the North Vietnamese side of the story. During the remainder of the war, newspapers that wanted to be neutral could refute charges of lack of patriotism with claims of subjectivity-balancing objectivity.

Most journalists forced into stenography were frustrated, though. Subjectivity-balancing satisfied parts of an ingenuous public, but it was unsatisfying to reporters who wanted to express themselves. As an article in *The Public Interest* noted in 1978, "A significant segment of the media has become impatient with its limited information dissemination role. It is not easy and frequently not exciting for an intelligent person simply to report events. The tendency, therefore, has been for imaginative and socially dedicated journalists to go beyond normal reporting in order to seek fuller expression of their talents or social values."[16]

The movement toward fuller expression of social values led in the 1960s to development of an explicitly subjective "new journalism." Magazine writers such as Tom Wolfe, Gay Talese, and (on the extreme) Hunter Thompson wrote themselves and their ideas into their stories, often with startling effect. New journalism stories often seemed more vivid and honest, with a writer's beliefs showing through.

Television stations and established newspapers, however, tended to oppose "new journalism" methodology. Stations by law, and newspapers by practice, had become by the 1960s very careful about giving obvious offense. For mainstream reporters, the "new journalism" officially could become a subject for gossip but not overt imitation.

PHASE FOUR OBJECTIVITY: DISGUISED SUBJECTIVITY

And yet, with subjectivity roaring through America over the past two decades, and each person supposedly an oracle unto himself, journalists inevitably were going to act in ways designed to more fully express their "social values." If they could not do it openly, they would make the world safe for duplicity by doctoring the subjectivity-balancing scales.

Readers and viewers could continue to believe that subjectivity-balancing gave them the opportunity to make up their own minds, but journalists would be sure to *select the evidence and structure the debate* to produce the desired conclusions. To some extent this had always been done in subjectivity-balancing, since no reporter could be completely neutral. During phase three, however, reporters were taught to have so much doubt about their own conclusions that they would not want to push their vision too far.[17]

Since the 1960s, though, journalists have been encouraged to think of themselves as more knowledgeable than the people they cover. Washington *Post* editor Ben Bradlee argued even two decades ago that "Nowadays, when a government expert gives a press briefing on news about economics, missiles, or Africa, there are four or five reporters in the room who know more about the subject than he does." (Maybe the journalists do and maybe they don't, but if they think they do they will write accordingly.)[18] "News analysis" articles became common, and were not always marked as such. As early as 1965 one correspondent was saying, "My instructions are not to write a story unless I can put into it at least some analysis and interpretation."

The 1980s have witnessed an extension of "strategic ritual" (pseudo-objectivity that provides defense against criticism).[19] A key aspect of strategic ritual is choice of sources and selection of quotations. Of half a dozen legitimate spokesmen on a particular issue, reporters can readily pick out one who expresses the reporter's own position. One reporter, Norma Quarles of NBC, has been honest enough to admit that she plays journalistic ventriloquism when she wants to make a point: "If I get the sense that things are boiling over, I can't really say it. I have to get somebody else to say it."[20]

Similarly, of the many statements an opponent may make during an interview, reporters can play up one that will make that opponent look foolish. The upshot is that, once again, a reporter often makes a story conform to the "pictures in his head," just as in the era of straightforward materialism. Now, though, the process can be far more effective, for readers and viewers have become used to thinking they actually are receiving the debate. When such attitudes are imbedded, millions of suckers are born during every minute of airtime.[21]

Some poker-faced reporters continue to proclaim that they merely present "information." Since they do not have to show their hands unless a libel suit results, many readers and viewers never see that they are bluffing. The abortion debate alone provides endless examples of journalistic strategic ritual. As ABC executive producer Av Westin has noted, network abortion stories during the early 1970s followed a formula: First, dramatic photos of bruised, "unwanted" babies, or shots of "a silhouetted woman telling how she nearly died after an illegal abortion"; then, "with the case for legalized abortion powerfully presented, an opponent of abortion would be given a chance to make the prolife side of the case, usually without dramatic pictures, inserted merely as a 'talking head.' "[22]

The game of strategic ritual is often unsatisfying to a reporter, but what alternative does he have? He cannot return to phase one, because he (and his editors) will perceive spiritual matters as grounded in opinion, not fact. He cannot return to phase two, because twentieth-century relativists have seen correctly that no man is a camera. Phase three is increasingly seen as forcing balance where there is none. (Rita Braver, covering health issues for CBS news, skillfully made the argument from absurdity: "When I cover drugs, it would be absurd for me to look for a person who says PCP is good for kids.")[23] Phase four is the last resort.

Yet, he who digs a pit falls into it. Strategic ritual is based on deception, the idea that reporters are smart enough to indoctrinate subtly and the assumption that readers or viewers are too stupid to get angry. But readers and viewers are getting angry, as we will see in the next several chapters. Strategic ritual alienates journalists from the communities they are supposed to serve and exhibits the arrogance that people hate.[24] Unless a reporter has extraordinary gifts or technical backing, readers seeking knowledge of the way the world works will eventually turn away from such contemptuous treatment.

NEW OBJECTIVITY, NEW SERVANTHOOD

There is a Christian solution to the problems of objectivity. It is based on a different understanding of the nature of man, the nature of God, and the nature of man's tasks and man's hopes.

First, the Christian solution is not based on confidence in man. It assumes that fallen man naturally distorts and lies, and it assumes that fallen man's wisdom will slide us even deeper into sin and misery. Objectivity in all its non-Christian phases assumes that the major check on pernicious news twisting is journalistic goodwill. As former Louisville *Courier-Journal* Editor James Pope put it, "Objectivity is a compass for fair reporting, a gyroscope, a little secret radar beam that stabs you when you start twisting news to your own fancy. . . ." But, given man's nature, is such a man-made belief likely to function in that way?

Second, the Christian solution is based on confidence in God's objectivity. God alone, the Christian knows, has given us a Biblical measuring rod built of true, godly objectivity. As the prophet Amos saw, "The Lord was standing by a wall that had been built true to plumb, with a plumb line in his hand." God then told Amos that he was "setting a plumb line among my people Israel" (Amos 7:7, 8). We have that plumb line today, the Bible. Thus, we know what man should do.

Third, the Christian solution is based on man's ability, with God's grace, to study God's objectivity and apply it to everyday situations. Christians know that our hope of arriving at accurate views is not to wipe our minds clean, because then we are at the mercy of our fallen vision, but to fill up our minds with God's vision. Walter Cronkite once said that he was a liberal, which he then defined as one "not bound by doctrines or committed to a point of view in advance."[25] But, given our fallen natures, we are all captive to sin unless we are committed to Christ.

Christians are skeptical of self-generated conclusions but sure of God's. When Christians understand the Bible and are able to apply Biblical principles, then there can be confidence to go beyond subjectivity by responding to problems with God's Word, which is objectivity. Since the Christian presuppositional structure is closer to reality than competing frameworks are, Christians can explain more accurately how the world truly works.

Furthermore, since Christians can measure with God's plumb line, Christians can use all the techniques of phases one, two, and three; there is much that Christians can learn from talented journalists who were philosophically wrong. Since spiritual causes are not always clear, pure material description will be all that is sure in some cases. For example, the Boston *Recorder* reminded readers of the results of Napoleonic ambition by printing, without editorial comment, the following report:

> More than a million bushels of human and inhuman bones were imported last year from the continent of Europe into the port

> of Hull. The neighborhood of Leipsic, Austerlitz, and Waterloo, and all of the places where during the late bloody war the principal battles were fought, have been swept alike of the bones of the horse and his rider, and shipped to England, where steam engines have been erected, with powerful machinery, for the purpose of granulating them. In this condition they are sent chiefly to Poncaster, one of the largest agricultural markets, and sold to farmers to manure their lands.[26]

Just as Christians may use straightforward description of material at times, so Christians may use phase three techniques of quoting various sides fully—as long as the context of actions also is shown, so that the relationship of lying promises and horrible deeds becomes evident.

God's inspired writers quoted adversaries often in the Bible. Almost entire chapters of 2 Kings (18) and Isaiah (36) were given over to the blandishments of a blaspheming Asssyrian general who demands surrender and promises exile to "a land of grain and new wine, a land of bread and vineyards, a land of olive trees and honey." The strategy involved in printing this offer was clear from the context: The Assyrian was merely imitating what God had told the Israelites concerning the land of milk and honey He was offering them in permanence. The Israelites remained silent.

Christian objectivity, then, consists not of a technique but of a plumb line. All kinds of stories can be Christian. Those that end in sadness often teach the wages of sin, those that end well may emphasize the wages of piety, and those that are unclear teach us that much of life is unpredictable and often confusing. Immediate justice often is not forthcoming, except in poetry. Poetic justice tells us what Heaven will be like, but an undue emphasis on good guys always winning might make us believe, falsely, that the present, shattered earth is our real home. Christian journalists like to "see what God is doing today"; they do not necessarily supply the didactic "why." Christian objectivity means having both eyes fastened on God.

CAN THIS BE TRUE OBJECTIVITY?

This type of objectivity will not be satisfying to the atheist. Yet, criticism of Christian objectivity must necessarily assume what it is trying to prove. If an atheist says that a Christian is being subjective by reporting God as reality, the atheist is insisting that God is merely an object of the Christian's consciousness; the atheist is thus assuming, without proof, that atheism is true. If an atheist says that a Christian is wrong to report God's activities as factual, then he is assuming that his own ability to report reality is accurate and the Christian is adding on something.

To the Christian, the atheist is leaving out basic fact due to his spiritual blindness. No easy compromise is possible when such fundamental presuppositions are battling each other. God shows Christians that He exists independently of our minds by acting on our minds from outside. Yet, if a person who had not had that experience is unwilling to accept the testimony of others, and thus assumes internally-generated psychological change rather than God's grace, he will see Christian fact as imagination, and Christian objectivity as subjectivity.

In the long run, journalistic differences between Christians and non-Christians are inevitable.

PART TWO

EXILE

Man without God is a beast, and never more beastly than when he is most intelligent about his beastliness.
(Whittaker Chambers)

FIVE

ETHICS WITHOUT CHRIST?

The hills are alive with the sound of musings. Almost everywhere, it seems, journalists and journalism professors are attending conferences on ethics or writing books on ethics. Some valuable work has illuminated the hazards for reporters in accepting bribes ("freebies"), overt or subtle, or in making up stories.[1] But the discussions of ethics have overlooked some deeper problems.

Part of the impetus for the ethics books and conferences may have come from the shocks to journalism which came in the early 1980s. Novelist John Hersey, writing in a 1980 issue of the *Yale Review*, criticized what he saw as "the great fallacy" of the new journalism, the movement noted in Chapter Four that turned its back on objectivity: "Since perfect objectivity in reporting what the eyes have seen and the ears have heard is impossible, there is no choice but to go all the way over to absolute subjectivity."[2]

Hersey argued that such a view "soon makes the reporter the center of interest rather than the real world he is supposed to be picturing, or interpreting." Events of the following year, though, showed there was more to it than even that: As the reporter became the center of interest the world's actual reality would become less important, with imagination (pretending to honesty) assuming the throne.

The best-known recent episode of journalistic dishonesty involved the awarding in 1981 of a Pulitzer Prize for a Washington *Post* story, "Jimmy's World." The story itself was a series of imaginary events and fabricated quotations about a supposed eight-year-old heroin addict. When *Post* reporter Janet Cooke lied once too often and was found out, the *Post* returned the award, explaining that one of its reporters had victimized the newspaper, and that no editor could be safe from a clever liar.

Some *Post* editors had been suspicious all along. One *Post* reporter drove Cooke through the neighborhood where she claimed Jimmy lived, and saw that she did not know the area. He reported that to the city editor, but there was no investigation. The story, true or false, was just too juicy to pass up. Cooke's editor, Bob Woodward, who was previously best-known for helping to break the story of Watergate, said "Jimmy's World" was "so well-written and tied together so well that my alarm bells simply didn't go off."[3]

Ironically, the prize Cooke had to return was awarded to another article that used what the National News Council called "overuse of unattributed sources" and "reckless and speculative construction." Then, a New York *Daily News* reporter admitted that he had made up "facts" in a column reporting on violence in Northern Ireland; the reporter, in his defense, said he had done the same thing three hundred times before. Meanwhile, the New York *Times* acknowledged that it had published an article about a trip inside Cambodia by a writer who had not gone to Cambodia, and had instead plagiarized passages from a novel written decades before.[4]

Journalists could see part of the problem behind those stories: The movement away from subjectivity-balancing to expression of the reporter's own subjective views, generally through subtle "strategic ritual." Editors tended to react by deploring inaccuracies, pledging to cut down on the remnants of "new journalism," and demanding more substantiation from reporters.

Stories such as "Jimmy's World," however, showed not only problems in "objectivity" as it has been most recently defined, but a lack of compassion. *Post* editors did not respond to readers' pleas to try to find "Jimmy" so that he could be helped. A former editor, Charles Seib, pointed out that *Post* editors would have saved themselves much subsequent recrimination if they had shown some compassion for Jimmy, because in searching for him they would have realized that the story was made up.

Deceptive stories have continued to emerge during the 1980s, along with many conferences decrying ethical "lapses" of journalists. Behind most of those deceptive stories, though, stand reporters who cared little about real people and real problems, and therefore let imagination reign. When John Hersey noted the present and impending triumph of journalistic subjectivity, he could have gone further and spoken of journalistic solipsism, with many reporters writing as if their private pursuit of stories was the only reality, or at least the only one that counts.

Newspaper treatment of Hilda Pate (she now has a new last name) provides a good example of the failure to place compassion for victims above journalistic cheap thrills. A 1982 court case revealed how Pate was abducted by her estranged husband. He came to her office and, at gunpoint, forced her to go with him to their former apartment in Cocoa Beach, Florida. There he beat her repeatedly and forced her to take off all her clothes.[5]

As police closed in Mr. Pate killed himself. The police entered, found Hilda Pate in a state of shock and emotional distress, and rushed her out of the house to a police car in full view of reporters, photographers, onlookers and other policemen. She was still naked, but was clutching a dish towel to her body. The local newspaper, *Cocoa Today*, published a photograph of Hilda Pate, her private parts barely covered by the dish towel. The photograph was distributed across the United States through the news services and published in newspapers throughout the country.

Pate sued for invasion of privacy and won a jury verdict, but a Florida appeals court ruled that the photographs were taken in public during a legitimate news event and showed only what a gawking onlooker at the spot could have seen. Photographers and editors were legally in the clear. According to an angry jury, though, journalists had re-victimized a sad victim, causing her "severe emotional distress and mental pain and anguish."[6]

The Pate case was typical of a pattern emerging in recent years: A victim rescued from an assailant, only to face a new victimizer—the press. For example, in 1980 the Burlington County (N.J.) *Times* printed the name of a rape victim in three separate stories about the rape, despite her request to police that it not be revealed. The victim sued both the newspaper and hospital which had supplied confidential information to reporters. She charged that identification of a rape victim was not necessary to a rape story but reflected "morbid desire." The *Times* defended its action, saying identification by name strengthened the impact of its stories, and the New Jersey Superior Court agreed.[7]

Similarly, a Florida rape victim testified at the 1982 trial of her assailant after receiving assurance by state authorities that her name and photograph would not be published or displayed. A television station, though, videotaped the trial proceedings and ran the rape victim's testimony on its evening news show. While the videotape ran, the newscaster identified the victim by name to the viewing audience. She sued the station for invasion of privacy, but a Florida appeals court had to note that the state, despite its promise to the rape victim, did not try to restrain the videotaping or use of the woman's name. Since the information was readily available to the public, the television station was legally in the clear.[8]

The station *was* an ethical derelict in the eyes of the judge. He let the station off "reluctantly," he wrote, "because the information disclosed during the television broadcast appears to us to have been completely unnecessary to the story being presented. Withholding the name and photograph of the victim in this case would in no way have interfered with or restricted publication of 'news of the day.' " He asked that journalists think about the "individual rights of others."[9]

Judge Campbell also noted the price of journalistic license: "The rape victim," he wrote, "had the unhappy circumstance of becoming a victim of a crime. The publication added little or nothing to the sordid and unhappy story; yet, that brief little-or-nothing addition may well affect appellant's well-being for years to come." The judge was not calling for courts to be closed, nor should Christians generally. Biblically, court proceedings generally were open. Yet, Campbell was asking for compassion. He deplored "the lack of sensitivity to the rights of others" evident among many journalists.[10]

A 1982 Supreme Court decision spotlighted that widespread lack of sensitivity. The Massachusetts legislature, hoping to protect the privacy of minor rape victims, had passed a law excluding the public from sexual assault trials during the testimony of victims under eighteen years of age. The Boston *Globe* wanted its reporters to be present for the victims' testimony during a trial in which the defendant was charged with raping three minor girls. The trial judge said no. The Supreme Judicial Court of Massachusetts refused to issue an injunction and later dismissed the *Globe*'s appeal.[11]

The *Globe* kept pushing, and finally found powerful protectors. In 1982 Justice Brennan and six other U.S. Supreme Court Justices overturned the Massachusetts ruling. Brennan wrote that the press could be barred only under "narrowly tailored" situations when "necessitated by a compelling government interest." Brennan wrote that the First Amendment did not "explicitly" justify the Supreme Court's ruling, "but we have long eschewed any 'narrow, literal conception' of the Amendment's terms."[12]

Former Chief Justice Warren Burger dissented, writing that the legislation was justified in trying "to prevent the risk of severe psychological damage caused by having to relate the details of the crime in front of a crowd which inevitably will include voyeuristic strangers." In most states, that crowd may be expanded to include a live television audience, with reruns on the evening news. That ordeal could be difficult for an adult; to a child, the experience can be devastating and leave permanent scars. Burger concluded that Brennan's opinion showed a "cavalier disregard of the reality of human experience."[13]

The cavalier disregard goes beyond coverage of rape. As we will see in Chapter Ten, nineteenth-century journalists at times would cover "successful" suicide attempts after they had happened, with the hope of trying to show others that suicide was brutal and nonheroic. Recently, though, some journalists have not acted to prevent suicides, and by their presence have even urged on those aspiring to a brief moment in the headlines.

One notorious instance "starred" a newspaper photographer in Oregon. He could have helped a woman on a bridge who was desperately gripping her husband in an attempt to restrain him from jumping one hundred feet into the Columbia River. The photographer, instead of grabbing on, took five pictures. The man broke loose from his wife and jumped to his death in the river.[14]

A well-publicized episode in 1983 began when a man called television station WHMA in Anniston, Alabama, to say that he planned to set fire to himself in a nearby town square at midnight. The station's news director dispatched a camera crew. When the news team arrived no one was visible, but when the cameraman climbed out of his car the apparently drunken man approached, poured charcoal-starter fluid over himself, lit a match, and started the fire. The cameraman continued to film as the burning began, but an eighteen-year-old who had a part-time job with the station did try to beat out the flames. The man survived, with serious burns.[15]

Some journalists expressed concern over that episode, and several others. Some attention was paid to the tale of a television camera crew following a man trying to pay a ransom to persons who had kidnapped his wife. Despite the man's pleas, the crew kept coming and—according to the FBI—"put that woman's life in danger." The newspaper trade magazine *Editor and Publisher* editorialized that the TV crew had been practicing not "enterprising reporting" but "sheer stupidity. . . . It is this sort of arrogance and brashness that gets media in trouble with the public."[16]

Overall, with ethics conferences wading in humanistic homilies, many non-Biblical journalists still were like Pavlov's dogs, salivating whenever the story bell sounded. This was certainly the public perception of the occupation. According to a survey by the American Society of Newspaper Editors, 78 percent of Americans believe that news reporters "are just concerned with getting a good story, and they don't worry much about hurting people." In the same study, 63 percent said that "the press often takes advantage of victims of circumstance who are ordinary people."[17]

That popular mood has contributed to vigorous criticism and occasional boycotts of local newspapers that print names of rape victims. The Commission on Women of Arlington, Virginia, asked readers to cancel their subscriptions to the *Northern Virginia Sun*, which had a policy of identification by name. The Durham, North Carolina, Rape Crisis Center picketed the Durham *Morning Herald* after it named a rape victim in a front-page story.

Some newspaper editors hit back, though. Michael Rouse of Durham argued that opponents to the printing of names were "seeking to coerce the free press." He wrote that the protesters "believed divine guidance was on their side," and added that "newspaper editors lacking the benefit of divine guidance usually call upon their own objective judgment when deciding such matters."[18]

Rouse apparently was sarcastic, but the difference between man's best "objective judgment" and divine guidance is clear. Many newspapers do not print names of rape victims, but others do. Major journalistic codes of ethics do not cover the question. Legally, newspapers covering details of rape are generally in the clear. One U.S. Circuit Court of Appeals decreed in very broad language that a reporter's privilege "extends to information concerning interesting phases of human activity." Man's judgment tends to approve of publishing whatever seems interesting.[19]

Real divine guidance, that found in the Bible, is very different. Yes, many things are interesting: "The words of a gossip are like choice morsels; they go down to a man's inmost parts" (Proverbs 18:8). Nevertheless, in Proverbs we are often told to be careful about what we report, for "When words are many, sin is not absent, but he who holds his tongue is wise" (10:19). Subsequent chapters of Proverbs note similarly that "a man of understanding holds his tongue," and that "He who guards his lips guards his soul, but he who speaks rashly will come to ruin" (11:12; 13:3).

The Bible often contrasts those who emphasize the educational with those who blurt out the merely interesting. Proverbs teaches that "A man of knowledge uses words with restraint" (17:27), but "He who winks maliciously causes grief, and a chattering fool comes to ruin" (10:10). Thoughtless reporting may have physical consequences: "A fool's lips bring him strife, and his mouth invites a beating" (18:6). It also may have consequences for a community: "A perverse man stirs up dissension, and a gossip separates close friends" (16:28). The reporter himself may suffer the spiritual consequences: "A fool's mouth is his undoing, and his lips are a snare to his soul" (18:7).

Development of a Biblical standard for coverage of rape trials involves three questions of increasing specificity. First, should information about the trials be available to the public? Second, should specific detail from testimony be published? Third, should victims be identified?

On the first question, Biblically the presumption is that most trials should be open to the public. Trials in the Bible were generally conducted by "elders at the gate," a prominent and public passageway (Deuteronomy 21:19; 22:15; 25:7-9; Ruth 4:1, 11).

On the second question, the Bible's refusal to shy away from harsh reality shows that depiction of evil can be useful, *if context is provided*. The Winfield, Kansas, *Daily Courier* was criticized for reporting testimony that after intercourse with one victim (unnamed) the rapist "entered her rectum." Publisher David Seaton, though, argued that citizens needed "to know how severe rape cases are. . . . It seemed to me that there was a sound case to be made for having people face the harsh realities."[20]

The third question, on naming the victim, highlights the question of compassion. Victims generally are powerless during a rape to control what is happening to them. Identification in a news story may be a second assault on privacy, a second situation in which the victim feels powerless to protect herself from consequences such as humiliation, embarrassment, and possible danger. Biblically, we are to have compassion toward widows, orphans, and others who are abandoned or left destitute in a variety of ways. Biblical compassion certainly is owed to rape victims.

The word *compassion*, however, "makes a lot of journalists squirm," according to former reporter Gene Goodwin: "It describes a condition that runs counter to the strong tradition in journalism of detachment." Harvard University's James C. Thomson wrote that among leading journalists taking sabbaticals under his supervision, "What is usually lacking is empathy or compassion for their subjects, those reported about, or even token nods toward those qualities." Robert Maynard, editor of the Oakland *Tribune*, noted that "when people see a TV person shoving a mike in front of a grieving relative," journalists "appear to be boorish and ghoulish." Appearances in this case may not be deceiving.[21]

Again, there are many newspapers that do not print names of rape victims, but—unless the person raped is of great prominence—it is hard to see *any* situation in which identifying the victim is vital. Possible apologia for printing names (for example, making the story more "real" for readers) are underwhelming in comparison to the detriments of such action.

The details of re-victimization are sad. When one newspaper printed the name of a rape victim without her consent or knowledge, her son learned about his mother's rape through taunting by his playmates. Not only more shame for the victim, but more physical danger as well, may be by-products of journalistic arrogance. Rape victims are far more liable to be threatened again than are victims of other crimes, if their names are revealed in newspapers.

Why, then, do journalistic codes of ethics not prohibit such noncompassionate treatment? To get at that answer, an apparent digression is in order: Comparison of the openness to naming rape victims with the blanket prohibition against identification of confidential sources.

The American Newspaper Guild's Code of Ethics states flatly, "The newspaperman shall refuse to reveal confidences or disclose sources of confidential information in court or before judicial or investigative bodies." The Society of Professional Journalists, Sigma Delta Chi Code of Ethics also presents "the newsman's ethic of protecting confidential sources of information." Journalists have frequently protested attempts by judges to make them reveal the names of sources with knowledge of crimes.

Journalistic organizations have made passage of "shield laws" (statutes protecting journalists) a top priority. They note that reporters vulnerable to subpoena might lose access to important information that helps them in performance of a "watchdog" function. They say a closet whistleblower with knowledge of official misconduct but concern for keeping his job might be unlikely to cooperate with a journalist for fear that his identity will be made public. They fear that other sources fearing identification would "dry up." They fear harassment of newspapers by subpoena-wielding officials. All of these concerns have some validity.

There is another side, though. Criminal defendants have an explicit Sixth Amendment right to compel the attendance of witnesses who could provide helpful information. Furthermore, courts and police like to prevent future crimes and catch fugitive felons. As Justice Byron White once put it, "We cannot seriously entertain the notion that the First Amendment protects a newsman's agreement to conceal the criminal conduct of his source, or evidence thereof, on the theory that it is better to write about crime than to do something about it."[22]

The Bible in its newspaper-less age, of course, never delved into the particulars of such questions, but it does provide clear principles. First, occupation does not allow a reporter to turn his back on crime: "If a person sins because he does not speak up when he hears a public charge to testify regarding something he has seen or learned about, he will be held responsible" (Leviticus 5:1).

Second, there is a strong presumption in favor of open accusation that allows witness and defendant to confront one another, and there is a requirement that at least two sources of indictment are necessary: "One witness is not enough" (Deuteronomy 19:15-18). Good reporters today should refuse to report without attribution accusations against or evaluations of a named person by a non-named "source." If they choose to use confidential material, it should be only to develop leads on stories and witnesses who will testify openly.[23]

Third, reporters can minimize problems by evaluating carefully all motives for requesting anonymity and fighting hard to have everything on the record. As Leviticus 5:4 notes, a person should not "thoughtlessly" take an oath "in any matter one might carelessly swear about." The books of Matthew (5:37) and James (5:12) both contain the essential lesson for reporters and many others: "Let your 'Yes' be 'Yes', and your 'No,' 'No.' "

When the reporter does promise confidentiality he should keep his promise, even at the cost of going to jail, for the honest person "keeps his oath even when it hurts" (Psalm 15:4). The Biblical presumption, though, is that such promises might only be given in very rare circumstances, and with full knowledge of the possible consequences. Shield laws that promise immunity from hurt may be easy ways out.

The Biblical presumption against reportorial immunity does not mean that state officials should be free to harass reporters or use them as spies. Justice generally does not require that journalistic sources be revealed. Yet, when the only way to prove that the defendant is innocent is to have the reporter testify, or when all alternative sources of obtaining information concerning a crime have been exhausted, then a reporter's claim to privilege becomes an assertion that his relations with sources are more important than the life or liberty of others.

CONNECTIONS

Some journalists, as we have seen, do not hesitate to publicize the names of rape victims. Most reporters, though, refuse to give police information relevant to crimes given them by sources. Why so much agony about protecting those sources and not the victim of rape?

One reason is that of the simple business decision: Protection of source yields future stories; protection of subject brings no dividends. It is the nature of man to use and discard others, in this case probably forgetting about them except as a press clipping or a film clip.

But a second reason proceeds from humanistic emphasis on man-made law and on ethics apart from Christ. The problems of the first emphasis are obvious: Law deals with short-term "can" and "cannot," not "should" and "should not" nor even the long-term implications of legal but unwise actions. The dangers of the second emphasis are more subtle: We might think that training the mind in "ethical reasoning" will create a higher standard of thought and conduct. The Bible, though, tells us that man's fallen mind will always be able to draw conclusions that appear logical, responsible—but wrong.

Paul said it succinctly: Our minds, without God's grace, "are darkened in their understanding" (Ephesians 4:18). Paul also explained to the Romans, "The mind of sinful man is death . . . the sinful mind is hostile to God. It does not submit to God's law, nor can it do so" (Romans 8:6, 7). Some commentators on these and other verses have made suggestions that media ethicists should take to heart. Gresham Machen noted that "Sin is not the brute in us; it is, rather, the man in us," and Augustus Strong suggested that "Every man, so far as he is apart from God, is morally insane."[24]

The production of "justifiable actions" is easy, because man is ingenious enough to justify all manner of activities. As one popular song described a murderous decision, "Do it in the name of justice. You can justify it in the end." Obviously, public opinion has some effect on what individuals do or do not do; many newspapers do not print names of rape victims. Journalists who arrive at justifications, though, feel hampered by such pressures, and sometimes look for ways around them. As Jesus said, "Out of the heart come evil thoughts, murder, adultery, sexual immorality, theft, false testimony, slander" (Matthew 15:19).

How do we overcome ethical anarchy? The media ethics textbook opposes "the imposing of moral principles," since that "shortcircuits the analytical process." But shortcircuiting our fallen analytical process is the only way we ever come to a godly analysis rather than our own self-serving justifications. We may claim that we are without sin and capable of coming to righteous conclusions through our own reasoning power, but John noted that in saying so "we deceive ourselves" (1 John 1:8, 10). The same message is clear in 1 Corinthians: "The man who thinks he knows something does not yet know as he ought to know" (8:2). Without God's mercy, we are dead in our transgressions and sins; we must ask Him graciously to make us alive through Christ (Ephesians 2:1, 4, 5).

We are not even able to think wisely of long-term consequences when we are dead in our sins; we tend toward short-term gratification and protection. For example, those shield laws that restrict a judge's ability to apply pressure to a recalcitrant reporter could have a long-term cost: Governments would have to "define those categories of newsmen who qualified for the privilege."[25] Shield laws, by giving the state power to sanction some and not others, could lead to that governmental control over the press which many journalists rightfully wish to avoid.

We can learn to act ethically, and wisely, only by first having our hearts changed, and by then following Biblical example. In Matthew 18, Jesus uses a parable about forgiveness to show the source of all deeply motivating compassion. He explains that "the kingdom of heaven is like a king who wanted to settle accounts with his servants. As he began the settlement, a man who owed him ten thousand talents [several million dollars] was brought to him. Since he was not able to pay, the master ordered that he and his wife and his children and all that he had be sold to repay the debt."

The parable continues: "The servant fell on his knees before him. 'Be patient with me,' he begged, 'and I will pay back everything.' The servant's master took pity on him, canceled the debt and let him go. But when that servant went out, he found one of his fellow servants who owed him a hundred denarii [a few dollars]. He grabbed him and began to choke him. 'Pay back what you owe me!' he demanded. "His fellow servant fell to his knees and begged him, 'Be patient with me, and I will pay you back.' "

The first servant refused: "Instead, he went off and had the man thrown into prison until he could pay the debt. When the other servants saw what had happened, they were greatly distressed and went and told their master everything that had happened. Then the master called the servant in. 'You wicked servant,' he said, 'I canceled all that debt of yours because you begged me to. Shouldn't you have had mercy on your fellow servant just as I had on you?' In anger his master turned him over to the jailers until he should pay back all he owed."

Compassion comes through our thankfulness for the Master's mercy and our following of that merciful pattern when we deal with others. Relying on the law (which requires payment of such debt) or our own devious ethical analysis is of no avail. Yet, we are unwilling and unable to act rightfully until God transforms our hearts through His saving grace. Journalistic ethics without Christ means arrogance and hypocrisy.

Time spent in most non-Christian ethics conferences would be better spent in reading the Bible and, through God's grace, learning who we are. Christians can benefit from discussion of practical applications of Biblical truth at Christian ethics conferences, but each of us also must apply David's words in Psalm 51 to our specific situations: "Have mercy on me, O God, according to your unfailing love. . . . For I know my transgressions, and my sin is always before me. . . . Surely you desire truth in the inner parts; you teach me wisdom in the inmost place. Cleanse me with hyssop, and I will be clean. . . . Then I will teach transgressors your ways, and sinners will turn back to you."

By reading the Bible and realizing our own sin, we might develop the self-awareness of a New Englander named Shanghai Pierce who moved to Texas, built a great ranch, and in his retirement hired a sculptor to memorialize him in a giant bronze statue set out in the pasture. The story is that Pierce would ride by on horseback, doff his sombrero politely, and say to the statue, "Morning, Shanghai, you old cow thief."

Few journalists are like Shanghai Pierce. Many know the law better than their own selves. The result of journalistic emphasis on externals has been the digging of the deep pit that will be described in the next two chapters.

SIX

LIBEL: UTILITARIAN JUSTICE *vs.* BIBLICAL TRUTH-TELLING

Money talks. Big-money court settlements are talked about. Fascination with cash changing hands has made libel law a hot topic among journalists. "Did you hear about the $4.5 million verdict against the San Francisco *Examiner*?" "What about the $9.2 million verdict that forced the *Telegraph* into bankruptcy court?" According to the Libel Defense Resource Center, before 1980 a jury had awarded over $1 million to a defendant only once. Since 1980 there have been more than two dozen of those awards, averaging over $2 million each.[1]

There is more to the money question than court-ordered settlements. Many press organizations lose when they win. When CBS attacked General William Westmoreland, he sued. CBS spent $6 million in lawyers' fees before Westmoreland gave up, realizing he could not *prove* that CBS had willfully lied. ABC spent about $7 million on another case. *Time* magazine survived the suit of Israel's Ariel Sharon, but at a cost of $3 million. Plaintiffs also pay: Westmoreland and his supporters spent $4 million in a fruitless search for vindication.[2]

Journalists see big defamation suits as "horror stories," but when the telescope is turned around, there is horror in what some publications have done. Healthy individuals have been said to have leprosy, venereal disease, or mental illness. A baton-twirling Miss Wyoming sued after a baton-twirling character with that title was depicted as sexually promiscuous and immoral. *Hustler* magazine lied in depicting Jerry Falwell as an incestuous drunkard.[3]

Some journalists cite instances of libel claimants who seemed more interested in political advantage or monetary gain than in justice. More impressive, though, are the number of instances of libel claimants being doubly abused—first by publication of defamatory falsehood, and second by the reaction of journalists when the claimants complain. According to a University of Iowa survey, many individuals seeking corrections or apologies are chased out of newspaper offices, with reporters screaming obscenities after them. No surprise, the Chicago *Tribune*'s city editor noted: "The rudeness in this business is legendary."[4]

Journalists who are neither reckless nor rude also are harmed by their defamatory brethren. Libel insurance rates for many newspapers doubled during 1986. One family-owned group of seven small newspapers in eastern Tennessee has never lost a lawsuit. Only one current case is requiring a lawyer. Yet, the newspaper's premiums for 1986 were increased by 99 percent. A small Christian magazine that has never had a libel suit cannot find even minimal libel insurance for less than $10,000.[5]

Libel has become such a deep pit for journalists that many are wondering about the continued existence of independent journalism. Soaring litigation costs threaten to put some publications out of business. Other publications are becoming so fearful of any possibility of libel that their editors look for soft soap rather than hard-hitting coverage. Independent journalism also is threatened by those suggesting government regulation of newspaper content, with the goal of bringing about "fairness" but more likely to introduce a form of state censorship.[6]

Three major nonlegal answers to the libel crisis, and many minor ones, are trotted out regularly.

First, some continue to propose development of national and local "news councils," groups of citizens that would, in a nonjudicial setting, listen to complaints about media coverage. If the news councils were to find media fault, potential litigants would feel vindicated and news organizations could publish retractions or corrections.

News council proposals have a lot going for them, since some defamed individuals (according to the University of Iowa study) are mainly looking for a way to have their names cleared quickly. But only a few news organizations have supported the news council approach. Many legitimately fear outside involvement in their editorial processes. Many wonder about self-appointed memberships of news councils. From the plaintiff side, the news council alternative is less satisfactory than efficient judicial proceedings would be, because news councils have no authority to enforce judgments or award damages.[7]

Second, some editors continue to advocate self-policing by journalists, with the emphasis on making full and immediate corrections whenever there is doubt about accuracy or fairness. But in the absence of spiritual changes among reporters and editors, the arrogance of newsroom power may make self-policing a delusion. A *Washington Journalism Review* article suggested that reporters "should be more polite, respectful, long-suffering and never even a bit arrogant, no matter how overbearing, boorish or criminal the abusive slob on the other end of the phone may be." As long as there is a tendency to think of the complainant, who may have been smeared unfairly, as an "abusive slob," not much will change.[8]

Third, some predict that changing policies of libel insurance companies will have an effect. The largest libel insurer now requires news organizations to pay 20 percent of all legal fees and expenses above the deductible, generally $2,500 to $20,000, depending on newspaper size. Insurance companies believe that co-insurance rules will force news organizations to keep a tighter rein on their legal firms' expenses, and will also encourage some quick out-of-court settlements.

The new libel insurance policies may change the behavior of some media litigants. Many news organizations have had no-settlement policies, contending that their refusal to compromise would deter frivolous suits and show a willingness to fight for truth to the last dollar (the insurance company's dollar, that is). Now that news organizations have to share the costs, industry leaders such as the Los Angeles *Times* risk manager say that when the going gets tough, "We'll find a way to settle." The drawback, though, is that financial compromise will not bring reputational restitution. Plaintiffs and their lawyers may walk off with some cash, but they will not have what the University of Iowa survey indicates some most want: A clear judicial statement that they were wronged.[9]

At journalistic conventions and meetings, other partial "solutions" have been discussed. Sooner or later, though, almost everyone comes back to the current state of libel law. That is an unhappy subject—a *Journalism Quarterly* article has decried "the disarray that is libel law today"—but an inescapable one. Courts are the only institutions with authority to present judgments and enforce penalties, and it is to the courts that we must now turn.[10]

DIGGING THE PIT

A 1964 Supreme Court decision, *New York Times v. Sullivan*, opened the door for disarray. The Court decided that a public official could no longer win a libel case by showing that published defamatory falsehood had injured his reputation. Justice William

Brennan, writing for the majority, specified that the plaintiff could win only by proving that the published story "was false, *and* that it was made with knowledge of its falsity or in reckless disregard of whether it was false or true."[11]

The "and" was key: Brennan was breaking with centuries of English and American common law tradition. Previously, defamatory falsehood by journalists always was potentially punishable, unless it was a generally accurate account of a public proceeding or record, or unless it was opinion based on facts truly stated (most opinions by their nature are not provably true or false). But Brennan was trying to transform what had been issues of right and wrong into utilitarian questions of the greatest good for the greatest number: How do we balance competing claims in order to protect press freedom?

Brennan's expressed concerns had some validity. He wanted to prevent government from using civil libel penalties to inhibit journalists who did have legitimate criticism of public officials. If reporters were to need full factual documentation to criticize officials, and if those officials withheld necessary facts or had the power to do so, then truth-telling would be hamstrung. But Brennan went further, arguing that even stories that could be proven false should be legally permissible as long as they concerned public officials. (Some errors might result in the process, but if omelets are to be made, eggs must be cracked.)

A majority of Justices agreed: After *Sullivan*, journalists could print defamatory falsehoods about public officials and rest easy, unless it could be *proven* that the journalists had deliberately lied. That was extremely difficult to do, unless the journalist had been foolish enough to proclaim before many witnesses, or in his notebooks, an intention to lie. There was also the "reckless disregard" clause to fall back on, but the Supreme Court soon interpreted that to mean "something much more than gross negligence; reckless disregard . . . approaches the level of deliberate fabrication" and "must reflect a conscious awareness of probable falsity." In other words, recklessness had to include malice.[12]

One law professor praised Brennan's decision for its willingness to uphold "the strategic sacrifice of some deserving plaintiffs to the more important, at least to society as a whole, goals of the first amendment."[13] That law professor, like a high priest two thousand years ago, evidently believed that it was right for one man to be defamed for the good of the people. But others have asked: Is this fair?

For instance, why did Leonard Damron have to be sacrificed?

Shortly after the *Sullivan* decision, a Florida newspaper falsely reported that Leonard Damron, small city mayor and candidate for tax assessor, was indicted for perjury in a local court. The indicted man actually was Leonard's brother, James, with whom Leonard had no official or business connections. Leonard Damron lost the election and convincingly showed harm to his business. A jury found libel. The Supreme Court let off the newspaper with no penalty at all, since the defamatory article related to qualifications of a public official and candidate for public office, and deliberate lying could not be proven.[14]

Was it good for Leonard Damron to be defamed for the good of the people? The Supreme Court said yes. But if Damron must be sacrificed, why not others? Looking through some recent cases, we see that public officials who have been sacrificed for the good of the people include a waterworks auditor, a county motor pool administrator, a county airport board member, and a county social worker.[15]

Was it good for those minor public officials to be sacrificed for the good of the people? If the answer is yes, what about "public figures," prominent individuals outside of government? The Supreme Court, in several early 1970s cases, declared that "public figures" also would have no recourse when they were victimized by published falsehoods, unless they could prove malicious lying.[16]

Again, looking through some recent cases: Public figures sacrificed for the good of the people include officers of a taxpayers' association involved in a controversy over an appropriation for a new firehouse; a person who circulated a petition regarding a voter referendum on county land acquisition and purchased newspaper ads concerning it; a member of a civic organization who wrote a letter to a newspaper editor concerning a public issue; and a physician who participated in a public debate concerning fluoridation.[17]

Some of the cases seemed particularly unjust, and particularly likely to inflame public resentment of news media. For example, the major figures in the taxpayers' association controversy were Alonzo Lawrence and James Simpson, two senior citizens who in 1974 were volunteer president and secretary-treasurer respectively of the Rahway (New Jersey) Taxpayers Association. Rahway municipal authorities wanted to build a new firehouse, but Lawrence and Simpson led a successful campaign to get over five thousand signatures on petitions requesting a referendum on appropriations for the firehouse.

It turned out that some of the signatures were illegitimate for reasons such as a husband signing for his wife or vice versa. Typically during petition drives many signatures are thrown out for such reasons. But this time, an inexperienced reporter on the Rahway *News-Record* thought she had a scoop, and the following headline resulted: "Forgery Charges May Loom for Lawrence, Simpson." A New Jersey jury found that headline and the accompanying story falsely defamatory, but the New Jersey Supreme Court decided that both Lawrence and Simpson were public figures who would have to prove actual malice or reckless disregard (in the sense of premeditated misstatement rather than mere incompetence).[18]

New Jersey Supreme Court Justice Schreiber filed a dissenting opinion, arguing that, because of the majority's decision, "Two highly motivated senior citizens are left without redress for libelous publications holding them up to contempt and ridicule in the community in which they have lived for many years. This is the result of their sincere attempt to participate in local government." But the U.S. Supreme Court refused to hear their case, as only Justice William Rehnquist was willing to grant review.[19]

Those who placed public officials and public figures in journalistic free fire zones were not entirely indifferent to their fate. Judges suggested that such individuals could use their positions or community prominence to defend themselves against false charges. It turned out, though, that some public officials or public figures had that capacity, but many did not. Lawrence and Simpson did not have much beyond a mimeograph machine to use in clearing their names. Even a major public official or public figure could be a big fish in a small barrel when "60 Minutes" comes shooting. Slowly, even some utilitarians started complaining about the inequity of governments protecting certain classes of individuals and not others.

FALLING INTO THE PIT

The questions were being raised, but many journalists were sanguine, until one other problem developed.

When the Supreme Court announced its *Sullivan* decision in 1964, philosopher Alexander Meiklejohn predicted that journalists freed from many libel concerns would be "dancing in the streets." It appeared to columnist Anthony Lewis and others that few public officials (and, later, public figures) would be foolish enough to bring suit: What reasonable individual faced with the difficulty of proving what Justice Brennan had defined as "actual malice"—that subjective intention to lie—would want to waste time and money? Even if someone made the effort, it appeared inevitable that judges would see the scanty evidence and make summary dismissals. Even if judges should allow jury trials, juries composed of reasonable men and women would learn the Court's easy-to-remember code words—"absence of malice"—and refuse to convict.[20]

There remained only one threat to journalists within the Brennan dispensation: What if plaintiffs, juries, lawyers, and even some judges were not reasonable? If plaintiffs went against the odds and actually tried to prove malice, then legal costs could become much greater than under the old system of truth or falsehood. After all, it does not take long to read and analyze a newspaper article; but if it is necessary to read through long files and take depositions on comments made and states of mind, legal bills mount. When lawyers have hourly rates of $190 to $250 in New York and San Francisco, or $80 to $125 in smaller markets, the bills mount fast.

The threat became reality, for four reasons.

First, many defamed individuals did not give up. They continued to bring suit, despite the odds against them imposed by the proof-of-malice gauntlet. The University of Iowa study showed how desperate many plaintiaffs are: "They know that victory is unlikely, and that the final decision is likely in any event to be ambiguous and distant." But they still sue, and not for money, according to the study: "Money is rarely the reason for suing. They sue to correct the record and to get even."[21]

Second, some juries showed their respect for attempts by defamed individuals to win despite the *Sullivan* odds. Realizing that "malice" was not provably present, they still refused to accept the idea that a writer or editor could get away with character murder. Such "runaway juries" found news organizations guilty and stipulated large awards to defendants. The verdicts generally would be thrown out by judges and appeals courts, but only after greatly increased legal costs. For instance, one Texas appeals court overturned a $2 million jury award against the Dallas *Morning News*, finding that the jury had acted out of "passion and prejudice against newspapers." As law professor Marc Franklin put it, juries are "manifesting general community resentment by imposing liability."[22]

Third, with runaway juries seeking a way to keep producers of defamatory falsehood from going free, trailblazing (or money-hungry) lawyers emerged. They began finding ways to circumvent restrictions on libel cases. Some brought right-to-privacy actions known as "false light." Others asserted that publications had unjustly enriched themselves by violating the property right that an individual holds to his own name. American ingenuity also came up with breach of implied warranty cases (a newspaper cheating its customers by representing as true information that which is false).[23]

Fourth, some judges, fascinated by jury uprisings, further encouraged such legal guerrilla warfare through their reluctance to issue summary judgments in libel cases. When Chief Justice Warren Burger chastised some judges in 1979 for being too quick to dismiss libel suits, the reluctance to issue summary judgments became general. More libel cases survived infancy. More legal bills accumulated. A 1986 Supreme Court decision, *Anderson v. Liberty Lobby*, tried to plug the hole in the dike by expanding a judge's discretion in making summary judgments, but the result of the new change is still unclear.[24]

With four squads of irregulars—angry plaintiffs, sympathetic juries, resourceful lawyers, and even some curious judges—not giving up in the face of *Sullivan* and its follow-up cases, news organizations and their insurers began suffering great financial losses. Cries of "if only" could be heard: If only plaintiffs would keep cool, if only jurors would abide by the *Sullivan* decision, millions of dollars could be saved. But a Biblical verse well describes the irony of initial journalistic praise for the *Sullivan* decision, and later concern: "If a man digs a pit, he will fall into it" (Proverbs 26:27).

Sullivan, in short, put in place a malice stop sign, rationalistically designed to free the press and prevent suits. That sign, though, has become an invitation to a Demolition (or Defamation) Derby. One side must attempt to prove actual malice. The other side must stop that attempt. Both must examine and evaluate internal memoranda among reporters and editors, reporters' notes, or anything else that might show journalists had material available to indicate that what they published was not what they knew. Eighty percent of the expense of defending libel suits is now made up of attorney's fees, with the other 20 percent going for awards, settlements and administrative fees. Meanwhile, journalists feel pried into and preyed upon. They stop being writers or editors and start being witnesses.[25]

A 1979 case, *Herbert v. Lando*, showed how far the process could go. CBS documentary producer Lando was deposed in twenty-eight long sessions lasting, on and off, more than a year. Three thousand transcript pages and 240 exhibits were generated. In some sessions Lando had to scrutinize hundreds of his handwritten notes. In others, he had to go into detail about his thought process.

CBS had to produce notes of interviews conducted with 130 people. Herbert had to produce more than twelve thousand pages of documents. Lawyers had to examine them, with the meter ticking.[26]

Other utilitarian drawbacks of the Supreme Court's utilitarian decision also have emerged. Journalists complain of intrusion into areas of editorial decision-making. They worry about attempts to compel identification of confidential sources. As long as *Sullivan* and its follow-ups were merely seen as sacrificing individuals in the "public interest," there were few calls for change. But when journalistic time and money began to be lost, there were agitated calls for extending the Supreme Court's barriers to libel trials even further.

Some journalists proposed a granting of absolute privilege to journalists in cases involving public officials and public figures. Some wanted to do away with libel law entirely, giving journalists absolute freedom (as long as they could stay two steps ahead of those who would tar and feather them).[27]

Virtually all of the journalistic proposals viewed libel as a problem to be solved by standing on *Times v. Sullivan* and taking it either a bit further or much further. That is like viewing teenage pregnancy as a problem to be solved merely by improving contraceptive technology. During the 1960s two innovations—*Times v. Sullivan* and birth control pills—appeared to be opening up an era of journalistic and sexual freedom. But both have had ironic consequences: More libel actions, more illegitimate children or abortions.

Both sets of unforeseen circumstances developed because the legal and medical innovations of the 1960s directly challenged centuries of belief concerning the existence of objective standards of right and wrong. Before *Times v. Sullivan*, press falsehood was considered wrong. Before the sexual revolution which birth control pills symbolized, extramarital sex was considered wrong. Suddenly, though, the Supreme Court was excusing reportorial falsehood concerning public officials (later, public figures also) whenever it was produced because of lust for a good story rather than the deliberate desire to smear. Similarly, societal leaders were smiling on physical lust whenever the state of mind of participants was right—that is, if they were "in love," or at least in heat.

Times v. Sullivan and birth control pills for pregnancy-free extramarital sex were both clever, rational innovations. They were designed to liberate individuals from the consequences of actions that had been considered wrongful. Such liberation, though, has enslaved many; that's the way it always is for "liberation" apart from Biblical principles. Perhaps in the area of libel some utilitarians are ready to examine the Biblical alternative.

THE BIBLICAL VIEW OF DEFAMATION

Defamation is taken very seriously in both the Old and New Testaments. At issue is slander, not libel, for the Bible describes primarily oral societies. If there is any ethical difference between libel and slander, though, it seems evident that published or broadcast material should be treated even more harshly than local speechifying, because such material has a wider range and longer life span.

The first slander reported in the Bible was that of Satan in his serpent form against God; the Greek word *diabolis* actually means "slanderer." When Eve listened to and acted upon that slander, in conjunction with Adam, there were tragic consequences for mankind and the world in general. The slanderer was punished in two ways: The serpent thereafter had to crawl upon its belly, and Satan was told that he will one day be crushed by Christ, a woman's son.

Other Old Testament false defamations of public officials or public figures, such as Aaron and Miriam's slander of Moses (Numbers 14:36), also resulted in punishment. But it is not necessary to trace descriptive passages throughout the Old Testament, because the prescriptions could not be clearer. Exodus 23:1 declares, "Do not spread false reports," and Psalm 15:3 notes that the one who may enter God's sanctuary is he "who has no slander on his tongue." Punishment for false defamation is inescapable, as Proverbs 19:5 and 19:9 note: "A false witness will not go unpunished."[28]

Prophets did not hesitate to engage in truthful defamation of corrupt public officials and public figures. For instance, Jeremiah vigorously and publicly criticized the priest Pashhur, the false prophet Hananiah, and many others (Jeremiah 20, 28, etc.) The seriousness of false defamation, though, was emphasized in Ezekiel's criticism of "slanderous men bent on shedding blood" (Ezekiel 22:9), as well as in the Levitical injunction, "Do not go about spreading slander among your people. Do not do anything that endangers your neighbor's life. I am the Lord" (Leviticus 19:16).

The New Testament similarly linked slander with other crimes. Jesus attached "evil thoughts, murder, adultery, sexual immorality, theft, false testimony, slander" (Matthew 15:19). Paul linked slanderers and God-haters, calling them "senseless, faithless, heartless, ruthless" (Romans 1:30, 31). In recent years, a certain amount of the "senseless, faithless, heartless, ruthless" has been seen as good for society, keeping public officials and public figures on their toes; but Paul had none of that. He noted that slanderers who remain unconverted not only keep up their slandering, but also provide ideological justifications for the practice, and approve of their colleagues in crime.

The Bible clearly takes false defamation more seriously than today's Supreme Court does: No involuntary victim is to be sacrificed for the supposed good of the people. Nor are there any grounds for a double standard, with public officials or public figures deprived of their rights. The Bible is filled with admonitions against unequal justice, whether it involves the showing of partiality to the insignificant or to the great (Exodus 23; Leviticus 19:15; etc.)

Today, we have unequal libel justice in two ways. First, we suffer from the distinction between public officials or public figures and private figures. Second, the frustration of jurors becomes so great that when they can find a way to punish defamation, they are likely to load into one damage award all the damages juries could not award to others. One plaintiff goes away empty-handed; another, perhaps with no stronger case but with an imaginative lawyer and a jury foreman or strong-minded individual who can convince other jurors to "sock it to them," emerges millions of dollars richer (until the appeals court, at least).

If we adopted Biblical justice, we would have a much fairer libel law system. Biblically, journalistic false defamation tends to be midway between false witness and gossip. False witness in a court of law, where the issue literally may be life or death, is very serious; treated less severely, as far as civil penalty, is gossip or talebearing. Since libelous journalists are not actually prosecuting anyong—they typically report on or draw conclusions from evidence supplied by sources—they tend to be bearers of tales, not false witnesses.

However, lack of truthfulness makes libel a very serious offense. It can be looked upon as a form of theft: Stealing a person's reputation, perhaps injuring him in his business or causing other financial harm, and also causing mental suffering. Thieves, after all, take property, but libel robs victims of reputation and peace, perhaps repeatedly as defamatory falsehoods circulate. Penalties need to be serious enough to promote journalistic care and caution.

BIBLICAL LIBEL PENALTIES

Biblical penalties for theft are well-defined, with the goal of "making whole," not satisfying an itch for vengeance. Precise restitution, not arbitrary court adjudication, is the goal. Normally, thieves would have to pay back double the amount of property stolen (Exodus 22:4, 7). If they deprived their victim of his livelihood, they would have to pay back four or five times the amount stolen (Exodus 22:1).

By applying the principle of multiple restitution to certain types of libel, we can ask the right questions. When Leonard Damron, the Florida public official sacrificed for the supposed good of the many, was damaged in his livelihood by libel, how much damage (including estimated loss of future earnings) did he sustain? When a Miss Wyoming who took chastity seriously had her sexual morality impugned, how much did that libel cost her?

The difficulty and partial irrelevance of that last question, though, indicates the difficulty of assessing many kinds of libel damages. Discussing reputational loss and psychological harassment in terms of dollars and cents is like mixing apples and oranges, or hatchets and hand grenades.

The Bible, however, leaves no doubt that there can be financial penalties for such hard-to-measure damages. Deuteronomy 22:13-19 discusses the situation of a man who defames his wife by saying (in open discussion, not in a courtroom) that she was not a virgin upon their wedding day. If he is proven wrong in that assertion, he could be fined one hundred shekels of silver (about one kilogram, or 2 ½ pounds). That was a large amount in those days, for the annual poll tax ranged from one third of a shekel (Nehemiah 10:32) to one-half (Exodus 30:15).

Such a serious defamation shows severe problems within a marriage, but the Biblical court proceedings that would follow such a charge are well worth considering. No depositions concerning state of mind are required. Obviously, the husband dislikes the wife, but the simple job of a defamed woman's parents is to "bring proof that she was a virgin to the town elders at the gate . . . her parents shall display the cloth before the elders of the town, and the elders shall take the man and punish him."

In this case, extreme though it is, resides a model for justice when defamation has occurred. There is no attempt to determine whether what Justice Brennan would call "actual malice" was present. In most cases, only God can know what a person was thinking. Mortals can see only visible evidence, such as blood on a sheet. We examine what is visible, and rest secure in the knowledge that God will do justice concerning what we cannot see. Applying this principle to current libel law, we could eliminate lengthy depositions concerning journalists' state of mind. Judges and juries simply could examine the published story. If it contained defamatory falsehood, an appropriate fine would be levied.

Such a fine could have two parts: One for direct economic injury, one for reputational injury. The latter would be harder to determine, because it depends not only on the particular charges made but on the way a particular society might regard those charges. (Imputation of unchastity might cause major damage in previous generations, and still would in Christian circles now, but might be of minor importance in other social groups.) But whatever the precise penalty, the goal would be restitution in some multiple. If there were only minor damage from a falsely defamatory story, there would be a minor award.

If the Biblical view of libel became common, news organizations would have large incentives to take quick action when defamatory falsehoods were uncovered. Biblically, if a thief confesses and voluntarily offers restitution prior to trial, his penalty is only return of the stolen item or its equivalent, plus 20 percent, not 100, 400, or 500 percent. As Numbers 5:5-7 notes: "When a man or woman wrongs another in any way and so is unfaithful to the Lord, that person is guilty and must confess the sin he has committed. He must make full restitution for this wrong, add one fifth to it and give it all to the person he has wronged."

Is this applicable to defamation? A parallel passage, Leviticus 6:2-5, gives specific detail on some of the offenses covered: If anyone "deceives his neighbor about something entrusted to him or left in his care or stolen, or if he cheats him, or if he finds lost property and lies about it, or if he swears falsely, or if he commits any such sin that people may do . . . He must make restitution in full, add a fifth of the value to it and give it all to the owner. . . ." Applicable to many other kinds of crime, that passage also describes exactly what libelous reporters do: Maliciously or unwittingly, they twist words entrusted to them by interviewees, cheat the subjects of their articles, and state or imply that their defamation is true.

Such action demands harsh judgment. But the Leviticus passage also shows God's mercy if a person "commits any such sin that people may do." God understands our fallenness: It is the nature of man to sin. It is the nature of reporters to sin.

This does not mean that the sins we commit are excusable: They are still sins. This does not mean that false defamation, even of public officials or public figures, is legitimate: It is still wrong. But just as punishment is mandatory in such cases, so punishment also is designed to teach, not annihilate. Using Biblical principles of libel law, almost all of the large jury awards of recent years would be greatly reduced.

God is a God of both justice and mercy. Some may believe that God is too merciful at times: Should someone who has acted maliciously get away with such a mild penalty, if he decides the legal odds are against him and settles before trial? Matthew 7:1, 2 is useful here: "Do not judge, or you too will be judged. For in the same way you judge others, you will be judged, and with the measure you use, it will be measured to you."

It is very difficult for us to establish motive or to know exactly when a reporter knew that a statement was untrue. The Brennan dispensation attempts to make judges and juries godlike. Only God, though, knows what is inside men's hearts.

Exact measures of punishment will vary from society to society, but the Biblical principles remain valid. Falsehood always brings some punishment. The goal is restitution, including a penalty for the wrongdoer. Since the loss resulting from false defamation is more than economic, reputational consequences must be taken into account. Quick restitution can save the thief much grief, as it can save the injured party much suffering.

CONCLUSION

At heart, libel is an ethical problem, not a legal one. The best way to deal with the libel problem is to train journalists to respect truth and never publish anything that has not been thoroughly checked and checked again. But, given our own fallenness and the congratulations for sin which are often forthcoming in a society where relativism reigns, the sword of the magistrate becomes crucial.

For that reason, good libel law is vital: It punishes, and it also pushes publications toward an emphasis on greater accuracy and fewer falsehoods. Legal penalties signal to both journalists and onlookers an understanding of what is right to do and what is not. Over time, the sword educates journalists, or wounds repeat offenders.

Adoption of the Biblical model of libel justice would lead to speed, equal treatment for all, and restitution but not extravagance. With legal fees reduced by the elimination of depositions and discovery proceedings concerning malice, it is unlikely that libel expenses to news organizations would increase, but it is very likely that libel awards to worthy plaintiffs would be spread around more evenly. Falsehood would be taken seriously, but one transgression would not send a newspaper to bankruptcy court.

Some consequences are predictable. Since falsehood would be always punishable, newspapers would be more careful to check accuracy. Fact-checkers would receive funds that now go to lawyers. Insurance companies would relate libel insurance rates to performance rather than circulation size, for a clear record of a newspaper's penchant for printing falsehood would be available.

Journalists, within the structure of Biblical libel law, would be able to spend more time working and less time involved in litigation or the fear of it. They would be freed of deposition misery, since lawyers once again would have to look only at the actual published materials. Since there would be enormous advantages to quick correction of error, and no legal liabilities down the road from admitting error, newspapers would rush to make corrections and apologies as quickly as they can.

The most important change would be that some individuals would not have to be sacrificed for the supposed good of the many. Because quick and prominent retraction would eliminate the possibility of fourfold of fivefold restitution, the innocent could have their names cleared more quickly. Citizens would no longer be giving up their right to a good reputation (if earned) merely by taking part in public debate or by becoming public officials.

We would have the Biblical pattern of objective justice tempered by the merciful opportunity to make quick correction.

SEVEN

PRESS *vs.* PUBLIC

In 1986 and 1987, journalists did not head toward the Biblical patterns of law and ethics. Instead, the Supreme Court seemed willing to try tinkering once again. In one case, the Court (with Justice Rehnquist writing a dissent) even refused to grasp a splendid opportunity to review *Times v. Sullivan.*

The case, *Coughlin v. Westinghouse Broadcasting*, was a blatant example of investigative reporting run amuck. A television station, investigating the alleged failure of Philadelphia police to enforce state liquor laws, hid a camera across the street from the bar and videotaped police officers entering and leaving the bar. On October 11, 1981, policeman James Coughlin, carrying an envelope, entered the bar to investigate a vandalism complaint. Finding that all was quiet, Coughlin came out a minute later.[1]

The television station ran film of Coughlin's entrance and exit, with a reporter saying, "The only paperwork we saw [Coughlin] doing was carrying this envelope out of the Club less than a minute after he went in." A freeze frame with a circle around the envelope emphasized the clear implication that Coughlin had accepted a bribe.

Actually, the envelope contained Coughlin's incident report book. He sued and received judicial sympathy, but no redress, because of *Times v. Sullivan.* As one appeals court judge wrote, "The New York Times standard makes it hard enough for a public figure to win a libel suit, even when faced, as here, with what any fair observer must agree is egregious conduct on the part of the media."[2]

In a second case, *Hepps v. Philadelphia Newspapers*, the Supreme Court on a 5-4 vote ruled that a news organization even in dealing with a private figure could make defamatory statements of supposed fact that could not be proven. This time, Justice John Paul Stevens wrote a ferocious dissent, calling the decision a "blueprint for character assassination . . . a wholly unwarranted protection for malicious gossip."[3] Stevens added, "In my opinion deliberate, malicious character assassination is not protected by the First Amendment to the United States Constitution."

In another case, *Anderson v. Liberty Lobby*, the Court ruled that judges should have more power to dismiss (without benefit of jury trial) most libel charges against the press. The majority opinion, written by Justice Byron White, declared that libel suits filed by public officials and public figures in federal courts must be dismissed before trial unless the evidence suggests plaintiffs can prove libel with "convincing clarity."[4]

White's language stressed the judge's right to decide whether a "fair-minded" or "reasonable" jury could side with the plaintiff. His opinion clearly was designed to reduce the opportunity for runaway juries to act in ways thought by journalists to be "unfair" or "unreasonable." But it was unlikely that the decision would lead to speedier trials. As U.S. Court of Appeals Judge Antonin Scalia (whose opinion was overturned by the Supreme Court) noted, under the new standards "disposing of a summary judgment motion would rarely be the relatively quick process it is supposed to be."[5]

Scalia (who was soon afterwards appointed to the Supreme Court) pointed out that the plaintiff would now have to "try his entire case in pretrial affidavits and depositions"; the defendant would also want to use all of his ammunition in response. The real difference would not be time and expense, but the movement of the trial from open court with jury to judge's chambers. Furthermore, it still seemed likely that smart lawyers would find a way around the latest attempt to stifle the popular anti-press uprising.[6]

Ironically, Justice William Brennan, who had unwrapped the Supreme Court's gift to well-paid libel lawyers with his *Times v. Sullivan* decision, was in dissent this time. He complained that the Court majority's decision could "erode the constitutionally enshrined role of the jury." Brennan argued the decision would be seen as "an invitation—if not an instruction—to trial courts to assess and weigh evidence much as a juror would."[7] A few reporters seemed to take Brennan's argument to heart, but even concerned journalists often said there was no choice if press freedom were to be saved: The citizenry from which juries are selected is no longer appreciative of the press.

Those who were historically-minded asked, "Why can't today's juries be like the Zenger jury?" They were referring to the famous 1735 trial of John Peter Zenger for criticism of New York's royal governor. During that fondly remembered episode of journalism history, the judges in their red robes and white wigs were ready to impose stiff penalties, and juries had little authority.

Defense attorney Andrew Hamilton, though, turned directly to the jurors and asked them to find Zenger innocent, since he had published the truth. The jury retired and returned quickly with a verdict of "not guilty," after which there were "huzzas in the hall." The angered Chief Justice threatened to put those cheering in jail. In the face of overwhelming popular support for an independent press, though, he could not safely set aside the verdict. Zenger was freed.[8]

The belief that journalists today are modern-day Zengers who are being let down by the public is one of the prevalent current press myths. This chapter, though, argues that the public—as measured by polls and jury reactions recently, and jury verdicts from several centuries ago—has been fairly consistent for three hundred years in its expectations concerning the press. It is the predominant journalistic ethic that has changed.

TRUTH AND JURY

In both England and its American colonies during most of the seventeenth and eighteenth centuries, newspapers legally were supposed to serve as public relations vehicles for government, with the goal of creating warm feelings toward state authorities. British Chief Justice Holt argued that "it is very necessary for all government that the people should have a good opinion of it," and it therefore would be wrong "to say that corrupt officials are appointed to administer affairs."[9]

Holt's legal concern was not truth or even factual accuracy, but maintenance of the status quo: "If people should not be called to account for possessing the people with an ill opinion of the government, no government can subsist." Holt and his brethren even developed the doctrine that has come down to us as, "the greater the truth, the greater the libel." Since something that is true is likely to do more damage to a person's reputation than something considered fantastic, judges saw a writer's claim to truth as no defense, and even increased offense.[10]

The political theology of English kings demanded such illogic. As J.F. Stephens explained in his definitive 1883 work, *History of Criminal Law in England*, "If the ruler is regarded as the superior of the subject, as being by the nature of his position presumably wise and good . . . it must necessarily follow that it is wrong to censure him openly. . . whether mistaken or not, no censure should be cast upon him likely or designed to diminish his authority." Common people were supposed to sit still before governmental officials, minding their manners.[11]

The crown's Court of the Star Chamber, beginning in 1542, was given the right to try without a jury those who published opinions considered seditious. It punished, among others, Dr. Alexander Leighton, a Scotsman who declared early in the 1600s that both king and Anglican state-church were under "laws from the scripture." The Star Chamber had both of Leighton's ears cut off, his nose slit, and his face branded.[12]

The Star Chamber was busy until the Puritans gained power. In 1637, for example, the Star Chamber cut off the ears of John Bastwick, Henry Burton, and William Prynne, three Puritans who also spoke openly of their resolution to follow the Bible only. Later John Twyn was hanged for writing that the king is accountable to the people under God.

The bravery of men such as Leighton, Bastwick, Burton, Prynne, and Twyn showed that, even as the law was hardening, a Protestant ethic opposed to such arbitrary state power was developing. It had arisen out of the Reformational belief that there were laws superior to the state or to any other human institution. The medieval Catholic Church had presented itself as a divine-human bond of Heaven and earth, *the* Kingdom of God on earth. Reformers such as Calvin and Knox, though, had denied that the Kingdom of God could be equated with state or church-state. Instead, the goal of journalists and others would be the application of God's truth, as found in the Bible only, to everyday events, regardless of personal consequences.[13]

Puritans, within the theological context of their era, increased the freedom to proclaim truth once they attained power in England. They abolished the Star Chamber in 1641, and allowed a broader range of discussion than had been possible under Henry VIII and his successors. John Milton, poet and Puritan leader, wrote in 1642 that truth and falsehood should be allowed to grapple in a freer press, for "who ever knew truth put to the worse in a free and open encounter?"[14]

The Puritans, and Milton himself, were not always consistent, and in any case the Puritan revolution ended in defeat in 1660, with the English monarchy restored. But the idea was on the record: Truth and falsehood should be allowed to fight each other openly. This was a startling view, especially in an age when many governments yearned for unlimited power.

Given that view, those who aspired to journalism faced hazards throughout Europe. In France, under Louis XIV, printers and writers were branded, imprisoned, strangled, burned at the stake, or given life sentences in the galleys. In Venice, Italy, in 1650, Ferrante Pallavicino was executed for "disrespectful remarks." England did have a Parliament, but that did not make British political theory all that different from its neighbors. Even when the king lost power to Parliament, it was in the interest not of checks and balances but a new locus of supreme authority. As the famous jurist Blackstone wrote, "The power and jurisdiction of parliament" is "transcendent and absolute . . . sovereign and uncontrollable." (English lawyers put it this way: "Parliament can do everything except make a woman a man, or a man a woman.")

In such a system, journalists had to fight for even the smallest bit of elbow room—and fight they did, with popular support. Juries primarily concerned with the ethics of truth rather than the law of libel sometimes ignored judges' instructions. As early as 1689, when William Bradford was tried for seditious libel, he was insisting that the jury should decide not only whether he had printed the publication considered offensive, but also whether it was seditious; the jury, against the judge's instructions, debated both questions and ended up deadlocked.[15]

Again, when William Maule was tried in 1696 in a Massachusetts court for publishing a book said to contain "wicked Lyes and Slanders . . . upon Government," the presiding judge asked the jury to return a verdict of guilty. A runaway jury, though, returned a verdict of not guilty.[16] A decade later, two Presbyterian ministers of New York, Francis Makemie and John Hampton, were arrested for sedition, but the jury returned a verdict of not guilty.[17]

The famous Zenger trial in 1735 also was a battle between state power and the Christian faith in truth-telling. Attorney Andrew Hamilton emphasized, in his noted speech to the jury, "The cause of liberty . . . the liberty both of exposing and opposing arbitrary power by speaking and writing Truth." Hamilton argued that "Truth ought to govern the whole Affair of Libels." The jury sided with Hamilton and Zenger, even though the law said otherwise.[18]

While there were some eighteenth-century atrocities in seditious libel cases, journalists who were able to demonstrate that their articles had been factual generally did well before juries. Thomas Fleet, publisher of the Boston *Evening Post*, was prosecuted in 1742 for "libelous Reflection upon his Majesty's Administration" that could "inflame the minds of his Majesty's subjects here and disaffect them to his Government."[19] Fleet produced witnesses who attested to the truth of his news item, and the prosecution was dropped. Also in the 1740s, William Parks of the Virginia *Gazette* was acquitted when he proved in court that the legislator he had criticized as a sheep-stealer actually had been convicted of that.[20]

Throughout the century in England as well, the number of jury revolts seemed to increase. In 1752, Chief Justice Lee told a London jury that bookseller William Owen was guilty, but the jury brought in a verdict of not guilty.[21] In 1770, during what became known as the Junius trials, Lord Chief Justice Mansfield told juries that they must find guilt if the defendants had published the piece said to be libelous. The defendants acknowledged that they had, but the jury still ignored the judge and declared the defendants not guilty. The issue for the jury, once again, was truth: When editors were able to show that their statements, though sharply critical, had a factual base, they often went free.[22]

Transcripts of the trials themselves readily show the political suppositions of prosecution and defense. In the Owen trial, Attorney General Dudley Rider berated those who spoke of a right to appeal judicial decisions to juries: "An Appeal! To whom? To a mob? Must justice be appealed? To whom? To injustice?" Solicitor-general Murray defined the legal situation: "The question is, whether the jury are satisfied that the defendant Owen published the pamphlet. The rest follows of course. If the fact is proved, the libel proves itself, sedition, disturbance, &c."[23]

Defense counsel Ford, however, responded by speaking directly to the jury—a jury made up of three merchants, three grocers, three linen-drapers, one baker, one hosier, and one oilman. He called the prosecution's emphasis on judicial power "a doctrine that may be full of the most fatal consequences to all sorts of men." Ford asked, "If legal courts do wrong, must our mouths be shut, and not complain or petition for redress? God forbid!"[24]

Ford then told the jury, "I understand not the shutting of men's mouths. Let every man clap his hand upon his heart and examine how he would like it, was it his own case. . . . Surely, gentlemen, your own breasts, your own consciences, must tell you, which you consider of it—and pray consider it as your own case, fancy each of yourselves here under a rigorous prosecution, like this poor man,—there is no crime proved."[25]

According to Chief Justice Lee, there was crime. He instructed the jury "to find the defendant guilty; for he thought the fact of publication was fully proved; and if so, they could not avoid bringing in the defendant guilty." The jury, however, returned after two hours with a verdict of "Not guilty." Lee then asked a leading question: "Gentlemen of the Jury, do you think the evidence laid before you, of Owen's publishing the book by selling it, is not sufficient to convince you that the said Owen did sell this book?"[26]

Here the jurors were in a fix. According to one commentator, "The Jury could not say, to the question, that the evidence of publishing was not clear, without perjury; and if the jury had answered Yes, and not found the defendant guilty, one does not know what might have been done to the jury." When the judge demanded an answer, "the foreman appeared a good deal flustered," but he did not answer. He merely kept repeating, "Not guilty, not guilty." Several other jurymen chimed in, "That is our verdict, my lord, and we abide by it." The attorney general wanted to ask more questions, but the crowd was cheering and the noise did not permit more dialogue; the judge gave up.[27]

Similarly, in the 1770 case of *Rex v. Miller*, Solicitor General Thurlow argued for the prosecution that the case was "so plain, and in so ordinary a course of justice, that it would absolutely be impossible to have mistaken, either the application of the proofs of the charges that are laid or the conclusion to be made from them."[28]

Defense counsel Davenport, though, exaggerated somewhat and told the jury to "consider the nature of this question that comes before you, and the full and the absolute power which you have over it; for no power in this kingdom has the least control over you." Davenport asked jurors to go beyond examination of the fact of printing: "It is for you, and you only, to determine whether this paper deserves all the branding epithets with which it is loaded."[29]

Near the end of the trial, Chief Justice Mansfield said with apparent resignation, "I am used to speeches made to juries, to captivate them, and carry them away from the point of enquiry." Nevertheless, he emphasized the legal point: The jurors were to concentrate on the question of publication.[30]

As it turned out, the jurors spent over seven hours discussing the supposedly open-and-shut case, then carried their verdict to Mansfield at his house in Bloomsbury Square: "His lordship met them at his parlour door, in the passage, and the foreman having pronounced their verdict, Not Guilty, his lordship went away without saying a word." Hundreds of people who had assembled outside, though, "testified their joy, by the loudest huzzas."[31]

The thrilling part of this history is the willingness of some jurors to produce verdicts suggesting that government was not a private preserve for rulers. Jurors often reacted harshly when confronted by arrogant demands for punishment of seditious libel, such as those coming from Chief Justice Hutchinson of Massachusetts in 1767 and thereafter. An English lawyer with the pen name Candor asked in 1764, "What business have private men to write or speak about public matters? Such kind of liberty leads to all sorts of license and obloquy."[32] But juries generally sided with the press against such a political theory, and the press, consequently, worked to extend jury power and restrict that of judges.

Jurors, when they saw individuals threatened by state power, even took direct action at times. When William Bradford had been on trial in 1689, he may have been saved by a juror who "accidentally" shoved with his cane the bottom of the typeform that Bradford had used to print the tract in question. When it collapsed and all the type spilled onto the floor, the evidence that Bradford had done the printing was gone. Similarly, when Henry Woodfall was tried for seditious libel in 1770, he escaped renewed prosecution when a juror walked off with the prosecutor's only copy of Woodfall's newspaper.[33]

Eventually the law was changed to conform to belief in the power of truth. In England, Fox's Libel Act of 1792 proclaimed truth as a defense and provided that the jury rather than the judge would rule on whether published material was seditious. In the United States in 1791, the passage of the First Amendment meant that newspapers would be free (except in extreme situations such as wartime) to publish what they chose without prior restraint. The New York legislature in 1805 spelled out the meaning of the First Amendment by erecting the doctrine of truth as a defense against libel, and other states followed.

One of the most ringing court decisions concerning the central issue of truth and falsehood came in *Commonwealth v. Clap* (1808), with the Massachusetts supreme court observing that publication of truths concerning the fitness and qualifications of a candidate for public office, "with the honest intention of informing the people, are not a libel. For it would be unreasonable to conclude that the publication of truths, which it is the interest of the people to know, should be an offense against their laws."[34]

The court also added sternly, though, that "For the same reason, the publication of falsehood and calumny against public officers, or candidates for public offices, is an offense most dangerous to the people, and deserves punishment, because the people may be deceived, and reject the best citizens, to their great injury, and it may be to the loss of their liberties." That court statement succinctly described the Christian ethic of publication freedom within limits: Truth was a defense against prosecution, but falsehood was no defense.[35]

That was the common understanding of press freedom throughout the nineteenth century.[36]

CHANGING SIDES

Why, then, in the late twentieth century, have jurors become the frequent enemies of journalistic media, rather than the devoted friends they once tended to be? Many hypotheses have been thrown around: Newspapers are now big, established powers. They are often monopolies within their communities. Television stations package news as entertainment and entertainment as news. The class composition of journalists has changed. The public cares less about freedom to tell the truth than it once did.

Most of those generalizations have much to be said for them. Some recent surveys, though, throw suspicion on that last one, the idea that somehow the public is losing faith in truth-telling. One Gallup-conducted survey posed this question to a cross-section of the American public: "Some people feel that in a free society news organizations should be able to say anything about a person, whether true or false, without having to face libel suits. Others believe that even in a free society news organizations should be subject to libel suits if they say critical things about people that are false. . . . Which position comes closer to your opinion?"[37]

Only 4 percent of those polled said that news organizations should be free to say anything without penalty, while 89 percent took the position pushed for in the eighteenth century and solidified in the nineteenth century by cases such as *Commonwealth v. Clap*: Truth is a defense, but falsehood is no defense. (Seven percent answered, "don't know.")

Other survey questions showed very large majorities of the populace also saying that truth is essential in stories involving public officials or public figures, as well as those concerning private individuals. This popular sentiment is evident in the actions of recent runaway juries as well. For example, the jury in one noted case of the 1980s, *Tavoulareas v. The Washington Post*, ignored the judge and found for the plaintiff because the *Post* had not proved that the story was true.[38]

So many runaway juries have decided against newspapers during the past few years, often against the leanings of judges, that journalists now want judges rather than juries to hear cases in which they are the defendants. That is exactly the opposite of the tendency that prevailed from the seventeenth through the nineteenth centuries. The change may say less about beliefs of the citizenry than beliefs among journalists. Opinion polls and jury verdicts tell us of continuing popular concern with basic questions of truth and falsehood—but what about the concerns of many journalists? Has the public abandoned the press, or has the press abandoned the public?

REVOLUTIONARY VS. RESPECTFUL JOURNALISM

Complaints about public unwillingness to follow the press have emerged at crucial turning points of the past. Historian James Billington has noted that for leaders of the French Revolution two centuries ago "journalism was the most important single professional activity." As Billington pointed out, "In revolutionary France journalism rapidly arrogated to itself the church's former role as the propagator of values, models, and symbols for society at large." Those citizens who would not go along were excommunicated from the new church of journalists, and sometimes decapitated.[39]

The centrality of the press to the French Revolution is indicated by a statement of Nicholas Bonneville, editor of *Le Tribun du Peuple*. Bonneville wrote that he looked for deliverance not to any political republic, but to "the republic of letters," a rallying of writers who would lead mankind.[40]

Bonneville saw his new journal as a "circle of light," with writers who would transform the world by constituting themselves as "simultaneously a centre of light and a body of resistance." They were to be "legislators of the universe," preparing a "vast plan of universal regeneration." Bonneville published a pledge of allegiance to the nation which began, "I Believe in the Infallibility of the People." But since the people were to be instructed by journalists, Bonneville and his colleagues were really saying that they believed in their own infallibility.

The French Revolution destroyed itself, as other revolutions since then also have, but it left a legacy. As Billington noted, "The new breed of intellectual journalist during the French Revolution created both the basic sense of legitimacy and the forms of expression for the modern revolutionary tradition." Marx, Lenin, and others spent much of their lives as journalists, both to produce some income and to recruit followers. They believed that journalism could work fast where government often was slow. As one revolutionary Frenchman put it, the press could build a "new democracy" by providing a tribunal for the people that was "higher than the tribunal of judges, the throne of kings, and, I shall say, even the altar of the living God."[41]

That revolutionary idea never caught fire in the United States. It had its moments early on, with a few editors during the 1790s imitating their French brethren. The best-known Francophile editor, Benjamin Franklin Bache, had been educated in France while living there with his grandfather Benjamin Franklin. Bache edited in the 1790s a newspaper filled with malicious gossip, unsubstantiated by fact, directed against American leaders.

Typically, Bache wrote of George Washington that "If ever a nation was debauched by a man, the American nation has been debauched by Washington. If ever a nation was deceived by a man, the American nation has been deceived by Washington. Let his conduct then be an example to future ages . . . that the masque of patriotism may be worn to conceal the foulest designs against the liberties of the people."[42]

Bache also attacked "bald, blind, crippled, toothless Adams." (Adams *was* bald, but one out of four was Bache's average for veracity.) Adams attacked Bache and others for "contaminating the country with the foul abomination of the French revolution" and conspiring to "prostrate liberties at the feet of France."

Adams' wife Abigail, blunter than her husband as she often was, complained of "this lying wretch of a Bache," and others called him a "dull-edged, dull-eyed, haggard-looking hireling of France." When only a few Americans backed Bache, he criticized the populace generally for not only letting him down, but for opposing press freedom as well.

Most famous of the journalists who tried to revolutionize the United States during the 1790s was Thomas Paine. Riding on his immense popularity during the American Revolution, when he wrote the pamphlet *Common Sense* with its stirring introductory words, "These are the times that try men's souls," Paine tried to agitate for a very different kind of revolution twenty years later.

Paine's belief in intellectual freedom was indicated by his statement to a French friend, Etienne Dumont: "He said to me if it were in his power to demolish all the libraries in existence, he would do it so as to destroy all the errors of which they were the depository." When Paine received little support, he also accused Americans of not caring for freedom of the press.[43]

A few Americans during the nineteenth century tried to popularize a concept of journalistic godliness. In 1833 Joseph Warren of Cincinnati argued that "public influence is the real government of the world," and that printing should "henceforth be the main arm of this governing power." But more typical was the Christian conception of the relationship of citizen, government, and press that was published in the Boston *Recorder*'s explanation of its editorial policy: When it "be necessary to disapprove of public measures, that respect for Government, which lies at the very foundation of civil society, will be cautiously preserved; and in such cases, a tone of regret and sorrow will best comport with the feelings of the Christian patriot."[44]

The same held for other established institutions: They could be criticized, but regretfully. A policy of that sort would be useful today. The press should not be seen by Christians as an enshrined fourth estate, legislating without portfolio. Instead, reporters should report without assuming that those in governmental authority are adversaries. As Paul wrote in Romans (13:2), "He who rebels against the authority is rebelling against what God has instituted, and those who do so will bring judgment on themselves." When leaders rebel against God's authority, though, Christians may advocate opposition.[45]

Some twenty years ago, though, the idea of "adversary journalism"—reflex-action opposition to governmental leaders—took root among leading American journalists. The idea in its modern form originated with the tendency of the French revolutionary press *never* to give authorities the benefit of the doubt. As noted in Chapter Three, publisher E. W. Scripps summarized well the ideology of revolutionary journalism, past and future; "Whatever is, is wrong." But Oakland *Tribune* editor Robert Maynard acknowledged the hard edge in practice when he spoke of journalists who are "hungry for blood—it sometimes seems to readers that we will not do the story unless we can do someone in."[46]

Adversary journalists assemble regularly to pat each other on the back. At the 1984 meeting in Miami of a group appropriately called IRE (Investigative Reporters and Editors), Geraldo Rivera orated, "We are part of the process of the positive social change."[47] David Halberstam brushed off criticism: "The more we do our job of questioning accepted norms, the more we can expect to be questioned." As former reporter Kurt Luedtke noted about such apologia, "The press is full of itself these days, and frequently, it is simply full of it."[48]

Recently, journalists such as former Washington *Post* editor Larry Stern have been praised for their hatred of America's "huge mindless institutions that devour our substance and corrupt our fundamental ideals." (Washington *Post* foreign editor Karen de Young's comment about leftist guerrilla groups also comes to mind: "You assume they must be the good guys.") Max Frankel of the New York *Times*, complaining about restrictions on press coverage during the Grenada invasion of 1983, expressed his astonishment at the "assumption by some of the public that the press wanted to get in, not to witness the invasion on behalf of the people, but to sabotage it." Given the precedent of the last years of the Vietnam war, the assumption was valid.[49]

Christians are not necessarily conservatives. For Christians, institutions such as the state have delegated authority, not absolute authority. Governmental leaders, as Peter wrote, are sent by God to punish those who do wrong and commend those who do right; when they do the opposite, they have no proper authority, and Christians may have to act in civil disobedience. (Samuel Rutherford, in his 1664 book *Lex Rex*, wrote that law is king, and when kings and governors disobey the law Christians may disobey them.)[50] Yet, Christians do not see it as their function to oppose government automatically; that is a last resort. For many contemporary journalists, though, opposition is the first resort.

According to adversary journalists, a writer in opposition has the right to break most of the Ten Commandments. Top investigative reporter Robert Scheer has stated strightforwardly that it is "the journalist's job" to break into offices or seduce people to get a story.[51] Others would not be as blunt, but the New York *Times* and other leading newspapers have had no compunction against publishing stolen documents. As the last chapter noted, media false witness is frequent.

Reporter Julius Dascha described how many elite journalists "look upon themselves almost with reverence, like they are protecting the world against the forces of evil." But for many, those forces are now arising mainly from the American middle class. Over and over again, the theme of liberation from middle America emerges. Nicholas von Hoffman of the Washington *Post* praised during the 1960s "now people," those who were "groovy, sexy, beautiful, swinging, mellow, hip and hep." He attacked those who were "old, ugly, square, plastic and out of it."[52]

Similarly, during the 1970s *Post* Editor William Greider acknowledged the bias that "turns up in the columns of the *Post*, *Times* and other members of the media axis. The core of it is the unspoken assumption that the rest of the country is filled with boobs." During the 1980s Tom Brokaw, in a *Mother Jones* magazine interview, called those middle-class values "pretty simplistic, pretty old-fashioned," without "much application to what's currently wrong or troubling a lot of people."[53]

Many journalists also seem to desire "liberation" from Christian roots. In 1980, Stanley Rothman of Smith College and Robert and Linda Lichter of George Washington University surveyed and interviewed a sample of the "media elite": 240 journalists at the three big television networks, the three leading news magazines, and the three most influential newspapers (the New York *Times*, the Washington *Post*, and *The Wall Street Journal*). They found that 86 percent of the elite seldom or never attended church, and only 25 percent favored prayers in public schools (74 percent of the American public favored such prayer).[54]

Polling on social issues that often have a theological component also showed that the journalistic elite had separated itself from the American mainstream. Ninety percent of the elite approved of abortion on demand. (The American public registers at about 20-30 percent on the question of abortion as a woman's "right.") Seventy-five percent of the elite saw nothing wrong with homosexuality. Over half thought adultery was fine (American public: 15 percent). While a good survey of journalists' deeper religious beliefs still needs to be taken, these statistics are evidence of the divide between press and public.[55]

The results of that divide are evident. Public opinion poll ratings of press performance have slipped to only 16 percent favorable. Juries found news organizations guilty in forty-two of forty-seven libel trials during the early 1980s. Journalists had to go running to judges for protection against "the people" whose tribunes they were supposed to be. As James K. Batten, president of Knight-Ridder newspapers, told fellow publishers, "A lot of the American public don't much like us or trust us. They think we're too big for our britches."[56]

It is sad to contemplate the decay of institutions which started off with such hopes and still possess enormous wealth and talent. But *U.S. News and World Report* noted that "America's press, which often views itself as a knight on a white horse, is finding that the public sees its once shining armor has badly tarnished." Even *Time* could see the reason for the tarnishing: Many journalists are "arrogant and self-righteous, brushing aside most criticism as the uninformed carping of cranks and ideologues."[57]

Christians can oppose that arrogance and self-righteousness through prayer, through establishment of alternative media, and through thoughtful criticism of mainline journalism; sometimes, we have to admit, some of us have engaged in "uninformed carping." The next chapter suggests several informed and specific ways of analyzing journalistic products.

E I G H T

PERCEPTIVE MEDIA WATCHING

Some Christians are so disgusted with mainline newspapers and news shows that they refuse to read or watch and merely engage in a general carping condemnation. Others understand the problems of "the media" in abstraction, but are news consumers who tend to accept what they read or see as generally accurate: "The camera doesn't lie, does it?"

Sadly, it does. Modern journalistic technology can produce products with great style even when there is ungodly substance, and many journalists have great knowledge and talent (although not the fear of God which is the beginning of wisdom). Using attention-grabbers, skillfully constructed stories, and careful placement of articles, such talented individuals are able to pull wool over untrained eyes. This chapter shows how those who attack can add specific detail to their criticism, and those who tend to accept can become more discerning.

NEWSPAPER HEADLINES, TELEVISION FRAMING

Boiling down a complicated story into a headline's few words or a television station's video graphic and introduction is no easy task. Not only is accuracy vital, but the quick message must be lively enough to sell the story to headline scanners or channel switchers. Ambiguities are common: Does the headline "Women Oppose Bork" mean that all or most women took that position, or were several individuals testifying? Headline choice is vital in newspapers, since most readers are headline scanners and the only information they will have about a particular event or situation is what is conveyed in the headline.

A recent report in Detroit about a nuclear plant closed for safety reasons shows the importance of headlines. Detroit's two highly competitive newspapers, the liberal *Free Press* and the moderately conservative *News*, had similar stories about safety improvements being made at Detroit Edison's Fermi plant, but the headlines reflected a half-empty *vs.* half-full psychology. The Detroit *Free Press* headline was "Panel: Edison Slow to Repair Flaws at Fermi." The *News* headline was, "Outline for Fermi Improves."[1]

Choices of television graphics are also important. When oil prices were rising, some petroleum stories had a graphic of a man in Arab clothing, thus implicitly blaming factors abroad for the price rise. Others had a montage of U.S. oil company logos, thus implicitly blaming corporations for the price rise. Introductions to filmed stories also are crucial to watch: "Tennessee parents are challenging school officials on textbook selection—here's the story from correspondent Jim Bartleby" is very different from "Tennessee fundamentalists are fighting educational authorities—Jim, what's going on there?"

A perceptive reader thinks first about the headline and then turns to the lead (or, in a television report, the "framing" of a story). Leads can be either "summary" (designed to present succinctly the most important information about the story) or feature (designed not so much to provide news as to grab the readers's attention and get him to read on). Questions to ask about both kinds include: What impression did the lead create? What was its "hook" (the connection to a newsworthy event)? What other angles were possible? Leads are vital because at least half the readers who start a story are likely to read no further.

Feature leads often take more work to get right, and reporters sometimes pour their souls into them; so the use of a serious feature lead in a hard news story might indicate that the reporter cares about what he is writing. For example, here are two ways of beginning a story on abortion. First, "Six Austin doctors today announced formation of a new anti-abortion group. They said they were 'sickened' by abortions they had performed and had resolved to do no more." Second, " 'I reached with my forceps and pulled out a perfectly formed, tiny leg,' Dr. X said quietly. 'It was then, as I pulled out the pieces one by one, that I decided not to do any more abortions.' At a quiet news conference yesterday, X and five other doctors announced. . ." Of course, getting any publicity whatever for pro-life activities in some major newspapers is a triumph, but the second story is clearly more evocative.

On a national story, it is also worth asking whether reporters took the time to localize it, or whether they reported it dutifully but held it at arm's length while wrinkling their nose. For example, when the Detroit *News* and the Detroit *Free Press* ran front-page stories on AIDS-contaminated blood in blood banks, the conservative *News* lead provided specific detail on how sixty-four donors to Michigan's three Red Cross centers had tested positive for the AIDS antibody. The liberal *Free Press* lead, however, was a general statement about blood banks tracing blood donations. Which lead might build the willingness to treat AIDS like other dangerous diseases, despite the pressures of interest-group politics?[2]

One final element to examine before scrutinizing the story itself is the story's setting. News organizations try to regularize news coverage through institution of beats, often associated with government: State Department, City Hall, courthouse. Routine channels of that sort account for most news; on local television, death watches (fires, crimes, accidents) account for most of the rest. A television station's decision to send a camera crew to a location that is neither routinized (the beat) nor sensational shows a conscious decision to expend resources in particular ways and not expend them in others. Whose demonstrations are covered, and whose are not? Who gets free publicity, and who does not? Those are key questions that often have ideological answers.

STORIES: WHAT TO LOOK FOR

Turning to the story itself, basic questions to ask include: What words and characterizations were used to describe controversial individuals, groups, or ideas? What hard evidence was given? How were the sources of evidence identified—as participants, citizens, or experts? How was evidence made credible or not? How was the credibility of particular individuals heightened or not? Were individuals interviewed, quoted, paraphrased, or merely referred to? Were statistics used? Were governmental officials cited? Was one side more identified with the public interest, with individual freedom, or with idealism? Did one side seem to be the underdog?

The best way to check coverage is to compare stories on the same news item in roughly comparable news outlets: Two local television stations, or (in those rare cases where this is possible) competitive newspapers. Detroit, again, is probably the finest city for this, and one that provides many wonderful examples of sharply conflicting coverage. For example, one day both the *Free Press* and the *News* had at the top right-hand corner of page 1—the most read spot of the newspaper—articles on a keynote speech by union president Owen Bieber at the United Auto Workers annual convention. The placement of the story was no surprise: the UAW is very important in Motown, and each newspaper sent its own reporter to the convention site near Disneyland, rather than relying on wire services.[3]

The headlines, though, made it seem as if two different speeches were being covered. The conservative *News* proclaimed, "UAW Chief Threatens Wage 'War.' " The liberal *Free Press* reported, "New UAW Group to Chart Future." Further reading did not lessen the confusion. The *Free Press*'s lead of thirty-four words was: "In a spirited keynote address to the first session of the UAW's 26th Constitutional Convention here Sunday, President Owen Bieber announced the establishment of a new commission to guide the union in the future." The *News* lead of thirty-five words was: "The United Auto Workers will 'go to war' with the Big Three auto makers unless substantial gains are made in wages and job security during next year's contract negotiations, UAW President Owen Bieber said Sunday." Same speech, same length of lead, but two very different impressions. The *Free Press*, in its headline and lead, stressed the positive message (in today's culture) of future-orientation, while the *News* provided the negative message of "wage war."[4]

Nor did succeeding paragraphs provide what the leads lacked. The *Free Press* story, continuing onto an inside page, contained twenty-two paragraphs, but nowhere was wage war even mentioned. The *News* story also went onto an inside page and was also twenty-two paragraphs long. It at least mentioned the commission, but not until the eighteenth paragraph, by which time most readers would be long gone to the comics, sports or lifestyle pages.

Sadly, few cities have such standout competition, so questions about subtle specific detail are necessary: What descriptive words or settings were used: Were seemingly trivial aspects included in the story? For what reason? Any pattern? In an age when abortion is labeled termination of pregnancy and abortionists are "pro-choice," evasive language should not be overlooked: Why are pornography shops, patronized by those in arrested stages of development, referred to as "adult bookstores"? Why do many major media outlets use the words "dictator" or "strongman" to describe autocrats allied to the United States, but the word "leader" to refer to Communist dictators such as Jaruzelski, Ortega, or Kim Il Sung?

Newspaper readers must remember that specific, descriptive detail is the guts of journalism. Reporters quickly learn how to load stories not by distinguishing explicitly their perceived good guys and bad guys, but through the use of evocative descriptives.

For example, when Tennessee parents in 1986 protested the

teaching of anti-Christian doctrines to their children in public schools, reporters for *Time*, *Newsweek*, and major newspapers did not say, "We think the parents are nutty." Instead, they reported that the parents were objecting to the reading of *Goldilocks and the Three Bears, Cinderella, The Wizarad of Oz, Jack and Jill*, and so on.[5] In actuality, the parents were objecting to stories that preach the acceptability of lying, stealing, cheating, and disobeying parents, preach that motherhood is an inferior activity, and so on. The parents also objected to children being instructed in the writing of witchcraft incantations or the use of New Age meditational exercises.

Newsweek mentioned none of this, but padded its story with description of how the school board's lawyer "spread his hands in exasperation" because the Christian parents apparently were impossible to please. Then the magazine added a bit of local color in the form of an ersatz public opinion poll: "Customers at The Ivory Thimble needlework shop in nearby Church Hill thought the parents were making 'mountains out of molehills.' " Reporters often use such unnamed sources to indicate their own impressions.[6]

Such loading is easier to spot in print than on videotape. News film tends to go by so fast that it is generally necessary to tape a story on a VCR and run it by several times, perhaps with the sound off, to see what subliminal impressions a particular story might have created. Did quick cuts from one activity to another suggest a causal link between the two? Were people interviewed at different times, with material spliced together so it appears that they were engaged in a debate (one that never happened)?

Bias in news coverage of demonstrations is relatively easy to spot. At a rally, were news cameras focusing on a few or on a crowd? Were viewers left with an accurate impression of how many people actually were there? (A large crowd can look small and a small one large simply by changing camera lenses.) Did cameras focus on kooky stuff or typical activities? It is easy to trivialize a demonstration through emphasis on the silly, or to marginalize it by suggesting that those involved are deviant or irrational.

Through camera work, impressions can be influenced in both obvious and subtle ways. The normal camera angle for news interviews is straight across, simulating the way one adult of average height meets and talks with another adult of average height. If the camera either looks up at the subject (that makes him seem more powerful) or down (that belittles him), the reason is either incompetence or ideology. Worm's-eye or bird's-eye views are such obvious slanting devices that they rarely are used. Differences in distancing are more frequent. Interviewees are typically shot in medium close-up (after perhaps an opening shot to "establish" the setting). Close-ups, though, are used to bring out emotion (in an accident victim) or to show sweat (during an unfriendly interview). On the other hand, a full-length or long shot of an individual during the middle of an interview generally depersonalizes him and distances viewers. Departures from the normal medium close-up should be examined carefully.

Freeze frames (also called Jack Ruby frames ever since they were used in November 1963 to stop the action at the moment Ruby's bullet hit Lee Harvey Oswald) have become fashionable. Freeze frames give the impression that an individual has been caught doing something significant at what journalists believe to be a particularly important moment. As the previous chapter's discussion of the case of patrolman Coughlin showed, that moment may be crucial only in the eyes of an ill-informed reporter.

Few nonjournalists realize how frequently "experts" and "statistics" are used to bulwark a reporter's ideological position. An "expert" almost always can be found to support virtually any position. Books with titles such as *How to Lie with Statistics* also are valuable. Regardless of the statistics involved, skilled makers of line graphs or pie and bar charts can create almost any impression they want. Verticals in line graphs can be compressed, bar charts can leave out center sections, and picture graphs can leave the impression of much greater change than actually occurred, since doubling height often quadruples bulk.

Statistics often are misused in articles trying to make political points. Some ten thousand U.S. draft evaders in Canada during the early 1970s were transformed by the Boston *Globe* into "over 50,000," by *Newsweek* into fifty thousand to seventy-five thousand, by CBS into one hundred thousand, and so on.[7] During the late 1950s and 1960s, several hundred abortion-related deaths of women each year were turned into annual totals of five to ten thousand, and several hundred thousand illegal abortions per year became one to two million.[8]

Even apparently straight question-and-answer segments may be open to distortion. Some interviewers have been known to change the questions they asked, for the camera, following conclusion of a taped interview. For example, Geraldo Rivera in one interview asked a subject, "Did you make a mistake?" During the refilming, though, he asked an implicitly more critical question:

"Do you *admit* that a mistake was made?" He used the original answer and thus made his respondent seem evasive.[9]

The viewer, of course, would never know about that type of hanky-panky. Careful watching, though, often raises suspicions, as does general knowledge of journalistic practices. Since the classic news story structure is "inverted pyramid," with the most important information in the opening paragraphs and successively less important material bringing up the rear, deviations from that order gain significance. Readers can learn to spot changes and ask "why" whenever something apparently unimportant is given top billing.

BEHIND THE STORY: GATEKEEPERS

Why does one particular story make the front page or network news, when hundreds of other possible stories end up circularly filed? Many scholars suggest that journalists have their prime influence on society not so much by coverage of particular stories as by the choice of what to cover; journalists are sometimes called "gatekeepers" or "agenda-setters." Readers and viewers should keep asking: Why was the story considered newsworthy? Was it tied to a particular event? Did it have dramatic elements, such as violence or conflict? Was it something unusual? Was it a new development in a continuing issue? Did the activity reported affect many people? Was there a celebrity involved?

A story should be examined in the context of an entire newspaper or program. Where was it placed? How much space or time did it receive? Was it treated as hard news or feature? Could it have been either? How did it compare in interest to stories given more prominent space or time, or less? One other question is hard to answer from the outside, but it is well worth asking: Who might have been behind the story? Did someone outside the news organization start the ball rolling, or shape the story as it developed? Who benefited from the story? Who was damaged?

The best way to see how much of news is discretionary, again, is to compare coverage in different publications, then ask questions about contrast in information and handling. Did a story appear in just one publication or on one program, or many? For example, one day the Detroit *News* gave big play to a report calling the Detroit mayor inactive concerning "hundreds of thousands of vacant and abandoned homes," "abandoned cars by the thousands with nowhere to store them," and serious problems with the water, sanitation and other departments. The liberal *Free Press*, which has given consistent support to Detroit's mayor, at first did not cover the charges at all, and the next day buried on page 18A a tiny article about the controversy.[10]

A CLASSIC: THE CHAMBERS-HISS AFFAIR

Leads, stories, and story selection: All the elements come together in a comparison of how the Chambers-Hiss affair mentioned in Chapter Two was covered in the liberal Washington *Post* and the conservative Chicago *Tribune*. A jury in January 1950 found Hiss guilty of perjury. Historians have no real doubt that the jury verdict was correct.[11] Yet, five of my journalism history students who read about the trial in the Washington *Post*, without any other knowledge of the case, concluded that Hiss was innocent. Five other journalism students who read only the *Tribune* came to the conclusion that Hiss was guilty.

How could that happen? In the *Post*, evidence against Hiss that was irrefutable in the courtoom—microfilm, stolen documents retyped on his typewriter—was downplayed.[12] Instead, *Post* readers were told of the personal battle between "tall, lean, 44-year-old Hiss," with character references from Supreme Court Justices, and "short, fat-faced" Chambers, with his "customary air of complete emotionless detachment." In the pages of the *Post*, Chambers wore a "supercilious expression" while Hiss "calmly strode to the stand" and was always "sure of himself, answering the barrage of questions without hesitation, showing no uneasiness or equivocation."[13] The *Tribune*, though, stressed the evidence and supported Chambers.[14]

On June 2, 1949, for instance, Chambers testified that Alger Hiss had furnished government secrets to the Soviets, and also admitted having himself lied while a Communist during the 1930s. The following day the Washington *Post* headline emphasized Chambers' past derelictions: "Lies Admitted by Chambers." The Chicago *Tribune*, though, spotlighted Hiss' activity: "Hiss Aided Reds: Chambers." Each newspaper also described the emotional state of Chambers as he was testifying: The liberal *Post* reported that "Chambers seemed to be showing discomfiture," while the conservative *Tribune* noted that Chambers "never lost his composure."[15]

On June 6 Chambers again provided two possible story emphases: He testified that another federal official had spied for the Soviets, and he also admitted additional lies. The *Post* again played the lying angle big, even running a banner headline across the top of page 1: "Chambers Admits He Lied to Congress," followed by a pro-Hiss lead: "Under vigorous cross-examination which sought to depict him as a confused neurotic, Whittaker Chambers admitted some further conflict in his account." The Chicago *Tribune*, though, headlined the day's new development: "Chambers Says Wadleigh Was 2d Spy Source."[16]

One week later the testimony of Whittaker Chambers' wife, Esther, became crucial to Chambers' contention, denied by Hiss, that Chambers and Hiss had been close friends during the 1930s. The Washington *Post* transformed one faltering moment on the witness stand—Esther Chambers could not remember whether she had seen the Hisses twelve years earlier at an anniversary party or a New Year's Eve party—into a front-page headline: "Chambers' Wife Alters Testimony."[17]

The Chicago *Tribune*, though, emphasized the main part of her testimony and even suggested comfortable cruelty among the Hisses: "Hiss, resplendent in a cream colored summer suit, and his wife, in a cotton frock and a pert green hat, beamed as the 49 year old witness grew pale and exhausted, hesitated and faltered . . . under a merciless, four hour cross-examination."[18]

Two days later newspapers reported the testimony of a State Department secretary who had worked for Hiss. Part of her testimony was damaging to Hiss' case: She testified that four memoranda in Hiss' handwriting on top secret subjects were not made in the course of regular State Department business. Part could be construed as supportive: She also noted that State Department employees other than Hiss had access to some of the documents Chambers said he had received from Hiss.

The Chicago *Tribune*'s lead was pro-Chambers, describing how the secretary had "stunned the defense at the Alger Hiss perjury trial today with a series of damaging assertions," most notably the one about Hiss' secret memoranda. The Washington *Post*'s story was pro-Hiss, beginning with the headline "State Secrets Open to Many, Hiss Trial Told," and continuing with a direct presentation of the spin put on the story by the Hiss camp: "Trial attorneys for Alger Hiss today emphasized that dozens of other State Department employees had access to documents which Whittaker Chambers said he received from Hiss in 1938."[19]

Throughout the trial, then, *Tribune* and *Post* readers would have received radically different impressions. It so happened in this case that readers of the conservative newspaper would have been much better informed than readers of the liberal *Post*. It is not always that way, since the key dividing point of our era is materialistic *vs.* theist, not liberal *vs.* conservative.

Furthermore, *Tribune* readers would have been no better informed of the theological implications of the story than were *Post* readers. Chambers, throughout the affair, had tried to teach that communism could not be defeated by American materialism; he argued that it was the near-religious vision of communism that attracted to its ranks persons like Alger Hiss. Chambers had stated that only faith in God could allow Americans to stand up to Marxist faith. The *Tribune*, though, generally ignored Chambers' message.

In retrospect, it is clear that Chambers' agenda and the conservative press agendas deviated as he emphasized Christian beliefs and criticized materialism of all stripes. After listening to Chambers' statements, one observer suggested that the question was "no longer whether Alger Hiss is guilty. The question now is whether God exists."[20] Many conservative journalists, like many of their liberal counterparts, seemed uncomfortable with the debate on those terms. They did not understand the deeper implications of the ideas of Chambers and the fall of Hiss.[21]

CONCLUSION: NEWS PERSPECTIVE

Christians should not assume that news pages are any less biased than editorial pages; sometimes the only significant difference is the degree of subtlety. It is always important to keep in mind the importance of what writer David Altheide has called "news perspective." As Altheide points out, most stories are too complex to fit into a dramatic and easily understood standard news format. Journalists look for a lead or theme which will help them to structure the story and determine which facts are important. Once that theme has been developed, subsequent news stories on the same subject will be reported according to the same theme. Details which do not fit will not be pursued.[22]

The Sherri Finkbine abortion story from 1962, discussed briefly in Chapter Two, provides a good example of journalistic grasping for a new theme. The problem of what to call the being in the womb was difficult. Even though the use of the word "baby" went against the thrust of most stories, the Finkbine articles early on were sprinkled with references to "unborn baby" and "child." The New York *Times* on July 26 reported that Finkbine "feared her child would be permanently affected."[23] The next day the *Times* referred to "Mrs. Sherri Finkbine, pregnant for three months with a baby she fears will be deformed."[24] The New York *Journal-Ameri-*

can mentioned "her baby" and "the unborn child."[25] The Los Angeles *Times* reported that Finkbine "wants to prevent the birth of her child."[26] The Chicago *Tribune* referred to the "expected child [who] is threatened with deformed birth."[27]

Medical language provided the eventual solution: Dump the word "baby" and substitute the neutral-sounding term "fetus."[28] Early on, the word "fetus" (and occasionally the word "embryo") found use when reporters focused on the medical aspects of the situation. After the abortion occurred, the *Journal-American* used the term "fetus" on August 18.[29] The New York *Times* reported on August 19 that, in the Finkbine case, "the fetus" was deformed.[30] Journalists needed this new vocabulary to avoid using language that contradicted themes. Reporters could create sympathy for the Finkbines by emphasizing their appearance, children, love for children, professions, etc., but implicitly pro-life language could create tension by making readers believe that the abortion would affect a baby and not a thing. The tension was reconciled when reporters focused on the possibility of deformity (suggesting that the baby was less than fully human) and took from the medical profession a neutral term, "fetus."

Use of a dehumanizing term allowed reporters to stress more consistently Finkbine's "unselfish" willingness to sacrifice her privacy to promote "more humane" abortion legislation. The Los Angeles *Times* quoted her as saying, "I hope that in a small way we have contributed toward achieving a more humane attitude toward this problem."[31] The Chicago *Tribune* quoted Robert Finkbine's observation that his wife went public to "help others who may get trapped in the same horrible thing."[32]

Clearly, a new story format for abortion incidents was emerging. The old "abortion as crime" structure viewed the aborted infant as a murder victim, but in the new format sympathy was with Finkbine. Coverage was always from her perspective.

Providentially, though, new developments in medicine are making it more difficult for journalists to use implicitly pro-abortion language. Recently, when doctors announced that they had opened a mother's womb by cesarean section, removed her twenty-three-week-old baby for three minutes to correct a urinary tract infection, and put the baby back in the womb, the word "fetus" did not sound quite right even to some hard-boiled reporters. Baby Mitchell, after all, had been a fetus with his own doctor, his own medical records, even his own medical bills. One network news show still referred to him five times as just a "fetus," but the New

York *Times* several times called the child in the womb an "unborn baby." That is not great progress, but it may indicate a turning of the tide.

In general, mainline American journalism is still stuck in the ruts of a modernism now grown old. The refusal of many journalists to change should come as no surprise to Christians who recall Psalm 73's description of those who have power without godliness: "They scoff, and speak with malice; in their arrogance they threaten oppression. Their mouths lay claim to heaven, and their tongues take possession of the earth." The refusal is still a sorrowful sight for journalists and for journalism, because God is not mocked.

We should mourn the present and future of leading denizens of the current journalistic night. We should be joyful, though, that God is now raising up new technology, new institutions, and new journalists to take the places of those fallen away. The next section discusses the coming opportunity for return.

PART THREE

RETURN?

Whenever we see ourselves as weak, we should not concentrate on our own frailty, but should gaze—both eyes—upon God's glory.

(John Calvin)

NINE

NETWORK NEWS AND LOCAL NEWSPAPERS: THE COMING ECONOMIC JUDGMENT?

Some media analysts, after examining economic and technological trends, develop reductionist explanations for change. Ignoring the spiritual in this way, as in others, is clearly a mistake. On the other hand, since God works through physical means as well as spiritual power, to ignore economics and technology returns us to the nature *vs.* grace division that sapped Christian energies during late medieval times.[1] This chapter examines economics and technology, not to suggest that they are dominant, but to see how, over time, God "brings princes to naught and reduces the rulers of this world to nothing" (Isaiah 40:23).

TELEVISION NETWORK NEWS

During the 1970s and early 1980s, news budgets of all three major networks shot upwards. The CBS news division grew from seven hundred employees in 1970 to fifteen hundred in 1983, even though requirements for technical staffing decreased due to the introduction of video equipment and simpler cameras/editing machines that took less time to use. ABC and NBC also found that some of their news shows, which had been loss leaders promoted for prestige purposes, were becoming profit centers.[2] Yet, the words of Isaiah 40:24 describe well the brief glory of the news divisions: "No sooner are they planted, no sooner are they sown, no sooner do they take root in the ground, than he blows on them and they wither, and a whirlwind sweeps them away like chaff."

The new winds began to blow in 1983. In that year all three

network news divisions cut staffs and budgets. The firings were real hardships, the reduction of allowable expenses a psychological blow for those who had become used to lordly treatment. At CBS, for example, first-class travel and catered meals for journalists were virtually eliminated. These troubles were seen as only temporary, but in subsequent years network news departments continued to stagger, with NBC losing $50 million a year on its news operation.

Losses of that kind would have been no problem during previous years of almost automatic profit increases for the networks. The three networks during the 1985-86 television season, though, had a combined 76 share (76 percent of households with televisions turned on had then turned to network shows) compared with an 87 share five years earlier. The financial impact of viewer decline became evident in 1985 when advertising revenues for all three networks decreased that year for the first time since 1971 (when a ban on cigarette advertising went into effect).

News division and general network problems were made worse by the growing sense that viewer drop-off would accelerate. Network viewership losses followed the advent of cable programming and a strengthening of independent stations. In 1987, half of American households still were without cable: What would happen as more viewers had more options?

Another long-term problem for the networks emerged in 1984 when Hubbard Broadcasting of St. Paul, Minnesota, organized Conus, a satellite news-gathering service. Conus lets local stations transmit and receive footage by direct satellite hookup, without going through the networks. By September 1985, when networks were asking for help from their local affiliates in covering a bad hurricane season, some of the local stations were saying they were too busy with their Conus feeds. In 1986 Conus signed an agreement with the Associated Press to form a television news service linking more than six hundred stations, and in 1987 local stations had even less need to rely on networks.

Local stations are allowed to develop their own linkages because of the nature of networks. CBS, NBC, and ABC each own only a few stations in major cities, while hundreds of others are "affiliates" of those companies but are owned and operated by others. For the most part the network corporations and their affiliates have had a friendly, symbiotic relationship, with years of tradition and profits behind them. Affiliates give the networks access to local airwaves; in return the networks pay the stations for use of their airtime and give them a core of popular programming around which to sell advertising. Yet, any station can refuse to use network programming at any time; as Elton Rule noted when he was president of the ABC broadcast division, "Station owners do pretty much what they want to do."[3]

Given that opportunity for decentralization, change is coming through God's instruments of technology, economics and politics. With easy satellite hookups and film-sharing arrangements, local television stations do not have to rely upon networks to get national news to their viewers. Much as local newspapers have been able to fill their pages with a choice of material from various wire services and syndicates, so local producers are becoming their own national and international news editors, picking what they want for their broadcasts.

Network news economic problems center on advertising income. Most ad time on network news shows is sold by the networks, but ad time on local broadcasts belongs to local stations. Local news shows often have become cash cows, with higher ratings than the national news and far more local profit. There is little reason for local stations to give up a half-hour to the network when they can pick up inexpensive material from Conus or other feeds and reap profits by selling their own ads.[4]

Another advantage of doing just that involves response to rumblings about the biases of network news shows. ABC reporter Sam Donaldson told one interviewer that he preferred Washington politics to the supposedly stifling thought of his El Paso background—but in El Paso, they are still in El Paso. Local station heads who did not like the network slant are now able to purchase material through independent satellite film transmission, edit as they see fit, and then have their own anchors narrate the material.[5]

The transition from network to local control of national news will take several decades, but it already has begun. Surveys have found that 70 percent of network news viewers know about the major news stories before seeing the network news shows; they have heard about them on the local shows. Some stations are sending their own anchors to cover summit meetings or report on international crises. For example, Sacramento station KCRA recently sent its own anchors and correspondents to the Soviet Union, Ethiopia, and other countries. Ratings of ambitious stations have zoomed; viewers apparently like to see hometown heroes strutting world stages and playing up local angles. The ratings lesson is percolating throughout the industry.[6]

Network news shows will not die, but networks may function

increasingly like newspaper wire services, feeding stations material to use or not use in their own productions as they see fit. Since the networks own some of the biggest stations, they will continue producing news shows if only to service themselves. During the 1990s, however, some local stations are likely to drop network news shows. KCRA's station manager Peter Langlois pointed out, "The public doesn't care where they get their news from. They care that it's accurate, complete and available when they want it. Ten years from now we could be providing a complete newscast covering the world from Sacramento."[7]

Given competition from the local stations, network news is likely to head more towards features and mini-documentaries rather than breaking news stories. In 1986 ABC Vice President Av Westin predicted, "A few years from now you're going to see a format where the anchors simply genuflect to the major headlines for a few minutes, then go into two, maybe three longer, in-depth reports. That's their strength now." With network news shows losing money but interview and "magazine" shows such as "Nightline" and "60 Minutes" successful both economically and critically, networks are likely to move towards a magazine format, perhaps even a non-Christian version of "The 700 Club."[8]

The underlying threat to all three networks (and, to some extent, their local affiliates) is the growth of cable, which by the end of 1986 was in more than forty-two million American households, or 48 percent of the total. That number was up 4 percent from the previous year. Penetration of some major cities was still low, though, and some older cable systems did not have room for many channels. Nevertheless, cable growth already has led to a greater variety of news options, particularly through CNN (Cable News Network), C-Span (Washington coverage), CBN (Christian Broadcasting Network), and specialized business and religious programming.

The advent of CNN in 1980 was the beginning of television news on a twenty-four hour per day basis. CNN now has over thirty-two million subscribers, but it was not an instant success when it began in 1980. It took time to alter viewing habits and to educate advertisers who had previously been paying attention only to network or local station programming. By mid-1985, though, the success of CNN and its headline news service, CNN-2, was attracting ample advertiser attention.[9]

The reduction in network power is not automatically good news for Christians; local control over many newspapers did not preserve journalists from spiking the spiritual. The change does mean that the need to develop better local and cable news programs is great. CNN has shown that cable news can find an audience and even generate profits. CBN early in 1986 tried a half-hour evening news show but pulled back after two months; as cable penetration increases, though, other attempts will be made, and some will succeed.[10]

Major network television up to now has had little toleration for presentations of real Christianity, not only for theological reasons but also because of economics: The cross is an offense to many, and the goal of network television has been to keep from losing viewers, rather than take chances in the hope of gaining some. The challenge of cable, though, means an end to lowest-common-denominator programming. Talented Christians will have the opportunity to show on television the extent of Christ's Lordship on public-policy questions and in every aspect of life.[11]

One potential roadblock to such vigorous presentation used to be the Federal Communications Commission (FCC). Providentially, the advent of cable, along with a changed political climate, has led to a substantial decrease in FCC activity. Cable operators are correctly seen as different from broadcasters, and spectrum scarcity is no longer a problem: Ideologically independent stations and networks now have the opportunity to push hard for their own points of view, instead of going along with political fashion.[12]

Even with the FCC largely inert, it will still take a while for the full impact of cable programming to be felt. Not until large cities finally arc tied in (through cable or alternative technologies such as SMATV or MDS)[13] and old systems are updated will satellite-distributed programming approach the uniform national coverage that has characterized commercial broadcast networks for three decades. Only then might a major news and information impact be seen, with Christian presuppositions underlying some news broadcasts. The diversity of cable programming will include—it already does include—much that follows Satan. But if Christians are active it will include, and already does, much that glorifies God.[14]

Av Westin of ABC perhaps best summarized the present and future of network television news: "The whole definition of what a story is, and the network's role in delivering that story, has been changed by the satellite. In the past, we have always referred to the evening news shows as our 'flagships.' Well, as many navies around the world have already discovered, the flagship may prove to be too expensive to maintain." When the flagships are mothballed, there will be enormous opportunities for Christians—if there is understanding of ways to win and keep an audience.[15]

THE BEHEMOTH LOCAL NEWSPAPER

Since 1940, the United States has suffered through a steep decline in the number of cities having competitive daily newspapers. Some of the largest American cities now have only two daily newspapers, and many are down to one. Cities with a half-million population, such as Austin, Texas, typically have one daily newspaper; early in the century, with a population only one-tenth as large, Austin had six newspapers. There are fully competitive newspapers in only thirty American cities, representing just 2 percent of the total of about fifteen hundred cities with dailies.

Clearly, newspapers have not held their ground as other media have emerged. The number of newspapers sold per household per day decreased from 1.32 in 1930 (when radio began making inroads) to 0.79 in 1980. In the twenty largest U.S. cities, newspaper circulation fell by 21 percent between 1970 and 1980. And yet, the daily local newspaper business has been, and remains, very profitable; in general, newspaper companies in recent years have done better financially than most other companies. Newspaper revenues grew 64 percent between 1979 and 1984, and pretax operating income margins increased from 16 to 18 percent. A typical newspaper without daily print competition in its community can convert a third of its revenue to operating profit.[16]

The statistics *should* suggest profitable opportunity for Christians, and others, to jump in with competing newspapers. There is a big catch, though. Usually, when competition is low and profits are high, new competitors are quick to enter a market. But that has not been the case with city daily newspapers, for one main reason: The advertising pattern.

Newspaper advertising typically produces 80 percent of newspaper revenue. The amount of advertising dollars spent on newspapers quadrupled from six million in 1970 to twenty-four million in 1984. Inflation accounted for easily half of that, but the real increase was still very healthy. Most advertising is local retail, and what those local retailers want is penetration of over 50 percent of the local market. Total circulation may be less important than density of penetration in a particular area, for when a newspaper reaches over half the households in an area, it often becomes a must buy for local advertisers. Advertising managers have a motto:

"When you get 51 percent of the circulation, you get 70 percent of the advertising."[17]

As the 51-70 rule of thumb would indicate, in recent decades newspaper circulation leaders within their communities have tended to become fatter with ads. Their competitors have tended to lose advertising inches and revenues. Generally, after a struggle, those competitors have gone out of business. The result has been daily newspaper monopoly in most American cities.

Those wishing to break the monopoly have had to face a Catch-22. Advertising revenues allow the existing newspaper to publish a fat edition for, typically, 25 cents. New newspapers cannot get the advertising until they have established themselves by grabbing a big chunk of the market. Yet, unless they have large enough cash resources to cover tremendous losses for several years, they cannot sell "full-service newspapers" (complete with columns, special features, and so on) at a competitive price and gain the necessary circulation, *until* they have the advertising subsidy.[18]

The peculiar economics of entry explain why there has not been a new, major city newspaper developed for many years, with the exception of the Washington *Times* (published with millions of Unification Church dollars). And yet, success has created weaknesses for behemoth city dailies. To get maximum penetration they have had to provide a little for everyone, but in so doing they often have cut down on detailed local news coverage. By providing a little for everyone they have produced customers but not supporters, readers who subscribe as long as there is no alternative. In many cases they are ripe for the plucking, if a real alternative could be provided.

The efficiency of daily newspaper distribution also is questionable. Large city newspapers, with their multiple specialized sections, have developed the cafeteria line approach to journalism: Pick what you want, don't pick the rest. But the comparison has a catch to it: Cafeteria customers do not get a tray with everything on it and then throw 90 percent of their food into the trash can. But most of the typical metropolitan newspaper (72 pages by day and 265 pages—three pounds—on Sunday) is thrown away without being read. Trees are cut down in the forest, gasoline is used to get newspaper trucks across town during rush hours, and most of the effort is a waste as far as news-gathering is concerned. A typical 50,000-circulation daily newspaper spends only about one-eighth of its budget on news-gathering and editing; about three times as much goes for paper and printing.[19]

Advertising revenues allow for payment of production and

circulation costs with profits left over. If newspaper advertising were reduced, mainline newspapers would be in serious trouble. Media analysts such as John McManus note that newspaper advertising probably already has passed its peak. In a paper entitled "The Media Environment of the '90s: A Period of Danger for Newspaper Journalism," McManus noted that many retailers are learning that advertising does not have to appear between news columns to be read by consumers; other means, particularly electronic ones, are likely to come on very strong. Mass-market newspapers will face a loss of revenue, and will either have to raise prices (with resultant decreases in circulation and advertising rates) or find some other way to avoid hard times.[20]

One of the newspaper industry's main competitors, direct mail, already has proven that it can target marketing groups demographically, or reach all households in a geographic market, far more efficiently than can newspapers. An equivalent electronic attack is coming soon. Telephone circuits could bring shopping and other information directly to desktop terminals. Electronic classified advertising, or electronic yellow pages with prices updated continually, could cut substantially into newspaper revenues.

Eventually, use of personal computers in homes will lead to a more efficient delivery system for news and features also. Newspaper material will be sent over wires to individual homes. There many subscribers will print out automatically those sections they want. Others will look at material on screen, store on a disk what is useful to them, and print out only crossword puzzles that they will enjoy figuring out or articles that they wish to post on bulletin boards.

Publishers already have tried a few "videotext" experiments, with entire newspapers put on television and viewers allowed to call up the pages they want. But such approaches have been slow going so far, partly because of expense and the lack of mass computerization. Technology, after all, is not adopted by most people for its own sake: the technology must fulfill a need. For instance, the Bell System's "Picture Phone" did not catch on, perhaps because there was no demand, perhaps because of cost. Technological feasibility and economic viability are two different things. Videotext cannot compete with newspapers at present when the newspapers, with advertising subsidy, still only cost a quarter.

Over time, due to production and transport costs, newspapers will have to get more expensive. As computers become as common in homes as televisions now are, advertisers will explore those possibilities for direct consumer contact. Behemoth daily newspapers have become highly dependent on advertising, and if advertisers should find another way to cover the market so cheaply, current news monopolies will be broken.

Development of computerized daily newspapers will be immensely beneficial to Christians, because the market will be wide open again to new approaches. But it took seventy years for the telephone to reach 50 percent of American households, and it might take that long until computer communication becomes an everyday household event. In the meantime, computers will provide Christians with opportunity in another way, through the development of what is called "desktop publishing."

CHRISTIAN OPPORTUNITIES: PUBLISHING

Charging head-on against behemoth newspapers is hard; outflanking them is becoming easy. It is certainly feasible for Christians of modest means to establish weekly or monthly newspapers capable of covering major stories in ways that point out inaccuracies and biases of the big media outlets, and take into account the spiritual as well as the material. Such publications can be produced by a very small staff with the aid of a computer package—computer, laser printer, and programs—costing under $5,000. Layout by computer replaces time-consuming and costly paste-up of articles and artwork to produce camera-ready copy.

A recent dollars-and-cents analysis of what it would take to start a Christian newspaper in one city of three hundred thousand displays the opportunities. Using desktop publishing methods, monthly production and editorial costs for a 10,000-circulation, thirty-two page monthly newspaper were estimated at $10,500 (that figure includes payment for freelance writers and editors, printing, postage, circulation help, office expenses, and promotional material). The first-year circulation target of ten thousand was projected to include five thousand subscriptions at $10 each and three thousand sales in Christian bookstores at $1.25 per issue (bookstores keeping 50 cents).[21]

Projected revenue from advertising then was filtered in, with rates below those of magazines but similar to those of newspaper supplements and shoppers with equivalent impact. Total revenue for sixteen pages of ads, based on delivery of 10,000-circulation, was projected at $7,450 per month. Adding that to $7,500 from subscription revenue and $2,250 from single copy sales led to projected monthly revenue of $17,200. Given anticipated expenses of $10,500 per month, a profit potential of $6,700 per month was claimed.

Given the amount of wine that tends to be spilled from cup to lip, especially in circulation and advertising estimates, such a projection may be optimistic—but not wildly so, if a publication with something to say can be produced, and Christians respond. Repeatedly in many cities, Christian newspapers or magazines have been begun, only to be discontinued swiftly. Although editors may complain about lack of support from the Christian community, in some instances publications have been so poorly written and designed that they produced scorn rather than glory for God, and deserved to die. The hard part is producing a quality product that can keep and hold an audience. If that is done, with God's grace advertising and circulation will follow.

The long-term goal for such Christian publications will be to develop deep roots by building a solid staff and community support. When mass computerization opens up new opportunities by making the three-pound newspaper package extinct, the Christian publication will be well-positioned to challenge non-Christian media services.

A short-range alternative for Christians whom God has blessed financially involves purchase of an existing newspaper that could, over time, be staffed with talented Christians capable of gradually accustoming their readers to think of the spiritual as well as the material. Individual businessmen, or small partnerships, could take such initiative in smaller cities. Although it sometimes is said that individual enterprises do not have much of a chance in the face of newspaper chains, the largest chain, Gannett, even with its publication of *USA Today*, still has only about 8 percent of nationwide circulation. That is a lot, but in 1935 William Randolph Hearst alone controlled 14 percent of daily circulation and 24 percent of Sunday circulation. Most chains are small, and owned by small businessmen; they are often very profitable. A Christian with money can do well by doing good.

CONCLUSIONS

Research into current trends in media economics and technology leads to optimism for Christians. Anyone who is feeling pessimistic about media opportunities should compare the current problems in journalism to those facing Christians in education. Powerful groups with anti-Christian worldviews dominate major media and major educational institutions. In both fields it is often difficult to develop financially sound alternatives. But the contest to reclaim education is much harder than the parallel battle in media, for the schooling contest is rigged. Those pressing for educational alternatives have to produce an expensive product so far superior that it can pull away educational consumers from what appears to be a free lunch, the state-funded schools and colleges. Christians have seen that state largesse often can lead to isolation and practical disenfranchisement of theological minorities.

Providentially, the public television system is of only minor importance in this country, and we do not have a system of public newspapers as we have one of public schools. God has given Christians the opportunity to engage in fair competition. The number of media outlets indicates the vastness of opportunity: About 1250 television stations, over ten thousand radio stations, 1700 daily newspapers, 7700 weekly newspapers, at least twelve thousand magazines, and newsletters as many as the sand on the seashore.[22]

Those numbers are growing in most categories. From 1975 to 1985, there was an increase of two hundred television stations, 1600 radio stations, two thousand magazines, and one hundred weekly newspapers; only the number of daily newspapers decreased, down fifty.[23] Almost all of these new outlets are free of state control or policy dictation from a state religion. These opportunities, though, are just that: Opportunities. Christians will not succeed on cable, on radio, in magazines and newsletters by offering readers or viewers more of the same. Offering more of the same, slightly cleaned up, accomplishes little.

At times during the 1980s, a defeatist moan has come out of some parts of Christendom: "An elitist group of secular humanists has seized monopolistic control of the networks and major newspapers. They are brainwashing the majority of decent Americans. We can't fight them." Over three thousand years ago, after Moses had sent twelve men to explore the land of Canaan, the majority came back with a similar whine: "We can't attack those people; they are stronger than we are. . . . All the people we saw there are of great size. We seemed like grasshoppers in our own eyes" (Numbers 13:31-33).

Because of that lack of trust, the Israelites spent forty years wandering in the wilderness. If Christians today spend time complaining instead of doing, Americans may spend more decades wandering in a media wasteland. Media pessimism is not only wrong in principle and tragic in practice, but unnecessary, for three reasons. First, the deck is not necessarily stacked against Christians in media, as it is in education. Second, technological change is opening up new possibilities for wider competition. Third, and most important, God is in control: With His blessing, mountains can be moved.[24]

Providentially, Americans have an unusual media system. In other countries, governments often own the television and radio stations. Even when they do not own the printing presses, governments frequently offer newspapers and magazines considerable economic support. The American tradition is different. Newspapers and magazines operate almost entirely without governmental support. Except for the relatively unimportant Public Broadcasting System, American television and radio stations also operate without government funds. Limited FCC regulation is becoming less significant year by year.[25]

As cable television takes charge, as diversity and decentralization among local television stations develops, as opportunities to chip away at behemoth newspapers emerge, as low-cost newsletters grow in importance, the question will be whether Christians can produce programs and publications that Americans choose to watch and read. Those who shirk from the task of doing something special, convinced that there are indestructible giants in the land, are not glorifying God. We need the Joshuas and Calebs. We need journalists trained to see that there are ways to gain and keep an audience. The next chapter will deal with one of those ways.

TEN

COVERAGE OF SENSATION AND DISASTER: THE GAINING AND KEEPING OF AUDIENCES

Criticism of journalistic "sensationalism" has been common in the United States throughout the twentieth century. Theodore Roosevelt in 1909 complained that "sensational" journalism "does as much to vulgarize and degrade the popular taste, to weaken the popular character, and to dull the edge of the popular conscience, as any influence under which the country can suffer." In attacking sensationalism he could point to top circulation newspapers such as the New York *American*. One of its typical issues featured on page 1 a large picture of men attacking women in Alaska. Page 2 was mainly devoted to an illustrated discussion of the question, "Is Woman Human or Animal?" Page 3 discussed a "Woman with a Past," page 4 a torture chamber, and page 5 "The Black Spectre That Frightens Fashionable Brides at the Altar."[1]

Many critics of sensationalism have castigated the desire of editors to appeal to a wide audience, as if popularity necessarily meant lower quality. Newspapers should be solemn, they said. Roosevelt, though, wisely blamed not the mode of presentation itself, but the editors behind the style: "These men sneer at the very idea of paying heed to the dictates of a sound morality." And so the battle is joined: Is sensationalism inevitably a sneer at sound morality? Do the supermarket tabloids represent the only possible kind of sensationalism? Or might there be a Christian variety?[2]

To answer such questions, we have to get our definitions straight. The *Oxford English Dictionary* defines "sensation" as "a condition of excited feeling produced in a community by some occurrence; a strong impression produced in an audience or body of spectators." Sensationalism, then, is the attempt "in works of literature or art" to produce such responses. One example given of usage, from 1863, is a comment on "the cheap publications which supply sensation for the millions in penny and halfpenny numbers." Sensational stories tend to emphasize death and destruction.

If sensationalism, properly defined, is an attempt to produce excited feelings and strong impressions, often through tales of trouble and disaster, then the inspired authors of the Bible were some of the prime early users of sensationalism. Moses quoted the first news report, Lamech's announcement in chapter 4 of Genesis that he "killed a man for wounding me." Later in Genesis come the original tales of sodomy, leading to the destruction of Sodom and Gomorrah, followed immediately by the incest of Lot and his daughters (Genesis 19).

Many more sensational events fill the pages of Genesis and the four following books of Moses. That part of the Bible culminates in the blessings for obedience and curses for disobedience found in chapter 28 of Deuteronomy. The culmination of the curses is especially vivid, with Israelites told that unfaithfulness will lead to terrible war and starvation in which "you will eat the fruit of the womb, the flesh of the sons and daughters the Lord your God has given you. . . . The most gentle and sensitive woman among you—so sensitive and gentle that she would not venture to touch the ground with the sole of her foot—will begrudge the husband she loves and her own son or daughter the afterbirth from her womb and the children she bears. For she intends to eat them secretly."

The slide downhill was speedy during the period described in the Book of Judges. When God wanted to show the effect of the Israelites ignoring Him—"There was no king in Israel"—His inspired author wrote of a man murdering his seventy brothers and half-brothers, and of a woman being gang-raped and killed, with her husband cutting her into twelve pieces and then sending the body parts throughout Israel (Judges 9:5; 19:25-30).

Specific detail was not left out in Judges: Jael's assassination of Sisera was described in five graphic ways (Judges 4:22; 5:26). Similarly, when Ehud plunged his sword into the belly of the king of Moab, pungent description follows: "Even the handle sank in after the blade, which came out his back. Ehud did not pull the sword out, and the fat closed in over it" (Judges 3:21, 22).

By the time of Ahab and his son Joram, some of the curses for disobedience already were being realized. One woman told the king of her neighborly arrangement (2 Kings 6:28, 29): "This woman said to me, 'Give up your son so we may eat him today, and tomorrow we'll eat my son.' So we cooked my son and ate him. The next day I said to her, 'Give up your son so we may eat him,' but she had hidden him." Ezekiel promoted similar disgust at what God's covenant people had become when, in 23:20, 21, he wrote of how Judah "lusted after her lovers, whose genitals were like those of donkeys and whose emission was like that of horses. So you longed for the lewdness of your youth, when in Egypt your bosom was caressed and your young breasts fondled."

Such characterization would not survive the word processors of today's newspapers, but Jeremiah explained God's methods simply in 19:3: "This is what the Lord Almighty, the God of Israel, says: Listen! I am going to bring a disaster on this place that will make the ears of everyone who hears of it tingle." How can ears tingle if descriptions are mellow?

Directness was carried over to the New Testament as well. Paul, in Romans 1:27, did not mince words when he noted that men had "abandoned natural relations with women and were inflamed with lust for one another. Men committed indecent acts with other men, and received in themselves the due penalty for their perversion." The Book of Revelation was war reporting at its most vivid. In the New Testament as in the Old, sensationalism showed the difference between God's holiness and man's depravity.[3]

Christians who wanted to produce their newspapers in the image of Scripture regularly practiced sensationalism also. For instance, the Connecticut *Courant* in 1765 sounded very much like Jeremiah in showing the consequences of sin in a land of "indolence and oppression" where the Bible is not read and "no provision is made but from hand to mouth." A famine developed, and "in many places children expired in the arms of their mothers, who devoured them as soon as they were dead." Men tried to sell their wives and children "for a few dollars, to procure a short respite from the pangs of hunger and the approach of death."[4]

The Boston *Recorder* during the 1820s regularly ran sensational accounts. For example, "Earthquake at Aleppo" included both a first-person account of destruction in Syria and an overall report. Benjamin Barker, on the scene, wrote that he was racing down the stairs of a crumbling house when another shock sent him flying through the air, his fall broken when he landed on a dead body. He saw "men and women clinging to the ruined walls of their houses, holding their children in their trembling arms; mangled bodies lying under my feet, and piercing cries of half buried people assailing my ears; Christians, Jews, and Turks, were imploring the

Almighty's mercy in their respective tongues, who a minute before did not perhaps acknowledge him."[5]

The *Recorder*'s overall report continued the theme of sudden destruction affecting hearts and minds as well as bodies. It began with a description of the poor but peaceful city of two hundred thousand that Aleppo then was, with "nothing remarkable in the weather, or in the state of the atmosphere." But "in ten or twelve seconds" the city was turned into "heaps of ruins," with "hundreds of decrepit parents half-buried in the ruins, imploring the succor of their sons," and "distracted mothers frantically lifting heavy stones from heaps that covered the bodies of lifeless infants."[6]

The *Recorder* noted that "the crash of falling walls, the shrieks, the groans, the accounts of agony and despair of that long night cannot be described." But the *Recorder* could describe the likely purpose behind such a sad event: "Earthquakes must be numbered amongst the 'terriblia Dei,' the 'terrible things of God,' in which His irresistible power to punish His sinful creatures is most awfully displayed: and which fill the human mind with greater terror than any other public calamity."[7]

The *Recorder* then described great earthquakes of 1638, 1692, 1755, and 1783 and brought the point home: "Should not these awful demonstrations of divine power cause us to fear Him who can so suddenly sweep away a whole city into destruction? Should not sinners tremble to think how awful it is to have such a God for an enemy? Should they not immediately seek reconciliation to Him through the Blood of the Lamb?"[8]

The *Recorder* stressed the material/spiritual interface of earthquakes, which it argued were sent as a general punishment for sin, allowing the survivors the opportunity for new reconciliation with God. At Aleppo, according to the newspaper's account, many persons were seen "falling on their knees and imploring the mercy of God; and shortly after crowding the places of worship, eager to learn what they must do to be saved. Thus was it also in London in the year 1755." The *Recorder* then asked why sinners, standing "on the brink of eternity, and liable by a thousand means as fatal to life as an earthquake, to be hurried into eternity," do not "seek the Lord while He may be found."[9]

Later in the nineteenth century many newspapers did not emphasize God's sovereignty explicitly, but they still used sensationalism to stress morals emphasized in books such as Proverbs. Stories about executions of criminals had Biblically-referenced headlines such as "The Gallows Too Good/The Unrelenting Fiend Should Go to Welcome Haman."[10] Coverage paralleled the assertion in Proverbs that criminals lose out not only in the next life, but this one also: "Do not envy a violent man or choose any of his ways," for "these men lie in wait for their own blood; they waylay only themselves! Such is the end of all who go after ill-gotten gain; it takes away the lives of those who get it" (Proverbs 3:31; 1:18, 19).

Editors sometimes followed Biblical example by stressing the consequences of adultery. Just as Proverbs compares a man who sleeps with another man's wife to the man who hopes to "walk on hot coals without his feet being scorched" (6:28), so articles headlined "Shocking Domestic Tragedy" laid out sensationally the "tragic outgrowth of marriage infidelity in high life."[11] As Proverbs compares a man sleeping with a prostitute to "a bird darting into a snare, little knowing it will cost him his life" (Proverbs 7:23), so the Houston *Daily Post* described how a man was hanged for a murder he committed in "a house of ill repute."[12] The newspaper was explicit: "The black cap was drawn over his face and the noose arranged, and at three o'clock the cord holding the weight was cut and Doran was hurled into eternity. The body was left hanging eighteen minutes."

Many nineteenth-century newspapers also provided specific examples of the proverbial rule that one crime leads to another, until the person who has strayed "comes to rest in the company of the dead" (Proverbs 21:16). Newspaper stories often described the downward spiral of wrong behavior: A man forged another's name on bank papers and then tried to poison him to avoid prosecution, or a husband quarreled with his wife and then killed her with a carving knife.[13]

Editors also applied the verse, "If a man digs a pit, he will fall into it" (Proverbs 26:27; see also Psalm 7:15; 9:15; Ecclesiastes 10:8). They ran headlines such as "A Shooter Shot Dead"[14] (concerning a bandit who prided himself on a quick draw) or "He Is Fixed for Life,"[15] concerning a person who had hoped to steal enough to become financially independent, but ended up receiving a life sentence.

Convention reports from organizations such as the Texas Press Association showed that many editors were aware of their responsibilities. One editor, E. E. Harris, argued that "the press fills its largest and holiest function as the great schoolmaster of the age . . . for the good of humanity and the glory of God." Another editor wrote that "the press is the fair handmaiden of the Christian religion." Editor S. J. Thomas suggested that "the journalist is as surely called by divinity to his trade as is the minister of the gospel."[16]

By the late nineteenth century in most parts of the United

States the tendency to use sensation to teach Biblical morality had diminished, as newspapers had departed from Christian moorings. Yet, a sense of objective right and wrong still found its way into newspaper coverage of some sensational stories.

For example, newspapers did not accept the idea of no-fault, individual-choice suicide, and instead editorialized that suicides should receive more than pity: "It is necessary that we should also take into account the long concatenation of causes which have culminated in the tragedy—follies intellectual, moral, and physical . . . vices which are undeniable tokens of selfishness; passions to which the bridle has been given until it cannot be resumed; with all the waywardness and misemployed persistence of which the race is capable."[17]

Underlying the harshness was a theological sensitivity revealed in this 1877 editorial: "The highest wisdom, therefore, even for a wretch whose life is saturated with sorrow, and for whom apparently there is no future, is to wait. Surely, considering how much we need them, faith and persistence should not be lightly abandoned. The very fact that we are not yet called from the scene of wearisome struggle and disaster, seemingly consummate, should prove to us that Providence has some design in continuing our existence."[18]

Throughout the late nineteenth century, suicide was condemned by newspapers. Suicide often was described as an act committed by a person who had done wrong, but was unwilling to admit responsibility and ask for forgiveness. Newspapers saw suicide as a frequent aftereffect of murder, adultery, or theft. For example, a man who committed suicide in a county jail was said to be receiving from his own hand the punishment he deserved for brutally kicking his aged mother to death three months previously.[19]

Newspapers also publicized suicide by murderers and adulterers. The New York *Tribune* explained how a convicted wife murderer hanged himself in jail with a handkerchief.[20] The Los Angeles *Times* ran a front-page story about a murderer hanging himself.[21] The Chicago *Tribune* reported that one man took arsenic after learning of his wife's adultery.[22] The New York *Times* had a man killing himself after his wife found love letters another woman had sent him.[23]

Theft also was a leading cause of suicide, a reader of late-nineteenth-century newspapers might conclude. A typical 1877 story dealt with the "Suicide of a Defaulting Cashier."[24] Similarly, the Dallas *Herald* noted the cyanide-taking of a bookkeeper arrested for theft.[25]

The physical end of suicidal thieves often was described with particular vividness. One front page story, "A Thief & A Suicide," showed how a bank robber shot himself and was found with "his face shattered and covered with blood."[26] Another man, who also had a record of wife beating, slit his throat in the courtroom after being convicted of grand larceny.[27] A bank defrauder was found "with half of his head blown off."[28]

Was the violence necessary? The answer to that might depend on whether we really want to follow Jeremiah's procedure of making ears tingle when we communicate the results of sin, and the Boston *Recorder*'s policy of emphasizing tribulation to increase awareness of God's sovereignty. As New York reporter Jacob Riis wrote, a murder story can "speak more eloquently to the minds of thousands than the sermon preached to a hundred in the church on Sunday." And yet, sensationalism frequently has been opposed by both materialists and Christians, although for different reasons.[29]

Materialists have tended to criticize the view of man's lowliness that often seems implicit in tales of murder, rape or other crime. Over 150 years ago the atheistic journalist and reformer Robert Owen wrote, "Do you ask me wherein I put my trust, if religious responsibilities are annihilated? In human goodness. Do ye enquire what I propose as a substitute for religion? Cultivation of the noble faculties of the human mind."[30] During all the years since, those in the Owen mold have been surprised by stories showing human goodness untrustworthy and faculties often ignoble.

Materialists also have proclaimed that children should not be exposed to reports of man's depravity, or else they might also disbelieve in those "noble faculties of the human mind" that are to save us. The Biblical view, though, is that children must quickly come to understand that man needs to depend on God for all things, and that man without God is sinful and miserable. In any case, as children learn the Bible they will come across the sensational stories inside, and as they get older they will learn the facts of tragedy. It is far better for them to learn in a Christian context than elsewhere that we are sinners in the hands of a righteous (and for that reason angry) God.

Christians tended to object not to all sensationalism, but to the kind which preached that sin was not always wrong. From newspaper accounts in the 1920s, for instance, it would sometimes seem as if criminals like Bonnie and Clyde had committed victimless murders; they were glamorized while their victims, and the families of those victims, were ignored. Headlines such as "He Beat Me—I Love Him" or "Thousands Applaud While Woman Is Tortured for Amusement" became typical on some front pages. Meanwhile, the newspapers that could provide Biblical sensationalism were either defunct or sunken into anti-sensational staidness.[31]

Modern sensationalism, in short, proclaims that there is no king in Israel, so every man is right in doing what he wishes, in being his own oracle. The troubles of others are spectator sport. As one newspaper critic noted about some typical early-twentieth-century articles, "Last night this man was worth millions; this morning he has not a cent. Interesting. Yesterday this man was a pillar of his church; today he has two wives. Amusing. Last night he was a respected bank cashier; this morning he is in Canada. Alarming. This morning she was selling lace in a big dry goods store; tonight she is in the East River. Shocking. He quietly entered the house and put a knife into his wife and three children. Horrible."[32]

Sensationalism, as the Bible and the nineteenth-century examples show, does not have to be like that. The type of sensationalism with which we in the twentieth century are most familiar shows the world groaning in sin, yet provides no explanation of why we have such troubles and what we can do about them. The lack of context is not surprising, since in the twentieth century many writers use their pens in an attempt to ink out God. But a Christian sensationalism could win readers while glorifying God.

CHRISTIAN SENSATIONALISM WITHOUT GUILT

The journalistic textbooks proclaim that sensationalism is wrong, and cite solemnity as a sign of seriousness. Given the requirements of the media marketplace, such belief ends up turning many current journalists into shamefaced sensationalists. A multiple murder, just in time for the 11 o'clock news, with good film, is impossible to resist, for ratings purposes if nothing else. Journalists give in grudgingly and feel they have sold out. Or, in some cases—as with a frequent lack of suicide coverage—journalists do not cover a story in depth, if at all, and for not taking that job they feel very righteous. The straight-laced New York *Times* is seen as newspaper heaven.

The journalistic goal, though, should not be self-righteousness, but the production of lively and edifying newspapers and news programs. Non-Christians are increasingly having trouble doing that, since humanistic sensationalism fosters feelings of journalistic guilt. Christians can provide salt, not by censoring coverage but by expanding it; by making newspapers not in our own image but in the image of God's newspaper, the Bible; by helping readers realize not that editors are godlike, but that only God is Godlike.

To contemplate sensationalism constructively, it is necessary to keep in mind Biblical journalistic purpose. The Christian reporter's goal should be to provide a complete account, material and spiritual, as best he can within the limits of everyday journalism. If a Christian wants to report only the elevating and not the depressing, he is forgetting that in Christianity there is no repentance without an awareness of sin, no triumph without suffering, and no resurrection without the cross. The proper use of sensationalism could help Christians win back an audience of readers from those who purvey tragedy as amusement rather than education.

Readers and viewers should be unashamed about wanting sensational stories of disaster and death. Such stories appeal to us, in part, because they are telling us something important about our post-fall human condition. If, though, sensational stories teach readers and viewers to believe that man is not responsible before God, that obedience is not a requirement, that man's sin results from forces outside his control, and that society is responsible for crime because revolution or evolution has not proceeded fast enough, then the stories are appealing to our depravity, our desire to live without God. Sometimes they may even appeal to our sinful tendencies to gloat or to enjoy the suffering of others.

Biblical sensationalism, however, can provide bad news and good news by showing sin and repentance, and the reasons for thanksgiving day by day. Biblical sensationalism can portray man as sinner, fully responsible before God who requires obedience. It can make ears tingle at the news of punishment for breaking God's law. It can educate readers or viewers and inoculate them against the belief that sin is without consequences.[33] It can be the two-by-four that is often necessary to gain our attention. And it can do all this in a way that people will read.

In addition, Christians can report as sorrowful participants rather than gleeful spectators. After all, Paul explained in Romans that all have sinned and fallen short of God's glory. Christians who understand man's tendencies toward evil realize that every murder or suicide is neither an exotic man-bites-dog story nor a result of environmental pressure. Christians know that the murderous thoughts inside all of us are akin to murder; so the tale of murder itself is not bizarre, but a reminder to all of us. (If "news" is defined as deviation from the norm, then good news—taken for granted by those with faith in man—is truly news for Bible-believing Christians.)

Furthermore, Christians should be among the best at producing human interest stories of all kinds, because Christians are commanded to be truly interested in humans. For non-Christian reporters coverage of the macro issues of politics is prestigious, while the crime beat is something for newcomers or those who could not hack it elsewhere. A prevalent non-Christian belief was summarized well by Lincoln Steffens, the muckraker capsuled in Chapter Three: The cause of trouble in the Garden of Eden was not Adam, Eve, or even Satan, but the apple.[34]

Steffens was arguing that the real story of man is economic; the personal just reflects the societal. People are victims of circumstance, not truly responsible for their own actions, not truly important. For Christians, though, the most important battles are not fought out in Washington: They are fought out in the human soul. "Big questions" are reflections of that largest-of-all struggle.

CAUTIONS AND CONCLUSIONS

Christians who wish to reinvigorate sensationalism must be careful to avoid malicious gossip. Human disasters cannot always be connected to specific, personal sins that may have preceded them. Those who force such connections are in the position of Job's friends giving bad advice because they did not know that the war in the heavens was claiming one more victim. Particularly when reporters are writing against deadline, discernment is vital if false inference from inadequate evidence is to be avoided.

Christian reporters are not inspired. In our zeal to apply Biblical explanations for tragedy, we must avoid premature explanation, exaggeration, or malicious whispering. Forcing an explanation that seems to agree with a particular doctrinal or ideological perspective is also a danger. Christian journalists must remember that true justice, not poetic justice, pervades the world. This means we know that the Judge of the whole world does right, but—with Satan still going to and fro in the world—many tragedies are unpredictable from our human vantage point and may not have a journalistically discernible cause.

To some, it might seem strange to mention coverage of sensational events and truth-telling in the same paragraph, since the two have so often seemed opposed in non-Christian publications. God's world, though, is full of wonderful and terrifying things, and Christians are often faced with the question of whether to downplay the latter. That temptation must be resisted if we are to witness fully to our faith in God's sovereignty and justice, come what may. We tell the truth about the type of creator God is when we do not try to apologize for Him.

Disciplined truth-telling cannot be based on our own character development alone, but on the belief in God's sovereignty that only faith can bring. Telling the truth about a sorrowful incident is not easy. Augustine, after describing some of the difficult situations a person must face, noted that he found it very difficult "to resist when someone says to me: 'Look, here is a patient whose life is endangered by a serious illness and whose strength will not hold out any longer if he is told of the death of his dearly beloved only son. He asks you whether the boy is still alive whose life you know is ended.' "

Augustine then posed the hard question: "What will you answer when, if you say anything except 'He is dead' or 'He is alive' or 'I don't know,' the patient will believe that he is dead, because he realizes that you are afraid to say and do not want to lie? It will be the same no matter how hard you try to say nothing. Of the three convincing answers, two are false: 'He is alive' and 'I don't know,' and you cannot utter them without lying. But, if you make the one true answer, namely, that he is dead, and the death of the anguished father follows hard upon it, people will cry that he was slain by you."

Augustine wrote that he was "moved by these arguments," but then he "put before my mind's eye the intellectual beauty of Him from whose mouth nothing false proceeded," and was "so inflamed by love of such great beauty that I despise all human considerations that call me back from there."[35]

In a hard case of that sort, it takes enormous discipline born of faith to think of the "intellectual beauty" of God's truth. Yet, those who see the beauty realize that our most vivid teaching about man's fallenness comes from the large and small disasters we see around us. The Boston *Recorder*, at the end of its coverage of the Aleppo earthquake, asked a hard question: "Must we tempt God to visit us also with an earthquake?" Sensational destruction forced many in Aleppo to consider their Creator; the *Recorder* suggested that God could use its sensational accounts to make some readers think of spiritual questions while they still could.[36]

We know, therefore, that even disaster accomplishes something. It requires faith to understand that God protects, in life or in death, those who believe in Him. In the words of Paul to the Colossians, Christ has "reconcile[d] to himself all things, whether things on earth or things in heaven, by making peace through his blood, shed on the cross" (1:20). But if news organizations do their job properly, disaster also brings edification for those who look on with wonder and horror. When even Christian news organizations play down news of fallenness and the long-term consequences of the original fall, they are denying a truth that Martin Luther proclaimed: "It is impossible for a human heart, without crosses and tribulations, to think upon God."[37]

Sensationalism, in short, gains audience, but it also can educate that audience. The inspired writers of the Bible wanted to make ears tingle. So did American Christian journalists in the early nineteenth century. Tingling ears often are learning ears. They tend to belong to people who will come back for more stories of life and death, sin and misery, repentance and revival.[38]

In the nineteenth century, pride—a refusal to take audience tastes into account—contributed to the fall of many Christian publications. Their refusal to employ sensationalism actually meant that some editors were thinking themselves better than God, who showed in the Bible that He wants many sensational things reported. We should not make that mistake again: With God's grace, Biblical sensationalism is the key to successful Christian publishing and programming.

E L E V E N

CRUSADING ON SOCIAL AND POLITICAL ISSUES: PERSONALIZATION AND PERSISTENCE

According to the leading journalism history textbook, "The crusading spirit is as old as journalism, but never in American history had there been more opportunity for 'the people's champions' than in the years following 1900."[1] Joseph Pulitzer's New York *World*, the textbook states, "commanded deep respect for its intelligent and fair-minded approaches to issues of public importance, for its progressive and hard-hitting crusades. . . ." The textbook also praises Scripps, Steffens, and other "famous crusading liberals."[2]

It is ironic that the words "crusade" or "crusading" should be used nine times in three pages to praise the efforts of atheists. According to the *Oxford English Dictionary*, the word "crusade" (originally croisade) found its way into the English language around 1575, from the French. The word first was used in reference to the military expeditions in Palestine from the eleventh through the thirteenth centuries; then it was used to designate any war fought for supposed Christian ends; only in relatively recent times has it been generalized to refer to any movement against something considered evil.[3]

The current usage is ironic for two reasons. The first irony lies in the history of the word "crusade," and its French connection with "*croisement*," being marked by the cross. The second and most important irony is that non-Christian editors who want to crusade against evil are unaware of where true evil resides: not in specific individuals or institutions, but in the nature of man apart from God.

Without understanding original sin, non-Christian crusaders may gain relatively rapid passage of new laws and eviction of old leaders, only to find, once victory is declared, that little has changed. With an understanding of man's nature, Christian crusaders find that reform takes longer to bring about, since the goal is not just the exchange of one leader for another, or passage of a government program. The goal is to make people aware that all of us are, to use Jonathan Edwards' phrase, "sinners in the hands of an angry God."[4]

One practical outworking of this belief in changed hearts rather than (as a primary goal) changed laws is that Christian journalistic crusading does not *emphasize* the work of civil government: Use of the state is a last resort. Paul told the Christians in Rome to subject themselves "to the governing authorit*ies*" (Romans 13:1)—plural. Parents, church leaders, employers, teachers, and so on are all representatives of different types of governing authority. There must be change in many different spheres for true reform to take root. Once accomplished, though, Christian reforms are likely to last longer, with God's grace.

How should Christian journalists today conduct crusades? Two of the outstanding nineteenth-century successes point the way.

EXAMPLE: DUELING

The Boston *Recorder*'s crusade against one early nineteenth century practice, dueling, was carried on within the context of its Biblical political views.[5] Politically, the *Recorder* had argued that man's sin required diffusion of power and decentralization. Comparing God's holiness to man's depravity, *Recorder* writers concluded that man could hardly be trusted to rule himself politically, and could not be trusted to rule others; therefore, the less civil government, the better. The *Recorder*'s goal was to bring the power of multiple governments to bear on manifestations of sin.[6]

In developing an anti-dueling crusade, the *Recorder* first emphasized use of family. Since family was seen as one type of government, the *Recorder* argued frequently that potential duelists should respect the wishes of parents and spouses, rather than satisfying their own vanity. Many stories of parental request to avoid duels were given, and tales of mothers mourning over sons who had violated their wishes also were frequent.[7]

Dozens of family-stressing, anti-dueling stories appeared in the *Recorder* during the 1820s. A typical tale in 1823 began with one man challenging another to a duel. The challenged man accepted, on condition that they should breakfast together at his house before going out to fight. After breakfast, the challenger asked if the host was ready. " 'No sir,' " replied he, 'not till we are more upon a par; that amiable woman, & those six innocent children, who just now breakfasted with us, depend solely upon my life for subsistence—and till you can stake something equal in my estimation to the welfare of seven persons, dearer to me than the apple of my eye, I cannot think we are equally matched.' 'We are not indeed!' replied the other, giving him his hand."[8]

Second, the *Recorder* proposed voluntary associations, schools, churches, and businesses criticize duelists at every opportunity; newspapers, for their part, were encouraged to print names of all those involved in duels. Since entering into a duel was seen as an heroic act, the *Recorder* suggested that societal leaders should poke fun at duelists at every opportunity. One of its own stories told of a man awaiting his opponent's arrival, until "he observed some bushes near him shaking, and supposing it was his adversary skulking," fired. The man found out he had shot a cow.[9]

Third, since all authority came from God, the *Recorder* argued that Christians governed by God's law, not their own, would avoid situations in which they might commit murder. The lesson of Admiral Stephen Decatur's fatal 1820 duel—"there is no honor, which is valuable and durable, save that which comes from God"—was stressed repeatedly.[10]

Other Christian newspapers, and some non-Christian ones, joined the anti-dueling crusade, first in the North, later in the South.[11] Like the *Recorder*, they did not merely quote Biblical verses against murder and preach an abstract sermonette; instead, they used *specific detail* to make their points. They did not emphasize governmental action. Dueling already was against the law, but anti-dueling laws, like others, were regularly breakable unless they were written in men's hearts.

As the early nineteenth-century Christian newspapers became less vigorous, the crusade was carried on by others. Social changes contributed to the demise of dueling, but newspaper coverage seems to have had an effect. By the late nineteenth century dueling pistols were still very much in demand, but as collector's items.

ABORTION

It is no accident that the abortion story comes into play in several chapters of this book. Abortion is not only a major manifestation of sin in our age, but a deadly fad whose rise and fall and rise again and prospective fall is interwoven with the history of American journalism.

Part of Chapter One discussed the role of one newspaper, the New York *Times*. Segments of Chapters Two and Eight noted treatment of one aborting mother, Sherri Finkbine. The goal in this chapter is to learn a lesson from the way in which abortionists themselves were treated. As Pulitzer and his contemporaries knew, *personalization* is vital to a successful crusade: To keep readers' or viewers' attention throughout a long campaign, they must be able to see a bad guy rather than an abstraction. Christian crusaders must learn how to personalize in a way that spotlights the activity and its reprehensibility, and does not ignore the nature of original sin.

In the nineteenth-century abortion battle, the chief bad guy for forty years was a woman, Madame Restell. Born Anna Trow in 1812, she worked in New York as a seamstress and occasional midwife, and married a printer. In the late 1830s she opened an abortion business and took the name Madame Restell (the French were considered most up-to-date in such matters).

Madame Restell found that word-of-mouth would take her business only so far. Hoping to get her message on abortion availability to thousands of pregnant women and desperate men, she began to advertise in New York's newspapers.[12] She had to be careful, because abortion was illegal by statute in New York; she did not have to be too careful, because anti-abortion laws rarely were enforced.[13] She ran euphemistic ads in non-Christian newspapers, such as this one in the New York *Sun*:

> MADAME RESTELL FEMALE PHYSICIAN, office and residence 148 Greenwich Street, between Courtlandt and Liberty St., where she can be consulted with the strictest confidence on complaints incidental to the female frame. Madame Restell's experience and knowledge in the treatment of cases of female irregularity, is such as to require but a few days to effect a perfect cure. Ladies desiring proper medical attendance will be accommodated during such time with private and respectable board.[14]

Madame Restell also publicized her "FEMALE MONTHLY REGULATING PILLS" that would cure "all cases of suppression, irregularity, or stoppage of the menses, however obdurate."[15] This was accurate in that the leading cause of menstrual stoppage among women of child-bearing age was pregnancy.

According to contemporary observers, "every schoolgirl" knew what references to "female irregularity" and "perfect cure" meant. While no financial records of her business are known to exist, response to her advertising was so great that she soon was able to open up a chain of abortion offices in New York, Boston and Philadelphia.[16]

Other abortionists began advertising their "willingness to treat the private ailments of women" in terms that clearly indicated the availability of abortion services. Advertising of generally ineffective abortifacients, like that of patent medicines, also boomed. "Dr. Peter's French Renovating Pills" were sold as "a blessing to mothers . . . and although very mild and prompt in their operations, pregnant women should not use them, as they invariably produce a miscarriage." Dr. Monroe's French Periodical Pills displayed prominently the "precaution" that they were "sure to produce a miscarriage." Dr. Melveau's Portuguese Female Pills alerted consumers that they were "certain to produce miscarriage."[17]

Those whose "blockages" were not removed by medication were likely to turn next to surgical methods. By the mid-1840s doctors were noticing a great upsurge in abortion. Amos Dean of the Albany Medical College, *Medical Jurisprudence* editor R. E. Griffith, and many others wrote of a dramatic increase. Changes in the intellectual and social climate had an effect on the abortion rate, but advertising clearly was important. When abortionists occasionally were arrested, pregnant and unmarried young women testified that they had seen abortion advertisements and had begun thinking about what appeared to be an easy way out of trouble.[18]

Some doctors fought back. Dr. Gunning Bedford, in *The New England Journal of Medicine*, called Madame Restell "a monster who speculates with human life with as much cruelness as if she were engaged in a game of chance." He wrote of one patient who told him that "Madame Restell, on previous occasions, had caused her to miscarry five times." The patient also described one Restell abortion in which the aborted baby "kicked several times after it was put into the bowl." Bedford wrote angrily that Restell's "advertisements are to be seen in our daily papers. . . . She tells publicly what she can do; and without the slightest scruple, urges all to call on her who might be anxious to avoid having children."[19]

In the 1840s the New York *Times* was not yet in existence, and other Christian newspapers seemed reluctant to become involved. One newspaper, the *National Police Gazette*, did begin an anti-abortion crusade; its name came from a willingness to specialize in news of crime at a time when other newspapers often refused to get their hands dirty. Later the *Gazette* went through several changes of ownership and began to glamorize crime rather than expose and oppose it. In the 1840s and the 1850s, though, the *Gazette* was the only newspaper consistently attacking abortion.[20]

The *Gazette* began its great crusade in 1845 by proclaiming that it would publish articles about abortion "because we believe that full expositions of the infamous practices of abortionists will tend to present these human fiends in a true light before the eyes of those who may become their dupes. We shall follow up this business until New York is rid of those child destroyers."[21] Even though Madame Restell originally saw such attacks as part of a day's work, and even claimed they were good publicity—those who wanted abortions would definitely know where to go—the *Gazette* persisted.

The *Gazette* emphasized community action; it complained in February 1846 that "Restell still roams at large through the influence of ill-gotten wealth and will probably still continue until public indignation drives her and her associates from our midst."[22] Week after week the *Gazette* kept after Madame Restell, predicting that a "day of vengeance" would arrive for her and other "fiends who have made a business of professional murder and who have reaped the bloody harvest in quenching the immortal spark in thousands of the unborn."[23] Week after week the *Gazette* attacked "Restell, the murderess paramount in the dark scheme of professional destruction, openly defying decency and the statute, and proclaiming to the world to stifle human life at so much per deed."[24]

With authorities still not acting, popular hostility fueled by *Gazette* accounts and anti-Restell handbills erupted. At noon on February 23, 1846, a crowd of perhaps seven hundred gathered in front of Madame Restell's house to "publicly protest the inertness of the authorities." Reporters quoted cries from the crowd of "Haul her out!," "Where's the thousand children murdered in this house!," "Hanging is too good for the monster." The New York *Morning News*, describing "a universal cry for vengeance and retribution," made comments about "wholesale female strangler . . . vital spark of the unborn . . . rude and savage butchery."[25]

Under great pressure, police finally arrested Madame Restell in 1847 for procuring an abortion. At the trial a young woman, Maria Bodine, testified that during the abortion Madame Restell "hurt me so that I halloed out and gripped hold of her hand; she told me to have patience, and I would call her 'mother' for it."[26]

Found guilty, Madame Restell was given a one-year jail term, but political connections preserved her from great misery. She was allowed to put aside the lumpy prison mattress and bring in her own fancy new featherbed instead. Madame Restell also brought into the "prison suite" her own easy chairs, rockers, and carpeting. Visiting hours were altered so that her husband was able to visit at will and "remain alone with her as long as suited his or her pleasure," according to Warden Jacob Acker.[27]

After release from such a jail, Madame Restell proclaimed that the trial and imprisonment were easily worth $100,000 to her in advertising. She moved to larger and better offices and in the 1850s was said to be spending $20,000 on advertising per year, at a time when eggs were six cents a dozen and decent apartments in New York City cost $5 or $6 a month. Madame Restell also became known as the favorite abortionist of the wealthy and powerful. She boasted that mistresses of senators, governors and other high officials used her services. One 1850 newspaper editorial explained her lenient treatment by police: "She held in her keeping the dread secrets of many a high-toned family, and fear of exposure led those people quickly to defend her when she got into the toils."[28]

Some newspapers would have given up, but the *Gazette* kept at it. Popular pressure led to a rearrest of Madame Restell in 1856; this time, though, her political connections were so strong that she was released at once. Growing still wealthier and continuing to expand her clientele, she moved to a mansion at Fifth Avenue and 52nd Street which, according to the New York *Times*, "never fails to attract the attention of the passerby, on account of its architectural beauty and magnificence." Madame Restell traveled the avenues behind a pair of matched grays and a driver with plum-colored facing on his coat lapels. According to one writer, she also carried a small muff of mink in which she hid her hands, much like the ones "famous pianists or violinists used to protect their hands from harm."[29]

By the mid-1860s she was said to be a millionaire. Other New York abortionists also had, in the words of the *British Medical Journal*, a "large and lucrative business," one in which they were "never in want of engagements." One anti-abortion doctor, J. H. Toner, had to admit that abortion "has become a regularly established, money making trade." Some opponents of abortion gave up, just as some give up now: The opposition seems too strong. And yet, the *Gazette* kept at it.[30]

In the 1860s the great crusade finally began to make real progress with the coming aboard of the New York *Times*, as described in Chapter One. Following the exposés by the *Times*, even the Greeley-edited New York *Tribune* ran anti-abortion editorials, examining the business aspects of "an infamous but unfortunately common crime—so common that it affords a lucrative support to a regular guild of professional murderers, so safe that its perpetrators advertise their calling in the newspapers, and parade their spoils on the fashionable avenues."[31]

The *Tribune* called for an end to newspaper advertising of abortion services: "Abortion at any period is homicide" and should not be "allowed to flourish openly as a recognized industry." Non-Christian newspapers, even the New York *Herald*, bowed to public pressure and at various points during the 1870s began refusing to run ads for known abortionists.[32] Madame Restell's business began to decrease, but as revenue slackened she seemed to spend more and more, putting part of her savings back into the Fifth Avenue house.[33]

Increasingly, though, her house itself became known as a symbol of ill-gotten gains. With newspapers attacking her *personally*, as a way of focusing attention on the issue, a new generation of officials did not automatically protect her. Assistant District Attorney Fellows complained that "Every brick in that splendid mansion might represent a little skull, and the blood that infamous woman has shed might have served to mix the mortar." Community pressure increased, and Madame Restell became isolated. Loud cries against "Madame Killer" would sometimes follow her carriage down Fifth Avenue. With anti-abortion laws not only tightened but, due to public sentiment, enforced, she began to lie low.[34]

Early in 1878, personalization and persistence finally paid off. The New York *Times* could report, "Mme Restell Arrested" for "selling drugs and articles to procure abortion." The *Times* noted that "The residence of Mme Restell is one of the best known in New York. . . . Her wealth is entirely the proceeds of her criminal profession. Her patrons are said to belong to the wealthiest families." But Madame Restell's patrons were not able to protect her from newspaper reporters who followed every detail of her arraignment and trial.[35]

Some of the developments were low comedy. Madame Restell could not immediately raise bail from her own funds, since her investments in bonds and real estate were illiquid. Bondsmen said they would put up sufficient funds only if the judge would order reporters not to print the bondsmen's names in the newspaper. The judge refused and the bondsmen refused. Madame Restell's lawyer turned to one bondsman and asked him to help out, saying, "Will you not allow a Christian feeling to govern you?" But there was nothing Christian about Madame Restell, the *Times* suggested, as it quoted the bondsman refusing not from opposition to abortion but from dislike of publicity: "I've got a wife and a family of girls, and I'll be hanged if I'm agoing to have my name in the papers as a bondsman for an abortionist."[36]

Madame Restell eventually left jail, but she could not leave behind newspaper attacks. She had lived by the press and was now dying by it. She asked her lawyers if there was some way to suppress the newspapers, but was told that nothing could be done, for the press was without standards. One of Madame Restell's colleagues complained angrily, "Money! We've plenty of that. But what good is it with the newspapers against us?" Madame Restell's lawyer asked both judge and editor to have mercy on his client, a "poor old woman," but he was laughed at. Madame Restell could not seem to understand the causes of the judgment she was facing: "I have never injured anybody," she complained: "Why should they bring this trouble upon me?"[37]

Madame Restell at age sixty-five became an avid newspaper reader, but she found no peace. The New York *Times* described how she was "driven to desperation at last by the public opinion she had so long defied." At night she paced her mansion halls like a latter-day Lady Macbeth, looking at her hands and bemoaning her plight. Early on the morning of the day trial was scheduled to begin, Madame Restell was discovered in her bathtub by a maid, with her throat cut from ear to ear, an apparent suicide.[38]

The end was sad; there is no evidence that Madame Restell ever repented. But she served during her life as the symbol of evil. She had flaunted wealth gained through murder. Just as the New York *Times* seized on the death of a young woman to drive home its abortion lesson, so the *Gazette* and then other newspapers concentrated on Madame Restell. Was the treatment of Madame Restell compassionate? Her only hope was to realize that abortion was wrong and to change, as Dr. Bernard Nathanson and many other former abortionists have done in recent years.[39]

Learning from their successful treatment of Madame Restell, and going with/contributing to the changed flow of opinion, many newspapers in the 1870s and 1880s emphasized the large monetary rewards many abortionists had received. They thus suggested "murder for profit" rather than an offering of professional services. Abortionists who were arrested were almost invariably described as rich.

At one abortion inquest, a "Madame Ihl" was "dressed handsomely in black silk." Another abortionist was "plainly but richly dressed in a costume of black silk."[40]

Always, the motto was personalization and persistence. In 1890 the New York *Times* wrote that an arrested abortionist, Dr. McGonegal, "has the appearance of a vulture. . . . His sharp eyes glitter from either side of his beaked nose, and cunning and greed are written all over his face." McGonegal's accomplice, Fannie Shaw, was described as "wholly repulsive in appearance, vice and disease having made her a disgusting object."[41]

The *Times* even sent a reporter to McGonegal's neighborhood in Harlem to learn how he was regarded by the people he said he was trying to help. The reporter concluded, "To the good people of Harlem, and especially to the poorer class, this grizzly old physician had long been an object of intense hatred. They were certain of his unholy practices, although he had escaped conviction, and when he drove through the streets in his old-fashioned, ramshackle gig, they hooted and jeered at him in derision."[42]

By 1900, though, the New York *Times* and other newspapers were not paying much attention to abortion. The practice had been driven underground, but it was far from ended. Magazine articles occasionally discussed abortion and abortionists, and slowly the slant of personalization began to change. *Time* magazine in 1936 called the pro-abortion gynecologist Frederick Taussig "a handsome man" who performs "strict and meticulous clinical work."[43] Eight years later *Time* was more forthright, reporting that "one of the best abortionists in the U.S. went to jail last week." "Best" was not just a slip of the pen; *Time* called the imprisoned abortionist a "good practitioner."[44]

By the end of the 1950s, with sweeping changes in the religious and intellectual climate, and in attitudes of doctors and many journalists, pro-abortion forces could reemerge. Conferences installed the intellectual carpeting. Then the techniques of persistence and personalization were used to sell abortion. A typical *Newsweek* article on abortion in 1960 was laced with quotations by pro-abortionist Alan Guttmacher, described by the magazine as a "strong-faced outspoken crusader." Guttmacher's book, *Babies by Choice Or by Chance*, was excerpted in the January 1960 *Reader's Digest*.[45]

The next step for pro-abortion personalization was television. In April 1962 the CBS show "The Defenders" aired an episode entitled "The Benefactor," with an abortionist as the hero of the title. This "benefactor" had become an abortionist not for profit but merely to help young women in trouble.[46] The idea that altruists could honorably kill unborn children was part of American popular culture. Shortly afterwards, the Sherri Finkbine incident hit the headlines.

A WILLINGNESS TO GIVE OFFENSE

To combat the perverse equation of abortion and altruism, Christian journalists and allies have to be willing to give offense when needed. Some Christians are uncomfortable with attempts to shock readers by providing unpleasant descriptions of the abortion itself, and sometimes even "bloody pictures" of aborted infants. There is also discomfort about the plastering of abortionists' names on billboards: Attack the institution but not individuals, some say.

The history of effective crusading shows the importance of personalization. So does the work of the best current anti-abortion newspaper in the United States, the *National Right to Life News*. One recent issue provided examples of all four types of stories useful in a persistent crusade: Bad news, good news, exposure of institutions, and exposure of individuals.[47]

The bad news story, "Murder Trial Set for Man Accused of Fatally Injuring Unborn Child," reported the follow-up to the death of a baby girl born prematurely after the accused man allegedly beat the baby's mother when she would not get an abortion. A California judge ordered the man to stand trial and rejected the defense attorney's motion to limit the charges to no more than second-degree murder.[48] This case seems like one taken almost directly out of Exodus 21:22, 23: In those verses, if a man hits a pregnant woman and she gives birth prematurely but there is no serious injury, a fine is in order; but if there is serious injury, more severe penalties go into effect, even up to life for life.

The good news story was of an operation in which doctors opened a mother's womb by cesarean section, removed her baby for three minutes to correct a urinary tract infection, and put the baby back in the womb. Nine weeks later a healthy baby named Mitchell was born. Doctors did not publicize the operation until a year after it took place. By then, according to Mitchell's mother, the baby could "walk holding on to the couch and he smiles all the time. We've decided he's an angel."[49]

The institutional exposé was of a cozy relationship between the most powerful pro-abortion group, Planned Parenthood, and the supposedly objective National Academy of Sciences; the Academy had just published a pro-abortion report, *Risking the Future*.

NRL News showed how the report came about: Planned Parenthood employees and allies "produced much of the 'research,' wrote the evaluation (of their own research), and critiqued their own findings and conclusions. Nice work, if you can get it."[50]

The individual exposé was the most gripping story on the front page. "Malpractice Result of 'Burnout,' from 2,600 Second-Trimester Abortions, Garrett Claims" told of a New Jersey abortionist who pleaded "no contest" to malpractice charges involving forty patients, including one fourteen-year-old girl who died. The abortionist, E. Wyman Garrett—*NRL News* published his picture—blamed his actions in the cases on stress caused by performing twenty thousand abortions, 2,612 of which were dilation and evacuation (D&E) abortions done in the second trimester. (In a D&E, the unborn child is crushed and dismembered before being removed from the mother's womb.)[51]

In at least one case, Garrett allegedly left the head of an aborted baby in the woman's body. Another abortionist, testifying in Garrett's defense, said he "could have predicted" that Garrett would suffer burnout from doing abortions because most doctors who specialize in obstetrics and gynecology (as Garrett did) do so to be part of the "life and birth" process, making abortion—especially D&E abortions—stressful.[52]

Did *NRL News* lack compassion to spotlight one particular individual? Did nineteenth-century newspapers lack compassion when they hounded Madame Restell? First, of course, we have to remember the mountain of tiny skulls on which abortionists stand. Second, we must pray for the abortionists: They also have souls which will never die, souls which are scarred anew when each abortion is performed. Trained to save life, they are taking it. They know, deep down, that what they do is wrong (Romans 1:32).

The best thing that could have happened to Madame Restell would have been for her to stop doing abortions; she kept on, and ended up committing suicide. The best thing that could happen to today's abortionists, for their own good as well as for the good of children, would be for them to cross over from death to life, physically and spiritually. Newspapers that pressure them could aid in the process.

In any case, compassion is not the only question worth considering. Augustine's emphasis on truth-telling is fundamental to good reporting. While we are concerned about the ultimate fates of Madame Restell and E. Wyman Garrett, truth and God's justice cannot be neglected. The inspired author of 2 Kings did not write with gentleness of the death of Jezebel, Ahab's queen: "They threw her down, and some of her blood spattered the wall and the horses as they trampled her underfoot." As Elijah had predicted, dogs quickly ate Jezebel's flesh: "When they went out to bury her, they found nothing except her skull, her feet and her hands" (2 Kings 9:33, 35).

FROM SPECIFIC TO GENERAL: THE NATURE OF CRUSADING

The four *NRL News* stories cited represent part of one issue. Every two weeks another issue is published, full of specific detail and personalization, not sermonettes and abstraction. Some Christian publications that style themselves newspapers are not: They present opinion, sometimes well-stated, but not much news. The essence of newspaper crusading, though, is *news*: Showing, not just talking about, the evil amidst us and the need for change.

The willingness to be specific, even if feelings are hurt, is based on some theological discernment. It is not enough for us to go around saying, "God loves you." He does, but Christ's sacrifice, the greatest love of all, can only be fully understood in terms of Adam's fall. Grace is a meaningless concept if sin is not taken seriously and condemned by journalists and others.

Crusading requires certain cautions, both in selection of issue—are we exposing something the Bible defines as evil, or just something we do not like?—and in method; carelessness may lead to ethical and legal problems, as indicated in Chapter Six's discussion of libel. Today's law allows some reporters to get away with character assassination, but Christians have a higher standard. A Christian journalistic crusader should never go to print unless his accusations are confirmed by the testimony of two witnesses.

Reporters must also remember that personalization is a dramatic technique; we should never think that if we depose one individual we have disposed of sin. Personalization, just like sensationalism, can be misused, if we do not remember that "all have sinned and fall short of the glory of God" (Romans 3:23). God's holiness and God's redemptive love go together. Paul's verse of bad news is followed by the Good News that we "are justified freely by his grace through the redemption that came by Christ Jesus" (Romans 3:24). Christian journalists who keep both verses in mind can avoid distortion while crusading.

The latter half of this chapter has given examples of crusading against abortion, one manifestation of sin. The same principles of specific detail, persistence and personalization may be applied journalistically in other social and political areas, and on economic issues as well. In every situation, it is vital to stress news rather than sermonettes, and to banish thoughts of easy victory.

T W E L V E

A CHRISTIAN JOURNALISM REVIVAL?

Technology provides the opportunity for a Christian comeback. Use of Biblical sensationalism and crusading personalization will allow Christians to gain and keep an audience. But none of this will make much difference unless Christian communities view journalism as a vital calling and Christian journalists as ministers worthy of spiritual and economic support. Christian editors and reporters, after all, are like fish in a lake. Some Christian newspapers made mistakes in the nineteenth century, as indicated in Chapter One, but the lake itself was drying up fast.

The water level of Christian lakes appears to be rising. The environment for successful Christian publications earlier in American history was a Christian population willing to fight on social and political issues. Jolted by the atheism of many French revolutionaries and their American supporters, Christians resolved to publish rather than perish. Jolted in recent decades by similar revolutionary doctrines in modern wineskins, Christians are relearning what the New York *Times* proclaimed during its abortion campaign of the 1870s: "The evil that is tolerated is aggressive," and the good "must be aggressive too."

A recent statement of the Coalition on Revival (COR) typifies the trend. (COR's leadership group includes individuals such as Edith Schaeffer, former *Christianity Today* editor Harold Lindsell, evangelists James Kennedy, Jack Van Impe and Tim LaHaye, and Southern Baptist Convention president Adrian Rogers.) The statement included admissions of sin such as, "We have neglected our God-ordained duties to be the world's salt, light, teacher, and example. . . . We, and our fathers, have settled for a sub-standard, false version of Christianity in our local churches and denominations. . . . We have allowed our churches to become irrelevant, powerless ghettos."[1]

The statement then asked for forgiveness by God, fellow Christians, and, significantly, non-Christians: "Forgive us for our failure to demonstrate to you Biblical answers for your difficulties and problems in life. Forgive us for failing to occupy our proper position as servants in the affairs of law, government, economics, business, education, media, the arts, medicine, and science as the Creator's salt and light to the world, so that those spheres of life might offer you more help, justice, hope, peace, and joy."

COR's Call to Action proclaimed several truths essential to the revival of Christian journalism: "We affirm that living under the total Lordship of Jesus Christ in every area of life is not optional for those who would call themselves Christians." Furthermore, we cannot be smiling all the time: COR stressed the "need for loving confrontation over matters of falsehood and unrighteousness in the Church and in the world." Regular confrontation, exhortation and rebuke are vital to the leading of Biblically obedient lives and the transforming of culture.

The statement concluded with an affirmation "that all Bible-believing Christians must take a non-neutral stance in opposing, praying against, and speaking against social moral evils." Among those evils listed were abortion, infanticide and euthanasia; adultery and homosexuality; unjust treatment of the poor and disadvantaged; state usurpation of parental rights and God-given liberties; and atheism, moral relativism, and evolutionism taught as a monopoly viewpoint in public schools.

Other Christian organizations also are speaking out forcefully. Some within the church are offended by such efforts. Jesus, though, said to His followers, "Do not suppose that I have come to bring peace to the earth. I did not come to bring peace, but a sword" (Matthew 10:34). Christians may be sure of peace in Heaven and peace in our consciences, but peace in our worldly dealings is rare.

The sword brought by Christ is twofold, as commentator Matthew Henry pointed out: The sword of the Word eventually conquers (Revelation 19:21), but God's truth often provokes such a hostile reaction among non-Christians that they apply the sword to believers. This effect of the preaching of the gospel is not the fault of the gospel, but of those who do not receive it. Because of this backlash effect, it is a mistake to think Christianity preserves its followers from trouble in this world. Becoming a Christian is not the end of the battle, but the real beginning.

The battle record of some established Christian publications is not good. Some now are public relations vehicles for their organizations, denominations, or peculiar beliefs. Some seem devoted largely to keeping up appearances and smiles. Editors who try to wield the sword on controversial issues sometimes have found that readers and contributors have exceptionally thin skins. One editor who tried to renovate a dull and declining magazine complained, following his pressured resignation, that "readers sometimes expect a magazine to be something for the whole family, with everything positive. Readers don't seem willing to tolerate a few articles they don't like."

Some Christian publications are willing to wield a sword. *World* magazine (Asheville, N.C.) covers hard news. *Twin Cities Christian (TCC),* a biweekly newspaper published in Minneapolis with a circulation of eight thousand and considerable advertising, has had front-page coverage of issues that "soil the breakfast cloth," in the words of the nineteenth-century New York *Times.* For example, when the Supreme Court struck down claims by homosexuals that the Constitution protects sodomy, *TCC* did not shy away from front-page sentences about oral and anal sex. When members of a pro-life action group were arrested for distributing literature in front of a hospital where abortions are performed, *TCC* published a photograph and a sympathetic article.[2]

TCC's coverage of local controversies includes three elements. First, the newspaper throws a spotlight on anti-Biblical activities. *TCC* gave front-page coverage to the sponsorship by a liberal church social services program of a program for sex offenders designed to help them "in the most important area of their lives, that of intimacy." To show what those nice words really meant, *TCC* had to quote charges from a responsible source that the program included use of explicit films portraying men and women masturbating to climax, having intercourse with animals, and engaging in a variety of homosexual and lesbian acts—the goal of the program apparently being not a consideration of right and wrong, but how-to training. The program concluded with a worship service featuring a pastor and his wife who were dressed as clowns. One clown wore huge glasses with obscene words written on the lenses.[3]

Second, *TCC* goes to bat for Christians facing discrimination. One headline stretching across the top of *TCC's* front page read, "Christian Students Suspended." According to the story's lead, "They weren't selling drugs, skipping class, or damaging school property. They didn't brawl in the halls or smoke in the bathroom. But last Thursday two Hopkins School seniors were suspended from classes." The students were "handing out religious literature.

Their action violated a school board policy." The story explained that the students had deliberately handed out free copies of a Christian magazine before classes began in order to test the school board policy: "We need to fight for our rights," one student said.[4]

TCC has used Biblically sensational headlines in coverage of stories involving such abridgment of First Amendment rights. "Bible-reading Grandma Kicked out of Mall" was the headline on a story of a grandmother talking with a young man about the Bible as they sat in a shopping mall rest area. "We were speaking quietly," she said. "When you're out in the world you're representing Jesus Christ, not only in your actions, but in how you're dressed and in how you talk. We were being careful not to offend anybody or to draw attention to ourselves. We were just talking one-on-one about the Lord." Then a security guard falsely accused the woman of selling religious literature, and escorted her off the mall property with orders not to return again.[5]

When the Bible-reading grandma protested and *TCC* investigated the incident, the mall management backed down, explaining that it was all a misunderstanding. "We had been picking up religious booklets that had been distributed in the mall, and when you were sitting discussing religious things with another person, we made an assumption that proved incorrect," the mall manager told the grandmother. "We apologize." She replied, "I'm not resentful, but people need to be warned about how our rights as Christians to worship God in public—even just reading a Bible—are being taken away from us." A loss of such rights can be more readily opposed when Christian journalists are present to blow the whistle.[6]

A third element of *TCC* coverage is also crucial: It will defend Christians who are suffering for Christ's sake, but it will also print critical evidence about Christians or Christian organizations engaged in unethical activity. The lead story in one issue concerned an evangelist accused of faking miracles at healing crusades for his own purposes. An editorial criticized a local Christian television organization for soliciting funds but not providing information on how the money was being spent. Other stories decried the fundraising tactics of some Christian organizations.[7]

Editor Doug Trouten defended his policy in a spirited editorial, "Why Write Bad Things About Good People?" He raised in print the questions that he had been asked: "When a ministry folds and its leaders leave town with its assets, why report it? When the leader of a ministry dependent on donations seems to live in unnecessary opulence, why tell the world? When an elected official strays from the Christian principles that were a part of campaign rhetoric, does somebody need to blow the whistle?"[8]

Trouten noted that "the Christian press often becomes a willing partner in efforts to cover up wrong-doing by religious leaders," but he argued that "this mentality runs contrary to Scriptural teaching. . . . Too often we are content to ignore unpleasant truths. Yet as Christians we worship a God of truth. We're not asked to follow our leaders blindly. The Bible says, 'I would not have you ignorant. . .' and 'My people are destroyed for lack of knowledge.' We need to know about those who lead us."[9]

TCC's willingness to cover sensation and take tough stands is essential to the establishing of real Christian journalism (rather than public relations) and the resultant strengthening of the Body of Christ. More Christian publications should take lessons from *TCC*—or from a Kentucky editor of the 1840s, the original Cassius Clay. (Muhammed Ali was named after him, but showed his theology by making a change.)

The original Clay, born in 1810, was a Christian who published in Kentucky an anti-slavery newspaper. When pro-slavery partisans threatened to destroy Clay's printing press, he made a fort out of his three-story, red-brick newspaper office: Clay purchased two small brass cannon, loaded them to the muzzle with bullets, slugs, and nails, and stationed them at the entrance, while his friends stockpiled muskets and Mexican lances.

Those measures forestalled the attack. Then Clay took the fight to the opposition, going before hostile crowds to speak his piece. Once, facing his enemies, Clay held up a Bible and said, "To those who respect God's word, I appeal to this book." Then he held up a copy of the Constitution and said, "To those who respect our fundamental law, I appeal to this document." Then he took out two pistols and his Bowie knife. He said, "To those who recognize only force. . ."[10]

Clay survived many fights and assassination attempts. Finally, he was seized by pro-slavery men and knifed. Gushing blood from a lung wound, Clay cried out, "I died in the defense of the liberties of the people," and then lost consciousness. He recovered, though, and helped to form the Republican Party during the 1850s. He had many political successes and personal adventures until he died in 1903, at age ninety-three.

The secret of Clay's strength may have been his belief in the power of God's law and personal faith. Clay saw even-handedness in the Bible: The rich should help the poor, and the poor should not envy or steal from the rich. Clay wrote, "Let true Christianity prevail, and earth will become the foreshadowing of Heaven." Clay also knew there is no such thing as neutrality in journalism. Knowing that all people, whether Christian or non-Christian, interpret the world through religious first principles, Clay openly acknowledged his beliefs and showed the willingness to fight for them.

The situation is a bit different now: In our daily business activities we can leave the Bowie knives home. Yet, the sword brought by Christ still flashes, and we need to be prepared to fight with our brains, pens, and computers. What keeps us from readiness to fight, often, is fear both obvious and subtle: Fear of ridicule and fear of audience are obvious problems; fear of distraction and, most crucially, fear of the Bible itself are the covert cripplers among Christians.

THE FOUR FEARS AND THEIR EFFECT UPON JOURNALISM

First, Christian journalists must not be afraid of boldly stating the Christian view of reality, which includes both material and spiritual dimensions. We must subdue our fear of what materialistic colleagues will think of us, not only because of the realization that Christ has come with a sword, but because the Biblical emphasis on truth-telling is fundamental to Christian journalism.

Some materialists will be tolerant of religious belief as long as it is privatized and equated with subjectivity: If it makes you feel good, believe it. Some also argue that Heaven, if there is such a place, must be an equal opportunity employer. Christians, though, know that subjective feelings are ephemeral: Our friends need to gain an accurate picture of the cosmos and then act accordingly, or else they are lost.

The Bible always emphasizes reporting of what actually happened. Luke began his Gospel by writing, "Since I myself have carefully investigated everything from the beginning, it seemed good also to me to write an orderly account . . . so that you may know the certainty of the things you have been taught." Paul told the Corinthians that they should not believe in the doctrine of Christ's resurrection because it might be comforting for some: The important question was, did it happen? Paul insisted that either Christ rose from the dead, or Christian hope is in vain.

In short, when a Christian reports spiritual happenings as fact, not subjective impression, he will be ridiculed by some. That is the price to pay for worshiping the God who really is there, not just a psychologically soothing idol.

Second, Christian journalists must not be afraid of audience. We should not turn inwards, nor be willing to accept a journalistic strategy that churches might find pleasant but the world will ignore. We should not be afraid of picking from the best of the methods of journalism, while always evaluating all means and ends in the light of God's Word (2 Corinthians 10:5).

After all, the authors of the Gospels knew how to produce the same message but with different emphases for those with different backgrounds. Paul, in speaking to the Athenians, was willing to make contact with them by pointing out their worship of an unknown God (Acts 17). A successful Christian journalist must similarly attract attention in order to affect intentions.

Third, Christians must not fear that a new emphasis on journalism will distract from either concern for evangelism or the godly education of those already within the church. That concern is short-sighted, since both evangelism and education become more difficult when both non-Christians and Christians are constantly being bombarded by messages on "non-religious" matters that assume materialism is true. Journalism is vital pre-evangelistic work, needed to prepare individuals to accept the reality of God's grace. Journalism also is post-justification work, helping those graced to construct godly lives.

Fourth, and most subtle of all, is the reluctance even among some Christians to acknowledge that all created things, including our own minds, are twisted by sin (Genesis 3:17-19; Romans 8:20-22). Our minds are not capable of creating a sound set of guidelines from either observation or pure reason. Our only hope lies in learning Biblical principles of thought and conduct, and trusting the Holy Spirit to help us make the right practical applications.

The Bible teaches that thought independent of God's special revelation is untrustworthy at best and eventually suicidal. Only the Word of God can give us principles for establishing a life pleasing to God. This vital concept is hard to swallow in a society with strong belief in existentialist creativity: Individuals supposedly develop new ideas and ways of conduct *ex nihilo,* as if they were gods unto themselves. The Bible, though, stresses God as Creator and man as image-bearer. We cannot create virtue or virtuous ideas apart from God's thoughts.

Sometimes, in short, Christians confronted by tough problems are afraid of Biblical truth. Why not abortion when there has been rape? Why not divorce when husband and wife fight? Why write a story that could lose the journalist his job? There are Biblical answers to such questions, but they require hard analytical and practical work. Sometimes even Christians fear the Bible because it does not give comfortable answers.

A TWO-PRONGED STRATEGY

If the four fears are overcome, Christian journalists will be strong enough, and will be receiving sufficient community support, to ask another question: Where can I best serve God?

Some may now have a tendency to choose working at publications or media outlets owned and operated by Christians because those positions seem "safer," removed from contact with the world. A Christian journalistic revival, though, would mean that no place would be safe: Christian journalistic organizations would be aggressively reporting on the contrast between man's depravity and God's holiness, and non-Christian organizations would be prime mission fields.

Christian journalists sometimes seem tempted into arguments about whether explicitly Christian or secular media represent better alternatives for service. Such debates can be equivalent to Jesus' disciples squabbling about primacy on earth and seating arrangements in Heaven. As bad as many public schools are today, a tough-minded, tenacious Christian teacher in the classroom can still be a Godsend to children. Similar considerations apply in journalism, where the influence of one person may be even more widespread.

Strong Christian publications and stations are vital, but salty Christians also are needed within today's influential, non-Christian media systems. As stories with overt theological dimensions continue to arise, and as the more subtle stories influenced by presuppositions cross newsroom desks, it is vital that there be Christian reporters and editors willing to speak up.

Christians in non-Christian media organizations can also serve as counselors and evangelists. Not only do the major media institutions have great power, but the individuals within them often have great problems. If we were to bring forward in time the series of mini-biographies in Chapter Three, we would see that many apparently secure contemporary journalists desperately need help. Smiling anchormen and women often are off-camera wrecks.

Christians who have thought through the nature of objectivity and sensationalism, and the ethical and legal problems of the field, can glorify God within such media outposts. Nor do well-prepared

Christians necessarily have to choose between mealy-mouthedness and unemployment. As the discussions of objectivity and sensationalism in Chapters Four and Ten indicated, Christians do not have to *preach* in stories. Instead, Christians can work toward honest selection of details, fair and ample quotation of Biblical Christian spokesmen, and examination of the spiritual/material interface.

Still, a Christian reporter should realize that even a small movement toward true objectivity might anger an atheistic editor. In such circumstances, firmness is essential. As soon as a worldview conflict becomes apparent, Christian journalists working for non-Christians have to decide which of two roads to potential success to follow: the way of the tough and talented Christian, or the path of the presuppositional sycophant. These two roads tend to divide early. A reporter who writes of fundamentalists with appropriate sarcasm will be praised; a reporter who quotes not only Darwinian scientists but creation scientists will be questioned. And yet, a skilled reporter will have some value to his editors even if he refuses to play the game. He may not receive fast promotions, but he will not necessarily be fired, for real talent is in short supply.

The danger of slow career progress is clear. Yet, the prayer that Christ gives us as a model includes the sentence, "Give us today our daily bread" (Matthew 6:11). The sentence is not, "Give us today our daily steak." Nor is it, "Give us today our daily starvation." We need bread: Good, healthy sustenance, both material and spiritual. If a Christian's career is not as visibly spectacular—at least in the short run—as that of a person who is crafty and corrupt, that is a relatively small cross to bear.

Christians working for unsympathetic employers can make some practical intellectual and financial preparations while they are on the job. A Christian journalist must know that a news organization is not a home. We are wayfarers and sojourners here on this earth generally, and in newspapers or broadcast stations specifically. If God's providence has put the Christian in a high-paying job, he must immediately calculate what he needs to live on, not what he is temporarily able to live on. Any extra money is a special gift from God and should not be squandered: Some of that money might support the journalist if he is forced to resign. Furthermore, the goal should always be to develop skills that will allow the Christian to become his own boss, if the possibility arises. For, in the long run, Christian journalists will need Christian publications.

In that long run, it is clear that only news organizations owned and staffed by Christians will be able to practice journalism consistent with strong Biblical faith. Only through independence can

Christians make sure that the Bible is taken seriously in journalism. Therefore, Christian entrepreneurs who start new publications now and have the talent and dedication to make a go of them are worthy of double honor. Support for such individuals is as important as support for those who preach within a church.

CONCLUSION

Joshua in his old age told the Israelites, "Choose for yourselves this day whom you will serve." The Israelites then promised that they would obey God, for they had learned that "It was the Lord our God himself who brought us and our forefathers up out of Egypt, from that land of slavery, and performed those great signs before our eyes. He protected us on our entire journey and among all the nations through which we traveled." The education of the Israelites, through God's grace, had enabled them to see events as they really occurred, with both material and spiritual dimensions.

Throughout the Bible, God's spokesmen and reporters constantly tried to explain to their listeners and readers the reality of His involvement in human history. Moses told the Israelites (Deuteronomy 29): "Your eyes have seen all that the Lord did in Egypt to Pharaoh, to all his officials and to all his land. With your own eyes you saw those great trials, those miraculous signs and great wonders. But to this day the Lord has not given you a mind that understands or eyes that see or ears that hear." Seeing was not believing; reporters had to provide context, and then pray for God's grace on eyes and ears. Psalm 78 reported "the praiseworthy deeds of the Lord," and Stephen testified before the Sanhedrin to God's continued working in human history (Acts 7).

Christian journalism, as history's first draft, should follow the Bible in depicting God's grace and man's sinfulness. Non-Christian journalism has led to attempts to make people happy, either by suggesting that things are right (the position of some non-Christian conservatives) or that man by his egoistical efforts can make all things right (the position of some liberals). Christians, though, know that things are not right, due to original sin, and will be made right only through Christ: "He is before all things, and in him all things hold together" (Colossians 1:17).

"Be strong and courageous," God commands Joshua repeatedly. Avoidance of the four fears, through the strength and courage that only God can give, is vital for Christian journalists.

If Christians are willing to cover all aspects of life, to soil the breakfast table, to deal honestly with evil, to avoid intellectual trendiness, to meet communication demands of a fast-paced marketplace, to hit hard in a compassionate way that does not libel individuals—then we have done as much as we can, and we can pray with clear consciences for God to grant us success.

If Christians are willing to report faithfully that God is sovereign, that Satan is active but under control, that man pursues evil by nature but can be transformed, and that God does answer prayers in the way that is best for our growth in grace—then, with God's grace, Christians will have the most insightful and exciting news publications and programs in the United States.

Gloria in Excelsis Deo.

APPENDIX

PUBLIC RELATIONS, THEOLOGY AND PRACTICE

This book up to now has not dealt with what is often the largest specialization within contemporary journalism schools: Public relations. It is an important specialty, the occupation of at least 120,000 men and women in the United States and the major or concentration of perhaps twenty thousand college and university students each year. It is also a vital amateur activity for hundreds of thousands of other men and women, particularly leaders of small groups who have to deal with the press and cannot afford professional counsel.[1]

Non-Christian presuppositions dominate the upper levels of current public relations practice, much as they do the field of journalism generally. Yet, some public relations techniques may be put to godly use by Christians. This appendix has two parts. Part One discusses the theology of public relations at its highest government and corporate levels, through an examination of the ideas of the key founder of modern American public relations, Edward Bernays. Part One does not condemn all of public relations or suggest that Christians should not work in the field; it does suggest that Christians should prepare to oppose Bernaysian public relations by developing a Biblical perspective. Part Two pulls out of one subset of public relations, "press relations," some useful advice for leaders of small Christian organizations.

PART ONE: PUBLIC RELATIONS vs. GODLY RELATIONS

Edward Bernays, known as "American's #1 public relations man" from the 1930s through the 1960s, was an intelligent ideologue as well as a crafty campaign director. When I interviewed Bernays at his home near Harvard University in 1984, he was still mentally alert at age ninety-two, and willing to talk about the consistency of his atheistic beliefs throughout a long career.

The basis of Bernaysian thinking was clear: He acknowledged that he did not believe in God. Bernays believed in himself and his ability to "manipulate public opinion," as he put it forthrightly in the title of one of his articles. Without faith in God, Bernays wrote often of how *chance* ruled the world. He said that public relations was necessary because, without it, society would be controlled by "the fortuitous and whimsical forces of life and chance." He wrote, "There is something appalling to the ordinary business man in the fact that his business lies at the mercy of uncontrollable forces of whim and chance." He said he met a need by showing others how "to control by means of propaganda what otherwise would be controlled disastrously by chance."[2]

Bernays did not believe in God, but he did believe in the worship of human idols, idols he himself could fashion: "Human beings need to have godhead symbols, and public relations counsels must help to create them." Bernays saw his idol-making as vital to the salvation of society: "We have no being in the air to watch over us. We must watch over ourselves, and that is where public relations counselors can prove their effectiveness, by making the public believe that human gods are watching over us for our own benefit." These human gods, created by astute public relations, would keep order by giving their followers reasons to live and goals to accomplish.[3]

Bernays also believed in the wisdom of his uncle, Sigmund Freud. Our interview was filled with comments such as, "My uncle expressed this very well: People need sacred dances. Public relations counsels should be trained to call the tunes." Developing such power would not be difficult for those who understood human desires, because human beings are not individuals made after God's image, according to Bernays: They are rubber stamps, "the duplicates of millions of others, so that when those millions are exposed to the same stimuli, all receive identical imprints."[4]

This view of man as responder to stimuli led to Bernays' doctrine of "social responsibility": Powerful individuals with "the public interest" at heart must do whatever is necessary to preserve society from "reactionaries," or those with religious goals. Thoroughly modern social saviors are obliged *not* to abide by the ordinary demands of ethics that might apply to them as individuals. Instead, they must subordinate individual behavior and conscience to the "progressive" needs of society. Bernays' "elite," he declared, must manipulate "so as to bring order out of chaos."[5]

For sixty years Bernays was consistent with this message. He argued from the 1920s onward that "The conscious and intelligent manipulation of the organized habits and opinions of the masses is an important element in democratic society." Strange: A democratic society is normally considered one in which "the people" in general do rule. An authoritarian society is often considered one in which a small group of people rule. Bernays was trying to square the circle by arguing, in effect, that we must kill democracy to save it. Strange: Yet, without the presence of God's "invisible hand," there was no choice, according to Bernays; wise men such as himself had to "pull the wires which control the public mind."[6]

Bernays, developing the rationale for a public relations style which prized manipulation, also argued for a new methodology. A sound public relations specialist, Bernays wrote, "takes account not merely of the individual, nor even of the mass mind alone, but also and especially of the anatomy of society, with its interlocking group formations and loyalties." The individual was "a cell organized into the social unit. Touch a nerve at a sensitive spot and you get an automatic response from certain specific members of the organism."[7]

The social Pavlovian nature of this procedure was, for Bernays, no exaggeration. Whether or not he and others could manipulate so mechanistically was and is open to question, but Bernays claimed that he could "effect some change in public opinion with a fair degree of accuracy by operating a certain mechanism, just as the motorist can regulate the speed of his car by manipulating the flow of gasoline." The way to that goal was through working on the leaders, and through them their followers, sometimes called "herds" by Bernays: "If you can influence the leaders, either with or without their conscious cooperation, you automatically influence the group which they sway."[8]

Bernays argued consistently that "the special pleader who seeks to create public acceptance for a particular idea or commodity" is a hero. Public relations, for Bernays, no longer needed to be defended as what sinful men do in a sinful society. Public relations, Bernays thought, was the service which saviors of that sinful society would take upon themselves to perform. It was hard work to be continuously "regimenting the public mind every bit as much as an army regiments the bodies of its soldiers," but someone had to do it.[9]

Who? Bernays' vision of the future of public relations was most attractive to status-seeking practitioners. Certainly, Bernays wrote, "There are invisible rulers who control the destinies of millions," but those were not the political leaders or big businessmen of common paranoia. No, Bernays insisted that "It is not generally realized to what extent the words and actions of our most influential public men are dictated by shrewd persons operating behind the scenes."[10]

The behind-the-scenes operators were necessary to the operation of a society, and there would not be many of them: "The invisible government tends to be concentrated in the hands of the few because of the expense of manipulating the social machinery which controls the opinions and habits of the masses." As to the job description and title of the behind-the-scenes operators, Bernays was precise: "There is an increasing tendency to concentrate the functions of propaganda in the hands of the propaganda specialist. This specialist is more and more assuming a distinct place and function in our national life. [He] has come to be known by the name of 'public relations counsel.' "[11]

"Public relations counsels"—leaders of the invisible government, taking upon themselves the responsibility of saving civilization from chaos. "Public relations counsels"—a brave new profession for a brave new world. Most low-level public relations specialists have never heard of Bernays, and many even in the highest reaches have never read his books; but those with experience in major public relations offices and a willingness to be candid admit that Bernays' doctrine has become almost the official theology of elite public relations.

Bernaysian public relations has come in for its share of scorn. Judge Learned Hand called the Bernays-style public relations of his time "a black art," and others have been harsher. But Judge Hand admitted ruefully, "It has come to stay. Every year adds to the potency, to the finality of its judgments." There are some public relations managers, though, who persist in doing honest jobs. Some, with consciously Christian worldviews, stand against Bernaysian ideas.[12]

THE ALTERNATIVE

The Biblical idea of public opinion, in one sense, is similar to that of Bernays. Biblically, there is little praise for the rationality of either individuals and groups of individuals, or for our ability to come to good judgments by following our natural tendencies. Rather, all of us are sinners, easily fooled by others or by ourselves, and ready to become a mob. Furthermore, our human tendency is always to proclaim ourselves autonomous, even though we know deep down that we are creatures and not Creator. Since the fantasy of autonomy can only be maintained when others go along with it, our human tendency, whenever we obtain power, is to attempt to manipulate public opinion in order to either make ourselves gods or to create gods of our own choosing.

Even in the first book of the Old Testament, some individuals and groups attempted to publicize themselves as well as certain physical symbols. Genesis 11:1-9 relates the construction of the tower of Babel by people whose goal was to "make a name for ourselves." Since the builders cared more for their names than for God's name, God responded by making understandable naming more difficult through a confusion of the languages of the whole world. The babblers failed in the effort to spread their glory throughout the world; they ended up without even a common name for themselves among themselves. So ended the first public relations campaign recorded in the Bible.

Other public relations campaigns followed, but one ran into stern opposition. In Genesis 14:21-24, Abraham showed understanding of the Sodomite strategy of image-building by refusing to take the spoils of war offered by the King of Sodom, so that the king "will never be able to say, 'I made Abram rich.' " Abraham realized that such a statement would be factually inaccurate, since it is God who made him rich. Abraham also avoided the possibility that others would perceive him to be in league with the Sodomites, either to the detriment of his own reputation or the building up of Sodom in the eyes of others who might think it innocent by association.

Throughout Biblical history, tension between public relations and godly relations increased. King Saul was so concerned about the crowd chanting, "Saul has slain his thousands, and David his tens of thousands," that he began spending his time trying to kill David rather than trying to follow God's commands; eventually, his kingdom was lost (1 Samuel 18). Later, a paid discrediting campaign at first was successful: Following the return from Babylon, opponents of the Jews "hired counselors to work against them and frustrate their plans during the entire reign of Cyrus king of Persia and down to the reign of Darius king of Persia" (Ezra 4:5). Eventually the walls and Temple of Jerusalem were rebuilt; once again, public relations concerns won out in the short run, but not in the end.

The climax of the battle between public relations and godly relations came in the New Testament, with manipulated public opinion demanding the crucifixion of Christ. As Matthew Henry wrote in his commentary on Matthew 27, "The chief priests had a great interest in the people, they called them Rabbi, Rabbi, made idols of them, and oracles of all they said."[13] At the same time, though, the chief priests and elders knew how to incite a crowd, so that the mob sentiment—"Crucify him! Crucify him!"—was as much a function of the public relations men of that time, having "persuaded the crowd to ask for Barabbas and to have Jesus executed," as it was of any uncoerced public opinion.

Bernays' ideas, innovative as they appeared to public relations managers in the twentieth century, were merely duplicating the strategies of the Pharisees: Leaders first manipulate the crowd and then cite the crowd's voice as evidence of "the will of the people" before which leaders must bow. The cycle worked with particular viciousness when the only person standing in the way of the leader-mob alliance was Pilate. Pilate knew "it was out of envy that the chief priests had handed Jesus over to him," but he nevertheless handed over Christ "to satisfy the crowd" (Mark 15:10, 15). For Pilate, public relations was more important than justice.

For Christ on the cross, however, public relations was so unimportant compared to godly relations that his dying words did not criticize Pilate, the priests and elders, or even the disciples who had abandoned Him at the end. Instead, Jesus focused on the only crucial issue: "My, God, my God, why have you forsaken me?" (Mark 15:34). By following godly relations despite Pilate's emphasis on public relations, Jesus, through His shed blood, empowered His followers to do the same. They would no longer be rubber stamps. They would be able to take to heart God's words to Abraham after the patriarch rose above the public relations plans of Sodom: "Do not be afraid . . . I am your shield, your very great reward" (Genesis 15:1).

The Holy Spirit provides similar power to Christians today. Rationales for manipulation "in the public interest" are always available. The decision about whether to practice deception regularly, though, depends on our understanding of how the world works: through "the whimsical forces of life and chance," as Bernays believed, or through God's Providence. If the former, then public relations officers who wish to avoid "social chaos" may feel self-righteous in taking whatever steps they consider necessary. They will often manipulate the public and then cite public opinion or even the public interest as reason for actions they take.

When we believe God's Word, though, we know that it is not man who prevents chaos, but God. There is no need to act out of desperation and prestidigitate for the supposed public good, because God has the whole world in His hands. In practice, a consistent espousal of godly relations rather than public relations requires a deep belief in God's sovereignty, and an adherence to objective, Biblical truth rather than an offering of incense to public opinion.

The starting-point for a public relations person who desires to practice godly relations rather than Bernays-style public relations is a willingness to witness to God's sovereignty and justice by not hesitating to tell the truth about God's creation, come what may.[14]

PART TWO: PRACTICAL STEPS FOR PRESS RELATIONS

If you are an officer of a small Christian organization you might be shocked if, for some reason, it comes under attack from the press. You should not be. Whether you are involved in a "controversial" issue such as abortion, or are "just" doing traditional evangelism, you may be on the enemies list of a reporter or editor who perceives Christians as closed-minded.

You need to be prepared to deal with unsolicited media attention, and you need to realize that, with God's grace, even a negative story often will end up helping your organization. This part of the Appendix, written in outline form, should help you to follow Mordecai's example and make better use of the gallows that may have been prepared for your organization (Esther 7:10).

A. Some General Considerations

1. Reporting is a young person's occupation: The reporter writing a story about your organization often will be in his twenties. It is also, generally, an unchurched occupation: One survey showed that 86 percent of the "media elite" seldom or never attend church. It is also an occupation with a training and reward structure that emphasizes investigative journalism.

2. Those general indications mean that the reporter covering a Christian organization's activities may be inexperienced. The reporter may be interested in the Christian organization because of contacts with anti-Christian groups. He may think Christian organizations have something to hide, something he will investigate and disclose.

3. Newspapers and television stations rarely employ fact-checkers. If a story smells right to an editor or producer, he will go with it. Current journalists often develop story ideas based on preconceived notions of potential conflict or reader interest. These notions may be based on what they have read in national magazines or seen on network television news shows, even if situations de-

scribed in those stories have little in common with the local situation.

4. Sometimes a reporter will have his story almost written before he ever talks to you: He is simply picking up facts and quotations to use as specific detail for the story already constructed, or a short piece of film to insert. Good writing with apparently accurate detail generally will get the story past an editor, even if facts and quotations are wrong and the entire story is misleading.

B. First Steps

1. Your organization should prepare a basic "press kit." The kit should contain information describing what the organization does, who it serves, how it was started, how it is funded, etc. The press kit should include the name and telephone number of the organization's media representative, with indication of a willingness to be called for further information.

2. Your organization should have a person designated as its media representative (hereafter, "M"). M should make sure that whoever answers the organization's telephone is instructed to tell the reporter to call him. There should also be back-up media representatives in case, in an emergency situation, M cannot be contacted. (For almost all organizations such circumstances are rare; in most cases, reporters can wait, even though they may not want to.)

3. M should prepare a "standby statement" containing questions and answers to frequently asked questions. Critical articles about other Christian groups, or criticism from local anti-Christian organizations, should be analyzed carefully to see what kinds of charges typically are made. Responses to those charges should be prepared.

C. When the Reporter Is On the Phone

1. At this point, assume the reporter has been put in contact with M. The reporter typically will say either, "I am doing a story on subject x and would like a comment from you," or "I want to do a story on your organization." If the standby statement is a good one, the organization's position on subject x will be covered; if not, M should be careful not to give off-the-cuff answers. If the subject is one on which the organization wants to comment, the reporter should be asked about his deadline and told he will be called back.

2. At this point, M should think through potential answers and discuss them with others. Then he should be sure to call back

before the deadline. If the subject is one the organization does not wish to comment on, M can say so. Reporters often will try to push interviewees into making a statement of some kind, but that pressure should be opposed. Reporters may say, "I just want to know how you feel about this," or "Can you tell me why you won't answer?" M should be steadfast in Biblical truth: "Let your yes be yes and your no be no."

3. If the reporter plans a story on the organization, M should find out if the story is so hot that the reporter is going to press immediately. That is unlikely. Assuming the organization is not involved in some scandal, M should set up an appointment with the reporter when it is mutually convenient.

4. The reporter may say, "I'd like to do this today," or in some other way push for an immediate response, but if the story centers on M's organization he *needs* an interview to make the story at least seem "objective." If M declines to be interviewed the reporter will print that in the story, but if the story is not explosive and M agrees to be interviewed within some reasonable period (say, several days), the reporter will have a hard time charging your organization with lack of cooperation.

D. Preparing For the Reporter's Visit

1. You and other leaders of your organization should choose a person to accompany M to the interview. The testimony of two witnesses is important, and it is easy to go off on a tangent in an interview; a second person can help steer the conversation back on track. Unless the reporter requests additional interviews or there is some pressing reason to the contrary, it is not a good idea to have three representatives of the Christian organization at the interview. That will look like either organizational timidity or a desire to gang up on the reporter.

2. Standby statements should be reviewed and updated. M should make an outline of important points. M and others might think of positive ways to answer negative questions. They might write out the answers to those difficult questions and show them to someone else. If M is unfamiliar with interviewing, he might want to role-play with another Christian, tape the role-playing interview, and listen to himself. He might practice keeping answers informative but concise: "He who holds his tongue is wise."

3. The organization should have a working tape recorder ready for the interview. Not taping leaves no protection against misquotations. Interviews for television news shows generally will

be short, but for print media interviews twice as much tape as seems necessary should be readily available; M will not want to miss the crucial closing remarks because tape ran out. The tape recorder should have a microphone that will pick up voices well, since many people during interviews tend to talk softly. A back-up tape recorder should be available.

4. If a hostile television interview is expected, you might think of videotaping the proceedings. (In normal situations, that might be considered overkill.)

E. Etiquette Of the Newspaper Or Magazine Interview

1. If the reporter is thorough, he will come with a tape recorder and ask permission to tape. M should say yes as he brings out the organization's tape recorder. If the reporter does not bring a tape recorder, it is possible (although unlikely) that he will object to M's taping, perhaps asking, "Is this really necessary?" or "Can't we trust each other?" Assure him that it is really necessary. Never submit to an interview with a potentially adversarial reporter without taping it.

2. If the reporter objects, do not go ahead with the interview; the reporter will be unable to write in his story that your organization refused comment, and he will be reluctant to write that he refused to ask questions with a tape recorder running.

3. If the circumstances of the interview are positive (such as a pattern of fair coverage of your organization in the news outlet requesting an interview), precautions must still be taken; but this may be the occasion for a favorable story that could be immensely helpful. M should be ready to suggest to a sympathetic reporter several possibilities for a positive and truthful feature story on the organization.

4. If the reporter is writing an article based on criticism of your organization, M should find out what that criticism is at the beginning of the interview. For example, if M is representing a Crisis Pregnancy Center, he should ask the reporter, while the tape is running, "How did you hear about the organization? Who made the complaints? How many complaints have there been? Will you investigate abortion businesses as well?" The reporter may say, "I'd like to start with . . ." It is perfectly appropriate to respond, "We will be happy to answer your questions, but we would first like to know . . ."

5. If the story is arising in a hostile environment, M and

others should beware of a reporter's requests for extensive personal background concerning organization leaders. The reporter should be told about professional credentials, but giving a testimony may backfire if the reporter wants to distort coverage by playing up in a sarcastic manner anything that sounds strange to him.

6. Following the interview, the tape should be transcribed immediately. The transcript may never be needed, but if it is, the organization will be prepared. The transcript also will be handy for in-house use, since the Holy Spirit may have made M especially articulate during the interview. Questions from the reporter on the transcript can be used to update standby statements. If some questions were answered poorly, M can learn from his mistakes.

F. Notes On Television Interviews

1. With television cameras, you are forced to make some kind of statement, or else your closed door probably will be filmed, with the reporter saying that your organization refused to talk to the press.

2. Typically, television crews have one camera shooting from behind the interviewer. The reporter will not be on camera during the interview. Following the interview, the crew will film the reporter asking questions. This means that sharp-edged questions during the interview, which might lead you to respond in kind, may be replaced by mellow questions, leaving you looking belligerent for no purpose. Therefore, answer every question in the positive way you want to answer it, regardless of the question's tone.

3. Remember that a press interview might last for several hours, while a television interview might last for ten minutes, of which thirty seconds might be used. You are at the mercy of the person who chooses which film to use; so do not let down toward the end of the interview: An antagonistic editor may show you at your weakest.

4. Occasionally cameras may be at your door, unannounced. For example, if your pro-life organization is picketed by a pro-abortion group, and a television reporter interviews demonstrators, he is likely to engage in "balancing" by coming to your office to interview your spokesman. This should be no problem if you have prepared and if you follow steps in Section E. Simply give concise statements based on your standby statement preparation.

5. Occasionally local stations taking after "60 Minutes" might burst into your office without warning. If your local television

station acts in this way, make sure that whoever is in the office is prepared to say, with a determined smile, "You are being extremely rude, and you are trespassing."

G. When the Story Appears

1. The story may be fair and helpful; if so, take advantage of the publicity. If it is a print medium story, tell others to read all about it, and reprint it in your newsletter. Show a videotape of the television story at your next general meeting. Coverage gives the organization legitimacy and, perhaps, added importance in the eyes of fence-sitters.

2. If the story is negative, examine your organization in its light. Is your organization being attacked because you and others are following in Christ's footsteps? Or were real weaknesses in the organization legitimately reported?

3. If the story is dishonest and defamatory, do not despair. It could be the beginning of a major victory. M and others will want to contact the news organization—but first, all evidence needs to be in order. A general discussion of slanting will get you nowhere, either in a news organizations office or (if it comes to this) in court. You have to have specific inaccuracies or misquotations to obtain a retraction, correction, or equal time/space.

H. Analyzing the Dishonest Newspaper Or Magazine Story

1. Compare the quoted statements in the article with the statements M and the other organizational representative actually made. If a statement is enclosed in quotation marks, it should be exactly what was said. If any words are missing, the exclusion should be indicated by an ellipsis (three dots). If a statement is a paraphrase, it should accurately reflect the meaning of what was said.

2. Examine any charges or statements against your organization. Are they demonstrably inaccurate? Was M given a chance to respond to the specific charges?

3. An article on a controversial question often will have some paragraphs that can be labeled "pro" one side or the other. Count the paragraphs. Within the common mode of journalistic "objectivity," your side and your critics' position should have received roughly equal space.

4. Examine the way in which "neutral expert witnesses" or "third party sources" are used. In a controversy story, use of such third parties is designed to help the reader sort out who's right and who's wrong. Are the witnesses actually neutral? Is their viewpoint

shown accurately? If you know the third party sources used, you might call to see if they were quoted correctly.

5. Only after determining that actual inaccuracies exist should you go on to the next steps. If the reporter has quoted M and others fairly, but you do not like the tone, and if he has taken facts out of context but has done so with subtlety, you have little recourse but a letter to the editor that probably will not be printed.

I. Analyzing the Television Story

1. The same general considerations hold. However, analyze not just the words, but the video segment, with great care, as indicated in Chapter Eight.

2. Observe reporters' and announcers' intonations and facial expressions. Raised eyebrows and a sarcastic tone are worth a thousand words.

J. Calling the Newspaper Office

1. A few words about organization: Typically, the publisher is a newspaper's CEO, with two people—a business manager and an editor-in-chief—reporting to him. The business manager handles finance, circulation, advertising, and other business aspects. The editor-in-chief (sometimes called executive editor or simply editor) is in charge of all the nonadvertising material in the newspaper. Do not go to the publisher, except as a last resort: That is going over the head of the person in charge of editorial content, and is likely to waste time or produce resentment. Also, do not go to someone you know on the business side of the newspaper.

2. Typically, leaders on the editorial side are the editor-in-chief, managing editor (who is concerned with day-to-day news and features), news editor (who is responsible for national and international news, but also for writing headlines and copyediting stories), and city editor (who assigns stories and supervises local coverage generally). Titles vary, but you probably will end up talking with one or more of those individuals.

3. Reporters are under the supervision of editors. Do not call the reporter who wrote the offending story. With ego invested in the story, and with less maturity than most editors, he is more likely to be belligerent.

4. Be aware of the role of the "ombudsman" (reader's advocate, public affairs editor, Mr. Go-Between, reader contact editor) if your newspaper has one. Don't let titles fool you: Unless the person filling the job is extraordinary, the ombudsman is not a

reader's advocate, but an employee of the organization that has treated you unfairly.

5. A few ombudsmen may be more independent. They may be individuals from outside the organization brought in temporarily, with a contract stipulating fixed terms of employment with no possibility of renewal. However, ombudsmen are selected by the newspaper's management and are likely to share the ideological presuppositions of that management. An ombudsman may be helpful, but he is not your friend.

6. In short, call the highest ranking person on the editorial side of the operation—not the business side. Do so with the expectation that you may end up talking with an editor slightly lower in the pecking order, but above the reporter. Remember to be careful with everyone you deal with in a news organization. Chances are, if the news organization had better fact-checking and higher ethical standards, you would not be there in the first place.

K. Calling the Television Station

1. Organization charts in television news often are functionally similar to those of newspapers, but staffs are smaller and titles are different. A producer rather than an editor decides which stories to use and how much time to give them. Often there will be different producers for morning, early evening, and late evening news shows. At some stations producers report to a news director, who in turn reports to a "general manager" or "station manager."

2. Many people think the anchorman (or woman) is tremendously influential. That is often not so. Within the studio his clout reaches only as far as his ratings. Organizationally on most local broadcasts, the anchor has little power. Only if he is so tremendously popular that his departure would cause ratings problems, can he throw his weight around effectively.

3. If you have a good complaint, do not call the anchor or the government. Call the news director or producer, if you know specific names and responsibilities. When in doubt, simply call the "general manager" or "station manager."

L. Preparing For Confrontation

1. After a defamatory story appears, an immediate meeting of your board of directors or other leadership group should be called, if possible. Before the meeting, a memo noting the article's factual inaccuracies and misquotations should be prepared. The memo should be free of church jargon, understandable on first reading or

hearing, and succinct. The act of composing the memo will help your organization to see whether it has a valid complaint. (At the end of this Appendix are notes on journalism codes of ethics that you may wish to cite.)

2. If your board of directors (or similar group) agrees that there are factual errors or misquotations damaging to the organization, the board should pass a resolution that it will consider libel action if the news organization does not act to correct the record. Libel suits are tricky and hard to win. They are not to be entered into lightly. They must be considered, though, if only because the news organization will take your complaint much more seriously if there may be dollar signs attached to it.

3. Once your board acts, M will call the editor, station manager, or other appropriate person. M should be prepared to say enough over the telephone to provoke the editor's concern. M should note that he has a tape of the interview and a detailed record of misquotations, inaccuracies, etc., and that the organization is considering libel action. He should not say, "We feel the article was unfair." The editor probably does not care what the organization thinks. He cares if his staff messed up and if there is cause for legal action. M should end the telephone call by setting up an appointment.

5. Two representatives of your organization, at least one of whom was at the interview, should go to the appointment. If you have a lawyer on your board, it might be good to send him. Your representatives should be prepared to play the tape for the editor. (This is especially effective if his reporter did not tape the interview.)

6. If the editor cannot listen to the tape that day, it should not be left with him, regardless of how many copies your organization has. Your representative should be present when the tape is played to point out specific problems. They also will want to see the editor's reactions when the quotations on the tape contradict the quotations in print.

M. Negotiating A Settlement

1. The news outlet probably will not make an offer at your first appointment. The editor will want to discuss the troublesome matter with his colleagues and probably his lawyer.

2. If the news outlet, after some thought, will not offer anything, then you must consult a lawyer knowledgeable about libel. News outlet now are very concerned about possible litigation. The

refusal to make an offer might mean that you do not have a case. On the other hand, the news outlet might be bluffing. See a knowledgeable lawyer.

3. The news organization may offer a retraction, a correction, an article to be written by you, or a letter to the editor. A retraction is an admission of error, generally combined with an apology. A correction is a restatement of the facts without explicit admission or apology.

4. Ideally, if you have been falsely defamed, there should be a prominent retraction and apology, in the same spot or time (preferably a better spot or time) as the original article.

5. Since we live in a fallen world, and since editors—like the rest of us—hate to be publicly embarrassed, you may be offered a mild correction, in which the news organizaion will correct specific errors but do nothing to remove the overall negative impression given by a skillfully biased article. In this situation, a mere correction might be as bad as seeing the story appear a second time, because it will remind readers of the initial charges. When the problems with the article are greater than a factual inaccuracy or two, be careful about accepting correction without retraction.

6. In such a situation, ask for space or time to present your own viewpoint, rather than a correction. You should have as much space and time to present your side of the story as the newspaper used to attack you.

7. If you are offered space on the editorial page, remember that such placement is not equivalent to space on a generally better-read news page. Negotiate on this point, at least asking for a boxed statement (in the same location as original article) pointing readers toward your rebuttal.

8. Do not settle for a letter to the editor. If that is all you are offered, examine the libel route.

N. To Sue Or Not To Sue

1. Jesus spoke of avoiding courts, and on this and other questions His words should be followed. As noted in Chapters Six and Seven, the search for American libel justice in recent years has become grossly expensive, time-consuming, and emotionally draining. Time spent on a libel suit could reduce your organization's effectiveness. Also, to defend themselves, news outlets might try to prove that your organization is as bad as they said it was. Complainants (and there are always some) will be pulled out of the woodwork.

2. On the other hand, if you have a strong case, and the news

outlet is stubborn, allowing it to stomp all over you will just encourage it to stomp all over other Christian organizations. Keeping in mind the great suffering that is likely to result, contact your local lawyer or national Christian legal organizations that might be willing to take your case.

3. If you are forced into libel action, keep track of any harm caused your organization by the defamatory news report. If volunteers or contributions decrease immediately after the article appears, this can be powerful evidence for damages.

O. COUNTER-ATTACK

1. Take advantage of the publicity your organization is getting, even if it is bad. If there is a Christian radio station, TV station, or newspaper in town, you need to bring them into the controversy right away. They will probably be interested in a story about how the paper was biased in a story about a Christian organization. A small organization against a big newspaper or television station makes for a good David *vs.* Goliath story.

2. Try to get on talk shows or other forums where you can take advantage of the publicity and get your story across. Develop or activate your speakers bureau. Use specific detail from your memo to show bias.

3. Discuss the article in your newsletter, and the steps taken to gain redress. Send out a fund-raising letter explaining how you were unjustly attacked. Remember that you are probably being attacked because you are effective.

NOTE ON JOURNALISTIC CODES OF ETHICS

Journalism ethics codes are at best semi-serious. There is no policing by journalism organizations, and not much in the way of penalties for violations. The codes are generalizations. They say little about practical application of principles, and offer no means for enforcement. Still, they are statements worth quoting when journalists do not take complaints seriously.

The Society of Professional Journalists, Sigma Delta Chi Code of Ethics was adopted in 1973. It states that "There is no excuse for inaccuracies or lack of thoroughness." It also stipulates, under the "Accuracy and Objectivity" heading, that:

> 5. Sound practice makes clear distinction between news reports and expressions of opinion. News reports should be free of opinion or bias and represent all sides of an issue. . . .

> 8. Special articles or presentations devoted to advocacy or the writer's own conclusions and interpretations should be labeled as such.

Under a "Fair Play" heading, the Code stipulates that:

> 1. The news media should not communicate unofficial charges affecting reputation or moral character without giving the accused a chance to reply. . . .
>
> 4. It is the duty of news media to make prompt and complete correction of their errors.
>
> 5. Journalists should be accountable to the public for their reports and the public should be encouraged to voice its grievances against the media.

The Code ends with a pledge: "Journalists should actively censure and try to prevent violations of these standards, and they should encourage their observance by all newspeople."[15] That means if the reporter or editor who has defamed you is not a member of Sigma Delta Chi, find someone who is: If he takes oaths seriously and a legitimate offense has occurred, he is bound to try to do something about it.

The other major code is the American Society of Newspaper Editors (ASNE) Statement of Principles. The particularly relevant sections of the statement, which was adopted on October 23, 1975, are as follows:

> ARTICLE IV: TRUTH AND ACCURACY
>
> Good faith with the reader is the foundation of good journalism. Every effort must be made to assure that the news content is accurate, free from bias and in context, and that all sides are presented fairly. Editorials, analytical articles and commentary should be held to the same standards of accuracy with respect to facts as news reports.
>
> Significant errors of fact, as well as errors of omission, should be corrected promptly and prominently.
>
> ARTICLE V: IMPARTIALITY
>
> To be impartial does not require the press to be unquestioning or to refrain from editorial expression. Sound practice, however, demands a clear distinction for the reader between news reports and opinion. Articles that contain opinion or personal interpretation should be clearly identified.

ARTICLE VI: FAIR PLAY

Journalists should respect the rights of people involved in the news, observe the common standards of decency and stand accountable to the public for the fairness and accuracy of their news reports.

Persons publicly accused should be given the earliest opportunity to respond.

Pledges of confidentiality to news sources must be honored at all costs, and therefore should not be given lightly. Unless there is clear and pressing need to maintain confidence, sources of information should be identified.[16]

N O T E S

INTRODUCTION

1. Jeremiah and the other prophets repeatedly describe the "spiritual adultery" involved in Israel's worship of other gods; similarly, physical adultery separates what God has covenantally united.
2. First Corinthians 7 notes that a husband's body belongs to his wife. If a husband steals from his wife, won't he steal from others?
3. A leader "must be above reproach, the husband of but one wife, temperate, self-controlled." Other qualifications may relate only to church elders, but the Biblical principle for all public leadership is clear: Above reproach, self-controlled.

CHAPTER ONE *The Decline of American Journalism*

1. Paul Vitz, *Religion and Traditional Values in Public Textbooks* (Washington, D.C.: National Institute of Education, 1986). For comments on Vitz's study, see *Newsweek*, July 28, 1986, p. 20; *Saturday Evening Post*, July-August 1986, p. 16; *Christianity Today*, January 17, 1986, p. 49; *Christianity Today*, March 7, 1986, p. 15.
2. Edwin and Michael Emery, *The Press and America*, fifth edition (Englewood Cliffs, NJ: Prentice-Hall, 1984), pp. 109-138.
3. Roberta Moore, *Development of Protestant Journalism in the United States, 1743-1850* (unpublished doctoral dissertation, Syracuse University, 1968), p. 237.
4. Frank Luther Mott's *American Journalism*, revised edition (New York: Macmillan, 1950) has one paragraph on p. 206 about the "religious newspapers" of the 1801-1833 period. According to Mott, about one hundred such publications, scattered across the country, covered both secular events and church activities: The newspapers were "a phenomenon of the times" and "often competed successfully with the secular papers." Mott noted that "many of these papers were conducted with great vigor and ability."

   Mott did not go into detail, but his brief mention was more than these newspapers have received in other journalism history textbooks written in the twentieth century, such as James M. Lee, *History of American Journalism* (Boston: Houghton Mifflin, 1917); George H. Payne, *History of Journalism in the United States* (New York: Appleton-Century-Crofts, 1920); or Sidney Kobre, *Development of American Journalism* (Dubuque,

IA: Wm. C. Brown Co., 1969). A history written in the late nineteenth century, Frederic Hudson, *Journalism in the United States from 1690 to 1872* (New York: Harper & Brothers, 1873), is also unsympathetic to the Christian press, but at least provides some information. A monograph by Wesley Norton, *Religious Newspapers in the Old Northwest to 1861* (Athens, OH: Ohio University Press, 1977), and dissertations by Moore and Kenberry, provide useful records.

5. Howard Kenberry, *The Rise of Religious Journalism in the United States* (unpublished dissertation, University of Chicago, 1920), p. 35.
6. New York *Observer*, June 23, 1849, p. 98.
7. *Puritan Recorder*, October 21, 1858; quoted in Hudson, p. 290. Willis had had no particular theological interests and did not attend church, "but spent my Sabbaths in roving about the fields and in reading newspapers."
8. Boston *Recorder*, January 3, 1816, p. 1.
9. *Ibid.*, September 11, 1819, p. 147. (The *Recorder* produced four-page issues but numbered its pages consecutively throughout the year.)
10. *Ibid.*, April 22, 1820, p. 57.
11. *Ibid.*, December 23, 1817, p. 202; August 25, 1826, p. 136. The *Recorder* is one of my favorite old newspapers; Chapters Four, Ten, and Eleven (on objectivity, sensationalism and crusading) provide more examples of *Recorder* news coverage.
12. Contents of the early publications could be almost as varied as those of newspapers. One early Christian magazine became a bit carried away in describing its variety: The *New England Magazine* contained, according to the editors, "Relations Wonderful, and Psalm, and Song,/Good Sense, Wit, Humour, Morals, all ding dong;/Poems and Speeches, Politicks, and News,/What Some will like, and other Some refuse;/Births, Deaths, and Dreams, and Apparitions, too . . . To Humour Him, and Her, and Me, and You" (Kenberry, p. 64).
13. *Presbyterian of the West*, December 30, 1858; *Northwestern Christian Advocate*, November 28, 1860; quoted in Norton, p. 2.
14. For details on Raymond, see New York *Times*. June 19, 1869, p. 4 (obituary); June 22, p. 1 (funeral); June 28, p. 8 (eulogy); also see Francis Brown, *Raymond of the Times* (New York: Norton, 1951), and Augustus Maverick, *Henry J. Raymond and the New York Press for Thirty Years* (Hartford: Hale, 1870).
15. See Emery and Emery, p. 215. When Raymond died in 1869 he was succeeded by his long-time partner George Jones in the business management of the *Times* and, after two short-lived appointments, by Louis Jennings as editor; both Jones and Jennings were Christians. When Jones turned down a $5 million bribe offered him by Boss Tweed, he said the Devil never again would offer him so high a price.
16. One pro-abortion article cited in the U.S. Supreme Court's *Roe v. Wade* decision suggests that newspaper stories contributed to a long-lasting abortion setback: See Cyril C. Means, "The Law of New York Concerning Abortion and the State of the Foetus, 1664-1968: A Case of Cessation of Constitutionality," *New York Law Forum*, Fall 1968, pp. 458-490.
17. New York *Times*, November 3, 1870, p. 4.
18. *Ibid.*, August 23, 1871, p. 6.
19. *Ibid.*
20. *Ibid.*

21. *Ibid.*, August 27, p. 1. The young lady was later identified as Alice Mowlsby, a poor orphan who lived with her aunt in Patterson, New Jersey.
22. *Ibid.*, August 28, 29, 30, p. 8. A boy who had helped carry the trunk into the station tried to find a man and a mysterious lady who had delivered the trunk. Readers daily absorbed the strategy of the detective in charge, Inspector Walling, who "issued orders which practically put every policeman in the force upon the case."
23. *Ibid.*, August 29, p. 8; August 30, p. 4.
24. *Ibid.*, August 30, p. 8.
25. *Ibid.* What would be called today a "free press *vs.* fair trial" issue does emerge here: With one of its own reporters giving a firsthand account, the *Times* sometimes seemed to be convicting the abortionist in the press.
26. *Ibid.*, December 8, 1871, p. 2. The *Times* did recommend passage of a bill "far-reaching enough to catch hold of all who assist, directly or indirectly, in the destruction of infant life," and gave its recommendation one additional populist thrust: "The people demand it." The New York legislature of 1872 passed tough new anti-abortion laws, with easier rules of evidence and a maximum penalty of twenty years imprisonment. Enforcement also was stepped up.
27. *Ibid.*, November 3, 1870, p. 4.
28. The New York *Times* continued to run anti-abortion stories through the remainder of the century. Chapter Eleven has more discussion of the overall anti-abortion campaign.
29. *Central Christian Herald*, September 2, 1852; quoted in Norton, p. 32.
30. Quoted in Kenberry, p. 158.
31. See p. 208 of each *Recorder* volume during the 1820s for a list of such articles. See also *Recorder*, January 27, 1837, p. 14.
32. Emerson's address is published in many books, including Volume 5 of the *Harvard Classics*, ed. Charles Eliot (New York: Collier, 1937), pp. 25-42.
33. This chapter has room to mention only in passing the major theological and social developments; it does not attempt to be anything more than a quick overview. For general discussions of the period, see Perry Miller, *The Life of the Mind in America: From the Revolution to the Civil War* (New York: Harcourt, Brace and World, 1965), and Sydney E. Ahlstrom, *A Religious History of the American People* (New Haven: Yale University Press, 1972). For a discussion of Unitarianism and the public schools, see Samuel Blumenfeld, *Is Public Education Necessary?* (Boise: Paradigm, 1985). For a discussion of the impact of evolutionism, see appendices to Gary North, *The Dominion Covenant* (Tyler, TX: Institute for Christian Economics, 1982), pp. 245-454.
34. Abbott's books include *The Evolution of Christianity* (Boston: Houghton Mifflin, 1900); *The Other Room* (New York: Grosset, Dunlap, 1903); *Christianity and Social Problems* (New York: Houghton Mifflin, 1896); and *Reminiscences* (Boston: Houghton Mifflin, 1915).
35. This discussion of Christian trends is, again, just a quick overview. For further information and perspective, see George Marsden, *The Evangelical Mind and the New School Presbyterian Experience* (New Haven: Yale University Press, 1970); Timothy L. Smith, *Revivalism and Social Reform in Mid-Nineteenth-Century America* (Nashville: Abingdon Press, 1957); James F. Findlay, Jr., *Dwight L. Moody, American Evangelist, 1837-1899* (Chicago: University of Chicago Press, 1969); John Woodbridge, Mark

Noll and Nathan Hatch, *The Gospel in America* (Grand Rapids: Zondervan, 1979).

36. As historian George Marsden has noted in *Fundamentalism and American Culture* (London: Oxford University Press, 1980), the 1860-1900 period brought with it "a transition from a basically 'Calvinistic' tradition, which saw politics as a significant means to advance the kingdom, to a 'pietistic' view of political action as no more than a means to restrain evil." This movement led to what Marsden calls the "Great Reversal" early in the twentieth century, with social concerns becoming suspect among revivalist evangelicals. Meanwhile, the older Reformed concern for social action was transmuted into a "social gospel" clung to by many who no longer held to the Biblical gospel.
37. See Abraham Kuyper, *Lectures on Calvinism* (Grand Rapids, MI: Eerdmans, 1983; first published in 1899). Also see Henry Van Til, *The Calvinistic Concept of Culture* (Grand Rapids: Baker, 1959), and John T. McNeill, *The History and Character of Calvinism* (London: Oxford University Press, 1954). Primarily see John Calvin, *Institutes of the Christian Religion*, 1559 edition, trans. Ford Lewis Battles, ed. John T. McNeill (Philadelphia: The Westminster Press, 1960).
38. Norton, p. 38.
39. Just as the Boston *Recorder* had been one of the first to see the entire society as a journalistic mission field, so it was one of the first to drop out under the twin pressures of Boston transcendentalism and the tendency to turn inwards. Circulation during the 1840s was stagnant at a time when non-Christian newspapers were soaring. A *Recorder* editorial in 1848 suggesting "encouraging prospects" for the newspaper was belied by both appearance and context. Type size was smaller, typography was muddy, and page size had decreased; those pages were filled with monthly, quarterly and annual reports of various church groups, indicating clearly that the *Recorder* had died as a newspaper and had become a public relations organ. In 1849 the *Recorder* officially merged with the *Puritan*, a ten-year-old newspaper. Examination of one advertisement in the last issue of the *Recorder*, though, makes the agreement seem more like a subscription list buyout than a merger. The little notice, placed by the *Recorder* itself, offered "the type and other printing materials which are now used in this office—the whole comprising all the fixtures of a weekly newspaper establishment" (*Recorder*, January 7, 1848, p. 2; May 4, 1849, p. 71).
40. An interesting test arose in 1899 and 1900, when international attention was focused on the battle in South Africa between Boers and British. Race was not an issue at the time, since neither side spoke much of the black inhabitants; the issue was social Darwinist "progress," and to the New York *Times* the Boers seemed least likely to succeed, due to their fundamentalist religious beliefs. "Poor, hidebound, Bible reading, otherwise illiterate Boers," the New York *Times* sniffed. The Boers' religion, according to the *Times*, makes them a "very stubborn people . . . in a state of arrested development. They are not much different from the Dutch of this island two centuries ago. That is to say, they are simple minded, Bible-reading, God-fearing people" with an "idiotic-heroic attitude" (August 24, 1899, p. 6; August 10, 1899, p. 6).
41. New York *Times*, July 26, 1925, Section II, p. 4. Leslie H. Allen, ed.,

Bryan and Darrow at Dayton: The Record and Documents of the Bible-Evolution Trial (New York: Russell & Russell, 1925), p. 1, conveniently assembles materials against which press reports may be checked.

42. The importance of the Dayton trial, for both prosecution and defense, lay in the chance to debate the issues of the case. The judicial proceedings themselves were not of great interest. The case was open-and-shut, deliberately designed for conviction on obvious law-breaking so that the decision could be appealed to the U.S. Supreme Court for a ruling on the act's constitutionality. (Ironically, although Scopes was convicted, as planned by the ACLU, and although the anti-evolution law itself was upheld by the Tennessee Supreme Court, the Tennessee Supreme Court also overturned the conviction on a technicality involving the imposition of a $100 fine without jury approval.)
43. Baltimore *Sun*, July 9, 1925, p. 1. Mencken attacked the Dayton creationists (before he had set foot in the town) as "local primates . . . yokels . . . morons . . . half-wits." Mencken put aside his typical amusement with life to ride Paul Revere-like through the land with dire warnings about the trial: "Let no one mistake it for comedy, farcical though it may be in all its details. It serves notice on the country that Neanderthal man is organizing in these forlorn backwaters of the land, led a by a fanatic, rid of sense and devoid of conscience" (Baltimore *Sun*, July 18, 1925, p. 1).

    Mencken's intolerance was parallel to that of many anti-evolution spokesmen. Columbia University dean Henry H. Rusby demanded that universities not recognize degrees from universities that did not accept evolution. A leading liberal minister, Charles Francis Potter, argued that "educated and enlightened men ought not to rest until the possibility of such dense mental darkness is removed." The New York *Times* then editorialized against "the mental and moral infection which has been let loose upon the land. . ." (New York *Times*, July 12, 1925, section I, p. 2; Arkansas *Gazette*, June 16, p. 2). Fundamentalists had some justification for believing that they were being told not "live and let live," but "your diseased religion does not deserve to exist."
44. Acid-tongued Westbrook Pegler, who covered the trial briefly, admired Mencken and imitated his coverage, but noted years later concerning the creationists, "They were intelligent people, including a fair proportion of college graduates. Nevertheless, the whole Blue Ridge country was ridiculed on religious grounds by an enormous claque of supercilious big town reporters." Such ridicule was not primarily a function of politics; it underlay the politics of liberal and conservative newspapers. The liberal New York *Times* editorialized that the creationist position represented a "breakdown of the reasoning powers. It is seeming evidence that the human mind can go into deliquescence without falling into stark lunacy" (July 13, p. 16). The conservative Chicago *Tribune* sneered at fundamentalists looking for "horns and forked tails and cloven hoofs" (July 19, p. 5).
45. New York *Times*, July 20, 1925, p. 14.
46. Arkansas *Gazette*, July 18, 1925, p. 5.
47. Baltimore *Sun*, July 10, 1925, p. 1. Also see Atlanta *Constitution*, July 9, p. 10.
48. Arkansas *Gazette*, July 12, p. 1. Also see Arkansas *Gazette*, June 23, p. 1, and June 28, p. 1; Washington *Post*, July 16, 1925, p. 6.

49. Arkansas *Gazette*, June 27, 1925, p. 1.
50. Atlanta *Constitution*, July 2, 1925, p. l; July 8, 1925, p. 22.
51. New York *American*, July 18, 1925, p. 1; July 14, p. 1; Arkansas *Gazette* (New York *Times*/Chicago *Tribune* news service), July 16, 1925, p. 3.
52. New York *American*, July 13, 1925, p. 1; July 15, p. 4; July 16, p. 2; July 17, p. 2.
53. New York *American*, July 12, 1925, p. 1; see also Arkansas *Gazette*, July 11, p. 1.
54. See Allen, *loc. cit.*
55. Baltimore *Sun*, July 17, 1925, p. 1.
56. Arkansas *Gazette*, July 12, 1925, p. 1; July 13, p. 1; July 17, p. 3.
57. Chicago *Tribune*. See also Arkansas *Gazette*, July 14, p. 5.
58. New York *American*, July 14, 1925, p. 1. One more bizarre twist to the trial deserves mentioning: the last Bryan-Darrow confrontation arose unexpectedly on the final day of the trial. Many reporters were off swimming or carousing, with the result that other reporters, after telegraphing their own stories, hastily rewrote parts and sent them to the missing reporters' newspapers in order to cover for their friends. Scopes himself was asked by several reporters to write parts of the new articles; so journalistic coverage of the trial concluded with a bizarre touch: the defendant reporting on his own case under someone else's byline. See John T. Scopes and James Presley, *Center of the Storm: Memoirs of John T. Scopes* (New York: Holt, Rinehart and Winston, 1967), p. 183.
59. Olive Clapper, *One Lucky Woman* (Garden City, NY: Doubleday, 1961), pp. 34, 51, 109.
60. *Ibid.*, p. 99.
61. The Atlanta *Constitution* editorialized about the trial coverage's potential effect: "Thousands of columns of newspaper debate have been published under Dayton date lines in the past two weeks, and from it all the cause of the religion of Jesus Christ has not been helped, but the world has been broadcast with the seeds of doubt and skepticism, and only the future can tell what the harvest will be . . . among the millions of people who congest the bumper ground between science and the Bible there may be thousands who will now find themselves drifting into the easy-going channels of agnosticism" (July 22, 1925, p. 6).

CHAPTER TWO *Spiking the Spiritual*

1. Some of the best books with a conservative perspective: Russ Braley, *Bad News: The Foreign Policy of the New York Times* (Chicago: Regnery, 1984); Tom Kelly, *The Imperial Post* (New York: William Morrow, 1983); James Tyson, *Target America* (Chicago: Regnery, 1981); Philip Lawler, *The Alternative Influence* (Lanham, MD: University Press of America, 1984); Herman Dinsmore, *All the News That Fits* (New Rochelle: Arlington House, 1969); Leopold Tyrmand, *The Media Shangri-La* (Rockford, IL: Rockford College Institute, 1975). Many book chapters—for instance, "The Media, Shield of the Utopians," in Rael Jean and Erich Isaac's *The Coercive Utopians* (Chicago: Regnery, 1984)—provide valuable perspective, as do essays by Irving Kristol, Paul Weaver and others in back issues of *The Public Interest*. In 1987 Reed Irvine's Accuracy in Media newsletter

and Tom Bethell's monthly columns in *The American Spectator* continued to provide useful and provocative criticism.

2. Boston *Recorder*, July 10, 1819, p. 116; March 15, 1823, p. 41; and other issues from the two decades beginning in 1816.
3. *Evangelical Beacon*, April 1986, p. 20.
4. *Ibid.*
5. *Ibid.* Our only totally reliable source of information and perspective is God's revealed will. Since Christians have been fooled before about international developments and leaders, it is vital not to leap to conclusions.
6. Quoted in William Rivers, *The Opinionmakers* (Boston: Beacon Press, 1965), p. 43.
7. Detroit *Free Press*, June 15, 1986, p. B1. For an excellent discussion of presuppositionalism, see Cornelius Van Til, *The Defense of the Faith* (Philadelphia: Presbyterian and Reformed Publishing Co., 1955).
8. Whittaker Chambers, a senior editor of *Time*, testified that he had been a courier during the 1930s between Soviet officials and several Roosevelt Administration officials who had agreed, for ideological reasons, to copy secret documents and have them delivered to the Soviets. One Administration official, Julian Wadleigh, confessed his role. Others had died or, when called to testify, took the Fifth Amendment.

   One of the accused, Alger Hiss, denied having been a Communist Party member, initially denied ever knowing Chambers, and later admitted an acquaintance but denied any participation in espionage. Hiss' alleged complicity was front-page news because he had been a highly-placed State Department official during the 1930s and most of the 1940s, and had then left the State Department to accept a prestigious position as head of the Carnegie Endowment for World Peace.

   Hiss stayed on the front pages for the next year and a half because he continued to deny any involvement with the Soviets, even as Chambers produced copies of secret State Department documents retyped on a typewriter Hiss had at his home, microfilm of secret State Department documents with Hiss' initials on them, and so on. Eventually a jury found Hiss guilty of perjury.
9. For examples of reporter's bias, see John Chabot Smith, *Alger Hiss: The True Story* (New York: Holt, Rinehart and Winston, 1976), p. 293, and Chalmers Roberts, *The Washington Post: The First 100 Years* (Boston: Houghton Mifflin, 1977), p. 277.
10. Whittaker Chambers, *Witness* (New York: Random House, 1952), p. 9.
11. *Ibid.* More details of the Chambers story will be provided in Chapter Eight.
12. Alexander Solzhenitsyn addresses the battle against communism much as Chambers did. Solzhenitsyn received considerable American media attention when he first arrived in this country—he was a "novelty" and his message seemed political—but he has now become a nonperson in the press, in part because many journalists will not grapple with his theological critique.
13. See Washington *Post*, July 7, 1949, pp. 1, 11; November 24, 1949, p. 6. Other Christians with well-publicized records of misconduct who have been "born again" since then—for example, Charles Colson and Eldridge Cleaver—have had to run a similar media gauntlet. While it is important

to test over time the firmness of faith among new believers, utter hostility among journalists shows an unwillingness to admit that new life is possible.

14. See, for example, Washington *Post,* June 27, 1962, p. 6, and June 28, pp. 1, 22; Los Angeles *Times*, June 26, p. 1, June 27, p. 21, June 28, p. 13; Chicago *Tribune*, June 26, pp. 1, 2, June 27, pp. 1, 12; Atlanta *Constitution*, June 28, p. 1.
15. More details of this story also will be provided in Chapter Eight.
16. *The Tablet*, August 4, 1962; clipping from *Journal-American* archives, Humanities Research Center, The University of Texas at Austin.
17. Los Angeles *Times*, August 4, 1962, p. 1; New York *Journal-American*, August 18, 1962, archives clipping; New York *Times*, August 1, 1962, p. 19; New York *Times*, August 19, p. 12.
18. For glimpses of the immediate impact of Finkbine coverage, see New York *Post*, August 20, 1962, p. 1; *The Gallup Poll, Public Opinion 1935-1971* (New York: Random House, 1972), p. 1984; Garrett Hardin, *Stalking the Wild Taboo* (Los Altos, CA: William Kaufmann, 1973), pp. 4, 11.
19. Forrest Boyd tells this story in his *Instant Analysis* (Atlanta: John Knox Press, 1974), pp. 79-86.
20. *Ibid.*
21. Quoted in Los Angeles *Times*, December 28, 1983; *Times* article by David Shaw reprinted in Ray Hiebert and Carol Reuss, eds., *Impact of Mass Media* (New York: Longman, 1985), p. 434. Actually, many reporters probably understood all too well what Huffman was saying—but they did not want to apply it to themselves.
22. Many Christians have shown God's love through compassion toward those who are ill; AIDS patients should also be helped in their time of greatest need. Homosexuality should not be condoned, though.
23. Detroit *Free Press*, June 16, 1985, p. 3A: "The most striking thing about the 1986 Michigan Lesbian Gay Pride Parade and rally was diversity. There were men and women of all ages, and some people brought their kids. Some men said they were gay dads; a couple of women said they were Lesbian moms. At least four parents showed up to support their gay sons. They were doctors and lawyers, waiters and writers." In one sense, this Detroit *Free Press* article was neutral. Nowhere did it state explicitly that homosexuality was right. But the reporter, in providing positive coverage similar to that given Easter parades, and in making homosexuality seem natural and normal, supported the objective of the parade sponsors: "To show the state that gay men and women are a visible group that should enjoy full civil rights."
24. Chapter Ten discusses the question of how far to go in providing gruesome detail about sin.
25. Detroit *Free Press*, June 13, 1985, p. 4A.
26. Concerned Women for America, 122 C St. N.W., Suite 800, Washington, D.C. 20001, an organization that provided legal help to the Tennessee parents, has a record of press coverage.
27. John Corry, *TV News and the Dominant Culture* (Washington: Media Institute, 1986).
28. Rivers, pp. 10, 126.
29. *Accuracy in Media Report*, May 1980, No. 2; July 1979, No. 1; quoted in Isaacs, *The Coercive Utopians*, pp. 262, 270. The power of the press to

tilt, for better or for worse, was obvious both to new arrivals and to experienced journalists. Alexander Solzhenitsyn came, saw, and commented that the press is "more powerful than the legislature, the executive, and the judiciary." A Washington *Post* editor boasted that, in the capitol, the practice of "not only getting it from the horse's mouth but being inside his mouth" is "almost a way of life." Former reporter William Rivers noted that journalists "sometimes are the prime promoters or offstage prompters of the Congressional hearings, legislative battles and other events they are chronicling, theoretically with detachment." For additional discussion of this, see William Rivers, *The Other Government: Power and the Washington Media* (New York: Universe, 1982).

30. Wheel-of-Fortune journalism often involves playing law-breaking for laughs. A typical story of this kind began, "Something went wrong for a 26-year-old Austin man suspected of processing methamphetamine Monday afternoon in a Barton Hills apartment. His laboratory blew up." The story notes that the man suffered minor burns and was arrested, but not until the ninth and last paragraph of the story were readers told that the man was on probation for a previous conviction of manufacturing methamphetamine. Only then would readers see that the explosion was not a question of bad luck or chance, but repeated law-breaking (Austin *American Statesman*, July 29, 1986, p. 1).

CHAPTER THREE *Not Without Personal Cost*

1. Examining the personal lives and careers of non-Christian journalists helps us to remember that the struggle from a Christian perspective is not Christians *vs.* non-Christians, us *vs.* them. Many non-Christian journalists are broken inside, looking for love in all the wrong places; they need compassion as well as correction.

   Jesus did warn, though, that His enemies would hate Christians also. Although the battle is not us *vs.* them, from the non-Christian perspective it may be them *vs.* us.
2. William Harlan Hale, *Horace Greeley: Voice of the People* (New York: Harper and Brothers, 1950), p. 83. See also A. Oakley Hall, *Horace Greeley, Decently Dissected* (New York: Ross and Tousey, 1862); L. D. Ingersoll, *The Life of Horace Greeley, Founder of the New York Tribune* (Chicago: Union Publishing Co., 1873); Henry Luther Stoddard, *Horace Greeley: Printer, Editor, Crusader* (New York: Putnam's 1946); Glyndon G. Van Deusen, *Horace Greeley, Nineteenth Century Crusader* (Philadelphia: University of Pennsylvania Press, 1953); and Greeley's autobiography, *Recollections of a Busy Life* (New York: J. B. Ford and Co., 1868). Greeley's three decades of editorials in the *Tribune* are the best source for an in-depth study.
3. Greeley, *Recollections*, pp. 68-74. Greeley was heavily influenced by early nineteenth-century Unitarian leaders such as William Ellery Channing, who argued that "Avarice was the chief obstacle to human progress. . . . The only way to eliminate it was to establish a community of property." Channing's view typified the materialistic approach to the problem of evil. Evil was created by the way society was organized, not by anything innately evil in man: Change society and evil could be eliminated.
4. Greeley received great individual renown for his work in promoting com-

munes. At one banquet he was toasted by Albert Brisbane, theoretician of the communalists, for having "done for us what we never could have done. He has created the cause on this continent. He has done the work of a century. Well, then, I will give a toast: 'One Continent, One Man!' " (Hale, p. 105).

Greeley gave Brisbane a column in the *Tribune*. Brisbane blamed the failure of the communes on the existence of a noncommunal society outside their boundaries. Many communalists, Brisbane wrote, "began to picture the broader, more independent fields of action in the great competitive life of the individual in civilization. This shows clearly that unless associative life is completely organized, so that all the sentiments and faculties of the soul find their normal development and action therein, it cannot stand. . . there must either be the complex harmony of a perfect organization, with a high order of spiritual activity, or man must remain in his little isolated, individual state." Brisbane, essentially, was saying he needed totalitarianism to succeed. Enter the Gulag.

5. Hale, p. xvi.
6. Van Deusen, p. 148.
7. As Greeley's family situation deteriorated, he became even a more driven man at work.
8. Detroit *Free Press*, October 20, 1855, p. 2.
9. Van Deusen, p. 423
10. For more examples of headlines, see Justin Walsh's biography of Storey, *To Print the News and Raise Hell* (Chapel Hill: University of North Carolina Press, 1968).
11. Chicago *Times*, November 21, 1871, p. 1.
12. *Ibid.*, January 16, 1873, p. 1.
13. Walsh, p. 206.
14. *Ibid.*, p. 212.
15. *Ibid.*, p. 236.
16. *Ibid.*, p. 261.
17. For more information, see Calder Pickett, *Ed Howe: Country Town Philosopher* (Lawrence, KS: University Press of Kansas, 1968), and Howe's autobiography, *Plain People* (New York: Dodd, Mead, 1929). See also Gerald Carson, "The Village Atheist," *Scribner's*, December 1928, and Gene A. Howe, "My Father Was the Most Wretchedly Unhappy Man I Ever Knew," *Saturday Evening Post*, October 25, 1941.
18. Pickett, p. 177.
19. E. W. Howe, *Plain People*, *op. cit.*
20. Gene Howe, *op. cit.*
21. Readable books about Pulitzer include James Barrett, *Joseph Pulitzer and His World* (New York: Vanguard Press, 1941); Don Seitz, *Joseph Pulitzer: His Life and Letters* (New York: Simon and Schuster, 1924); W. A. Swanberg, *Pulitzer* (New York: Scribner's, 1967).
22. Swanberg, pp. 131, 197.
23. Henry Watterson, "*Marse Henry*": *An Autobiography*, Vol. 1 (New York: Doran, 1919), p. 209.
24. Swanberg, pp. 223, 181, 386.
25. *Ibid.*, pp. 389-393.
26. *Ibid.*, p. 433.
27. The best sources for Scripps are two books of his writings: *Damned Old*

Crank (New York: Harper and Brothers, 1951) and *I Protest*, ed. Oliver Knight (Madison: University of Wisconsin Press, 1966). Here, *Damned Old Crank*, p. 101.

28. Scripps, *I Protest*, p. 178.
29. Scripps, *Damned Old Crank*, p. 137.
30. *Ibid.*
31. Scripps, *I Protest*, p. 434.
32. Much of my sense of Hearst comes from reading his lively San Francisco *Examiner* and New York *Journal* and *American*. Some of Hearst's editorials are contained in a public relations book edited by Edmund Coblentz, one of his executives: *William Randolph Hearst: A Portrait in His Own Words* (New York: Simon and Schuster, 1952). Biographies include Oliver Carlson and Ernest Sutherland Bates, *Hearst: Lord of San Simeon* (New York: Viking Press, 1936); Ferdinand Lundberg, *Imperial Hearst: A Social Biography* (New York: Equinox, 1936); John Tebbel, *The Life and Good Times of William Randolph Hearst* (New York: Dutton, 1952); W. A. Swanberg, *Citizen Hearst* (New York: Scribner's, 1961).
33. For other Hearst anecdotes, see Allen Churchill, *Park Row* (New York: Rinehart, 1958).
34. Descriptions quoted often by biographers, including by Carlson, p. 111.
35. Lundberg, p. 141.
36. *Ibid.*, p. 310.
37. Sources for Steffens include *The Autobiography of Lincoln Steffens* (New York: Harcourt, Brace, 1931) and *The Letters of Lincoln Steffens* (New York: Harcourt, Brace, 1938). Biographies include Justin Kaplan, *Lincoln Steffens* (New York: Simon & Schuster, 1974), and Russell Horton, *Lincoln Steffens* (New York: Twayne, 1974).
38. Columnist Mark Sullivan liked Steffens but said, "I felt that when one tried to hold him down to any orderly sequence of logical argument he took refuge in some evasive, grinning paradox . . . he was in part a poseur—possibly a sincere poseur, that is, a poseur to himself."
39. Steffens portrayed himself in his autobiography as a man of constant honesty and integrity, one with true love for all mankind. Toward the end of his life Steffens wore a small gold cross from his watch chain and called himself "the only Christian on earth" (Horton, p. 85). The autobiography was a best-seller. For seven months of 1931 so was a Soviet book, *New Russia's Primer*, an explanation for children of the Five Year Plan.
40. Kaplan lays out best the grisly details of Steffens' political end.
41. Steffens, *Autobiography*, p. 872.
42. Duranty information is drawn from his writing and from James Crowl's *Angels in Stalin's Paradise* (Washington: University Press of America, 1982). A documentary about the famine shown on PBS during 1986—due to PBS politicization it ended up on a special evening edition of William F. Buckley's "Firing Line"—supports Crowl's view.
43. Duranty certainly liked to play, in his way. In 1922, Crowl notes, Duranty brought to Moscow a Buick; he obtained "a fearless driver named Grisha and a screeching horn that was undistinguishable from that used by the G.P.U. For many, the sight of Duranty's Buick plunging through the streets with Grisha's hand against the horn was a terrifying experience. Duranty delighted in making such forays at dusk when the police made their raids, and, on one occasion, his friends efused to unbolt their door for fifteen

minutes while they disposed of some possibly incriminating foreign journals" (Crowl, pp. 34, 35).

44. Just as Satan quotes Scripture for his own purposes, so many pro-Soviet journalists liked to use Biblical references. Steffens called Lenin "Moses in Red."
45. Crowl, p. 139.
46. Steffens and Duranty may have been at the extreme, but many other journalists during the 1930s were not far behind. In *Bovard of the Post-Dispatch* (Baton Rouge: Louisiana State University Press, 1954), James Markham tells how Oliver Bovard, editor of the influential, Pulitzer-family-owned St. Louis *Post Dispatch*, believed that the Constitution should be amended to abolish guarantees of property rights and due process, so that socialism could speedily be enacted. "To educate readers," Markham writes, Bovard "gave space to Stanlin's addresses and the full text of the Soviet constitution," and sent a reporter to the Soviet Union with instructions to stress the theme in his writing that "economically the United States was going to the left, while Russia was tending to the right." Bovard believed, as did others on the left, that Franklin Roosevelt was "a mere schoolboy tinkering instead of getting down to cases, the 'Kerensky of the American revolution.' "

    The political climate of the 1930s and the ideology of many journalists make Duranty appear less an anomaly and more the iceberg's tip. According to Malcolm Muggeridge, "If the New York *Times* went on all those years giving great prominence to Duranty's messages, building him and them up when they were so evidently nonsensically untrue, to the point that he came to be accepted as the great Russian expert in America, and played a major part in shaping President Roosevelt's policies vis-a-vis the USSR—this was not, we may be sure, because the *Times* was deceived. Rather it *wanted* to be so deceived, and Duranty provided the requisite deception material" (Muggeridge, *Chronicles of a Wasted Time: The Green Stick* [New York: William Morrow, 1973], p. 255).
47. *Ibid.*
48. Duranty, *I Write As I Please* (New York: Simon and Schuster, 1935), p. 340.

CHAPTER FOUR *Man's Subjectivity vs. God's Plumb Line*

1. Quoted in Michael Schudson, *Discovering the News* (New York: Basic Books, 1978), p. 161.
2. Quoted in J. Herbert Altschull, *Agents of Power* (New York: Longman, 1984), p. 130.
3. Dinesh D'Souza, "Mr. Donaldson Goes to Washington," *Policy Review*, Summer 1986, pp. 24-31.
4. Harris published only one issue of his newspaper; he had not obtained a license from governmental authorities, and two of his stories did not fit British public relations goals. The first continuing American newspaper was the Boston *News Letter*, published in 1704. Bartholomew Green, editor of the *News Letter* from 1722 to 1733, was explicit about his desire to cover the spiritual so that those "who have the state of religion in the world very much at heart" will better know "how to order their prayers and praises to the great God" (January 21, 1723).

5. Boston *Recorder*, January 25, 1823, p. 13.
6. *Ibid*., March 15, 1823, p. 41.
7. *Ibid*., p. 40.
8. Schudson, pp. 78, 86.
9. Walter Lippmann, *Public Opinion* (New York: Harcourt, Brace, 1922), p. 21. Lippmann's ideas of subjectivity were picked up by professors and journalists but proclaimed infrequently. One reason might be that widespread acceptance of ideas of reportorial subjectivity would have undermined one of the key reporter's campaigns of the 1930s: the campaign against the publishers. Publishers, often conservative and Republican during the 1930s, tried to rein in their Washington correspondents, often liberal and Democratic. In 1936, when Leo Rosten asked Washington reporters whether they had "had stories played down, cut, or killed for 'policy' reasons, 56% said yes." The reporters tried to maintain that they were objective and scientific in their coverage, and thus should not be overwhelmed by the publishers' political considerations. Had they admitted that they tilted as much as the publishers did, but in a different political direction, their defense would have become untenable.
10. Ivy Lee, *Publicity* (New York: Industries Publishing, 1925), p. 21; Schudson, p. 149.
11. "Objectively" quoting the most articulate and convincing proponents of both sides in as even-handed a way as possible places reporters and readers in the position of Eve, who in the Garden of Eden did the first balancing act. Wanting to be "objective" in the sense of hearing both sides, she had first heard God's view. Then Satan gave Eve a different set of facts and asked her to be the judge as to which she should accept. As philosopher Cornelius Van Til noted, "The acceptance of this position of judge constituted the fall of man. . . . Before Eve could listen to the tempter she had to take for granted that the devil was perhaps a person who knew as much about reality as God knew about it. Eve was compelled to assume the equal ultimacy of the minds of God, of the devil, and of herself. And this surely excluded the exclusive ultimacy of God." See Van Til, *The Defense of the Faith* (Philadelphia: Presbyterian and Reformed Publishing, 1955), pp. 48-52.
12. Objectivity as traditionally understood—holding up a mirror to the area of coverage—began to receive fewer verbal plaudits during the 1960s. By then, the war of reporters' independence was won. For instance, a Washington correspondent from St. Louis could accurately proclaim, concerning his relationship with newspaper management, "I make a hundred decisions where they make one." Only 7 percent of Washington correspondents during the 1960s, according to William Rivers, ever had any disagreements with the "home office." By 1978, Stephen Hess (*The Washington Reporters* [Washington: Brookings, 1981]) could state bluntly that publishers' throwing around of their weight had simply disappeared as an issue of reporters' concern. In part, this was because many publishers had moved leftward also; in part, because publishers had been trained to keep hands off the news pages.
13. Michael Parenti, *Inventing Reality* (New York: St. Martin's Press, 1986), pp. 52, 53.
14. Quoted in William Rivers, *The Opinionmakers* (Boston: Beacon Press, 1965), p. 59. The post-World War II Commission on Freedom of the Press

had argued, "It is no longer enough to report *the fact* truthfully. It is now necessary to report *the truth about the fact.*" Reston continued that theme, writing that "You cannot merely report the literal truth. You have to explain it."

15. See Edward Jay Epstein, *News from Nowhere: Television and the News* (New York: Random House, 1973).
16. Max Kampleman in *The Public Interest*, Fall 1978, p. 18; quoted in Isaacs' *The Coercive Utopians*, p. 274.
17. Some journalists claim that they are just telling the story lucidly, giving more room to smart people and less to the befuddled. Give true equality to Bible thumpers? How is that possible if we are to improve mankind? In this sense, Wes Gallagher of the Associated Press may have been right in a less obvious way when he spoke of objectivity as journalism's Holy Grail: Not only was the Holy Grail never found, but after a time knights apparently had little desire to find it. They could use the search as an excuse to go gallivanting around wherever they chose.
18. Rivers, p. 13.
19. Gaye Tuchman, *Making News* (New York: The Free Press, 1978).
20. D'Souza, *loc. cit.*
21. Even when readers and viewers do receive some real debate, it is likely to be liberal materialist *vs.* conservative materialist.
22. Av Westin, *Newswatch* (New York: Simon and Schuster, 1982), p. 233.
23. D'Souza, *loc. cit.*
24. Strategic ritual receives particular scorn from those who have been libeled in stories that pretend to be objective. Rodney Smolla, in *Suing the Press* (New York: Oxford University Press, 1986), pp. 191, 192, examined the reaction of one defamed individual, William Tavoulareas: "People like William Tavoulareas do not seem to take offense when reporters draw personal conclusions, as long as they make it clear that they are drawing them. Nor do they take offense when the 'straight' news story neutrally lays out raw facts, leaving all conclusions to the reader. What appeared to irk Tavoulareas and the Washington D.C. jury was the subtle infiltration of judgmental conclusions by the *Post* in what on its face purported to be neutral reportage. What Tavoulareas lashed out against was advocacy wrapped up in the disguise of neutrality—the news story presented as pure fact that was really a selection of facts to support a predetermined opinion." Smolla himself criticizes the *Post* for not having "the courage of its own conviction—the courage to make its editorializing explicit. . . . The Post slipped into a wimpish middle ground, hinting that Tavoulareas had cheated the public interest, but putting the story in an objective voice."
25. Quoted in Epstein, p. 214.
26. Boston *Recorder*, January 18, 1823, p. 11.

CHAPTER FIVE *Ethics Without Christ?*

1. Some of the better books on journalistic ethics are: Clifford Christians, Kim Rotzoll and Mark Fackler, *Media Ethics: Cases and Moral Reasoning* (New York: Longman, 1983); Nelson Crawford, *The Ethics of Journalism* (New York: Knopf, 1924); Tom Goldstein, *The News at Any Cost* (New York: Simon and Schuster, 1985); Gene Goodwin, *Groping for Ethics in Journalism* (Ames, IA: Iowa State University Press, 1983); John Hulteng,

The Messenger's Motives: Ethical Problems of the News Media (Englewood Cliffs, NJ: Prentice-Hall, second edition 1985); Edmund Lambeth, *Committed Journalism: An Ethic for the Profession* (Bloomington: Indiana University Press, 1986).

2. John Hersey, "The Legend of the License," *Yale Review*, Autumn 1980, p. 2.
3. The sad story of Janet Cooke has been told in many books and articles; one of the fuller accounts is in Normal Isaacs, *Untended Gates* (New York: Columbia University Press, 1986), pp. 63-81. When the scandal broke, *Post* editors explained that they had not checked the story's facts more carefully or gone looking for Jimmy because a drug dealer had threatened Cooke's life if she identified him. One former editor, Charles Seib, reacted to that explanation by wondering publicly why the editors were "so willing to let Jimmy die." Seib noted that "There was deep concern for Cooke's safety. But not a thought for Jimmy" (Goldstein, p. 29).
4. "News Watchdog Group Scores 'Voice' Pulitzer Prize Winner," Washington *Post,* June 12, 1981, p. A2; Michael Kramer, "Just the Facts, Please," *New York*, May 25, 1981, p. 19; James Markham, "Writer Admits He Fabricated an Article in Times Magazine," New York *Times*, February 22, 1982, pp. 1Y, 4Y.
5. *Cape Publications v. Bridges*, 6 Media Law Reporter 1884; 8 Med. L. Rptr. 2525.
6. *Ibid.*
7. *Griffith v. Rancocas Valley Hospital*, 8 Med. L. Rptr. 1760.
8. *Doe v. Sarasota-Bradenton Television*, 9 Med. L. Rptr. 2074.
9. *Ibid.*
10. *Ibid.*
11. *Globe Newspapers v. Superior Court*, 457 U.S. 596, 102 S. Ct. 2613 (1984), 8 Med. Law Rptr. 1689.
12. *Ibid.*, pp. 1692, 1693.
13. *Ibid.*, p. 1699. The current legal confusion came out clearly in *Eversole v. Sonoma County Superior Court* (9 Med. L. Rptr. 2436). In that case, fourteen-year-old and sixteen-year-old victims were witnesses against a man charged with three counts of rape and unlawful sexual intercourse, and one count of oral copulation. The sixteen-year-old was willing to testify publicly in a preliminary hearing, but fourteen-year-old Laurie had been talking and crying in her sleep following the attack. She had headaches. She would start crying when asked detailed questions about the attack. The trial judge closed the preliminary hearing during her testimony. The man she testified against was convicted.

    The convicted rapist and his lawyer then appealed, arguing that Laurie should have had to testify publicly. A California Superior Court agreed that closing of the preliminary hearing had violated the prisoner's rights, because there was insufficient showing that "testimony before the general public would threaten serious psychological harm to the witness. . . ." Besides, the appeals court noted that closing of hearings would not avoid that part of the psychological harm which could be created by graphic press accounts of the rape, because closure would not prevent the press from promptly obtaining a transcript of the testimony.

    The convicted rapist was freed. The courts appeared to be offering alleged rapists the potential for a win-win situation. If there was an exciting preliminary hearing, with a fourteen-year-old rape victim fainting on the stand, resultant headlines could lead to appeals based on prejudicial pre-trial publicity. If the trial court attempted (as much as possible under current legal rulings and the need to bring out the truth) to protect the privacy of a rape victim, appeals based on the lack of public testimony could be forthcoming.

14. Gene Goodwin, "The Ethics of Compassion," in Ray Hiebert and Carol Reuss, eds., *Impact of Mass Media* (New York: Longman, 1985), p. 85.
15. Some television stations, while not acting in such grotesque ways, have turned suffering to promotional advantage. The Oregon Supreme Court in 1986 reviewed an invasion of privacy case that grew out of a news story. A television cameraman had photographed the scene of an automobile accident in which a man was injured. The evening news showed the man bleeding and in pain while receiving emergency medical treatment. This was legitimate news and the man recognized it as such, but the television station began using the clip for promotional spots in self-advertising; he sued. Oregon judges decided for the television station, thus ruling that the bloodied faces and bodies of accident victims are fair game for television use, not just as immediate news but again, again, and again (*Anderson v. Fisher*, 12 Med. L. Rptr. 1604).
16. *Editor & Publisher*, July 18, 1979, p. 6.
17. Public opinion polls record mixed definitions of "invasion of privacy." In one poll, 70 percent of those questioned said that publication of a photograph of a well-known politician entering a pornographic book shop was invasion of privacy; 26 percent said privacy had not been invaded. Should names of men arrested for soliciting prostitutes be published? 49 percent said that would constitute an invasion of privacy, 47 percent had no objection. Was publication of names of persons under sixteen years old accused of committing crimes an invasion of privacy? 51 percent said yes, 44 percent no (*The People and the Press*, Los Angeles: Times Mirror Co., 1986).
18. Michael Rouse, "Rape," *ASNE Bulletin*, February 1982; reprinted in George Rodman, *Mass Media Issues* (New York: Science Research Associates, 1984), pp. 300-303. See also Zena Beth McGlashan, "By Reporting the Name, Aren't We Victimizing the Rape Victim Twice?," *ASNE Bulletin*, April 1982, reprinted in Rodman, pp. 304-307.
19. *Campbell v. Seabury Press*, 614 F. 2d 395 (5th Cir. 1980), 5 Med. L. Rptr. 1803, 1829.
20. Rouse, p. 302.
21. Quoted in William A. Henry III, "Journalism Under Fire," *Time* (December 12, 1983), pp. 76-93. While invading the privacy of victims is poor practice, there is no need to give special privacy protection to those responsible for their predicaments. In *Holman v. Central Arkansas Broadcasting Co.* (1979), a man had been arrested for drunk driving. For five hours at a police station he was "hitting and banging on his cell door, hollering and cursing." A local radio reporter taped some of the noise and broadcast it. That seems fine.
22. *Branzburg v. Hayes*, 408 U.S. 665 (1972).
23. Many press subpoenas may damage source relationships primarily by compromising the reporter's independent or compatriot status in the eyes of sources, not by forcing revelation of sensitive information. Reporters

should limit areas of vulnerability by offering protection only for a certain amount of time, or until after certain events take place. Blanket assurances of confidentiality should be given very rarely.

24. Asserting that exposure to ethics courses will enable us to do better, naturally, misses one of the main points of the Bible. Ethics courses could do wonders if man's will and reason were unaffected by the fall, but that is not what the Bible says. An ethics course for non-Christian reporters could most usefully increase their understanding of public reaction to journalistic arrogance. An ethics course for Christians could be useful in making practical applications of Biblical truth.
25. Justice White argued in *Branzburg v. Hayes* that protection for reporters at major newspapers but not for independent journalists would be "questionable procedure in light of the traditional doctrine that liberty of the press is the right of the lonely pamphleteer who uses carbon paper or a mimeograph just as much as of the large metropolitan publisher." He mulled over the possibilities for confusion beyond even news publishing: "The informative function asserted by representatives of the organized press in the present cases is also performed by lecturers, political pollsters, novelists, academic researchers, and dramatists. Almost any author may quite accurately assert that he is contributing to the flow of information to the public, that he relies on confidential sources of information, and that these sources will be silenced if he is forced to make disclosures before a grand jury."

CHAPTER SIX *Libel: Utilitarian Justice vs. Biblical Truth-Telling*

1. *The Cost of Libel* (New York: Gannett Center for Media Studies, 1986), p. 2.
2. *Time*, February 4, 1985, p. 64; New York *Times*, February 19, 1985, p. 1; February 20, 1985, p. 13; James Goodale, "Survey of Recent Media Verdicts, Their Disposition on Appeal, and Media Defense Costs," in *Media Insurance and Risk Management* (New York: Practicing Law Institute, 1985); Rodney Smolla, *Suing the Press* (New York: Columbia University Press, 1986), pp. 80-99, 198-237.
3. *Pring v. Penthouse*, 695 F. 2d 438 (10th Cir. 1982), 8 Med. L. Rptr. 2409; New York *Times*, December 10, 1984, p. 15; Smolla, pp. 160-181.
4. Randall Bezanson, Gilbert Cranberg, John Soloski, "Libel and the Press: Setting the Record Straight," The 1985 Silha Lecture, University of Minnesota, May 15, 1985, pp. 26, 27.

   Michael Gartner, formerly of the Des Moines Register and Tribune Company, said wryly in 1984, "We'd sooner drown our children" than admit error. "What do many papers and editors—and their lawyers, I should add—do when a paper errs? We equivocate. We bluster. We alibi. We hide behind technicalities. We hide behind secretaries."
5. *The Cost of Libel*, *loc. cit.*; Michael Massing, "Libel Insurance: Scrambling for Coverage," *Columbia Journalism Review*, January/February 1986, pp. 35-38.
6. *Ibid.*; Michael Massing, "The Libel Chill: How Cold Is It Out There?," *Columbia Journalism Review*, May/June 1985, pp. 31-43; *New York Times v. Sullivan: The Next Twenty Years* (New York: Practicing Law Institute, 1984), pp. 87, 450, 507, 527, 528.

7. Interviews by author at Gannett Ethics Conference, University of Kentucky, 1985.
8. *The Cost of Libel, loc. cit.*; *Washington Journalism Review*, January 1986, p. 35.
9. *Ibid.*; Massing, "Libel Insurance," *loc. cit.*
10. Interviews at Gannett Ethics Conference and at annual convention of the Association for Education in Journalism and Mass Communication, Norman, Oklahoma, 1986.
11. *New York Times v. Sullivan*, 376 U.S. 254 (1964).
12. *St. Amant v. Thompson*, 390 U.S. 727 (1968).
13. Schauer, "Public Figures," 25 *William and Mary Law Review*, (1984), pp. 905, 910.
14. *Ocala Star-Banner Co. v. Damron*, 401 U.S. 285 (1971); cited in Schauer, *ibid.*
15. *Kruteck v. Schimmel*, 27 A.D. 2d 837, 278 N.Y.S. 2d 25 (N.Y. Appl. 1967); *Clawson v. Longview Pub. Co.*, 91 Wash. 2d 408, 589 P. 2d 1223, 4 Med. L. Rptr. 2163 (1979); *McMurry v. Howard Pub., Inc.*, 612 P. 2d 14, 6 Med. L. Rptr. 1814 (Wyo. 1980); *Press Inc. v. Verran*, 569 S.W. 2d 435, 4 Med. L. Rptr. 1229 (Tenn. 1978).
16. *Rosenbloom v. Metromedia, Inc.*, 403 U.S. 29 (1971); *Gertz v. Robert Welch, Inc.*, 418 U.S. 323 (1974). For more on the logic of extension from public official to public figure, see Daniels, "Public Figures Revisited," 25 *William and Mary Law Review* (1984), pp. 957, 965.
17. *Lawrence v. Bauer Pub.*, 89 N.J. 451, 446 A. 2d 469 (1982); *Cloyd v. Press*, 629 S.W. 2d 24 (Tenn. App. 1981); *Wright v. Haas*, 586 P. 2d 1093 (Okla. 1978); *Exner v. AMA*, 12 Wash. App. 215, 529 P. 2d 863 (1974).
18. *Lawrence v. Bauer Pub.*, *ibid.*
19. *Ibid.*
20. See Goodale, "Centuries of Libel Law Erased by Times-Sullivan," 191 *New York Law Journal* 49 (1984).
21. Bezanson, *et. al.*, p. 9.
22. Franklin, "Good Names and Bad Law: A Critique of Libel Law and a Proposal," 18 U.S.F.L. Rev. 1, 10 (1983).
23. For examples, see Libel Defense Resource Center Bulletin 11, Summer-Fall 1984, pp. 1, 2.
24. *Anderson v. Liberty Lobby*, 12 Med. L. Rptr. 2297 (1986).
25. *The Cost of Libel*, p. 3; Ethics Workshop interviews.
26. *Herbert v. Lando*, 441 U.S. 153 (1979).
27. See *Congressional Record*, July 24, 1985, p. E3478; Floyd Abrams, "Why We Should Change the Libel Law," New York *Times Magazine*, September 29, 1985, pp. 34, 87, 90-92.
28. The specific injunctions against defamation are all subsets of the Ninth Commandment: "You shall not give false testimony against your neighbor" (Exodus 20:16). Rousas Rushdoony provides a useful discussion of the many aspects of that commandment in his important book *The Institutes of Biblical Law* (Philadelphia: Presbyterian and Reformed, 1973), pp. 542-631.

CHAPTER SEVEN *Press vs. Public*

1. *Coughlin v. Westinghouse Broadcasting*, 12 Med. L. Rptr. 2263 (1986).
2. *Ibid.*

3. *Hepps v. Philadelphia Newspapers*, 12 Med. L. Rptr. 1977 (1986).
4. *Ibid.*
5. *Anderson v. Liberty Lobby*, 12 Med. L. Rptr. 2297 (1986). See also prior U.S. Court of Appeals decision, 11 Med. L. Rptr. 1005.
6. *Ibid.*
7. *Ibid.*
8. James Alexander, ed., *A Brief Narrative of the Case and Tryal of John Peter Zenger, Printer of the New-York Weekly Journal*, second edition, ed. Stanley Nider Katz (Cambridge: Harvard University Press, 1972), p. 101. See also Livingston Rutherford, *John Peter Zenger* (New York: Dodd, Mead, 1904), and David Paul Nord, "The Authority of Truth: Religion and the John Peter Zenger Case," *Journalism Quarterly*, Summer 1985, p. 227.
9. *Rex v. Tutchin*, in Thomas Bayly Howell, compiler, *A Complete Collection of [British] State Trials to 1783. Continued by T. J. Howell to 1820*, Vol. 14 (London, 1816-1828), p. 1095.
10. *Ibid.*
11. J. F. Stephens, *History of Criminal Law in England*, Vol. 2 (London: 1883), p. 299.
12. For descriptions of these and other cases, see Frederick Siebert, *Freedom of the Press in England 1476-1776* (Urbana: University of Illinois Press, 1952).
13. For an example of this application of the thought of Calvin and Knox, see Samuel Rutherford, *Lex Rex* (Harrisonburg, VA: Sprinkle Publications, 1982; orig. pub. 1644).
14. John Milton, *Areopagitica*, reprinted in Henry Morley, ed., *English Prose Writings of John Milton* (London: George Routledge and Sons, 1889), p. 345.
15. Isaiah Thomas, *The History of Printing in America*, Vol. 2 (Worcester: Isaiah Thomas, Jr., 1810), p. 12.
16. Matt Bushnell Jones, *Thomas Maule, The Salem Quaker and Free Speech in Massacahusetts Bay* (Salem: The Essex Institute, 1936), p. 30.
17. *A Narrative of a New and Unusual American Imprisonment of Two Presbyterian Ministers: And Prosecution of Mr. Francis Makemie, 1707, by a Learner of Law, and Lover of Liberty*, reprinted in Peter Force, ed., *Tracts and Other Papers Relating Principally to the Origin . . . of the Colonies in North America*, Vol. 4, No. 4 (New York: P. Smith, 1947 ed.), p. 24.
18. Alexander, p. 99.
19. Thomas, Volume 2, pp. 234, 473. See also Clyde Augustus Duniway, *The Development of Freedom of the Press in Massachusetts* (New York: Longmans, Green, 1906), pp. 112-115.
20. Thomas, Volume 2, pp. 143, 144.
21. *Rex v. Owen*, in Howell, Volume 18, p. 1203.
22. *Rex v. Miller*, in Howell, Volume 20, p. 870.
23. *Rex v. Owen, op. cit.*
24. *Ibid.*
25. *Ibid.*
26. *Ibid.*
27. *Ibid.*
28. *Rex v. Miller, op. cit.*

29. *Ibid.*
30. *Ibid.*
31. *Ibid.*
32. *A Letter from Candor to the Public Advertiser* (London, 1764).
33. Thomas, Volume 2, p. 12.
34. *Commonwealth v. Clap*, 4 Tyng 183.
35. *Ibid.*
36. See, for instance, *Henderson v. Fox*, 83 Ga. 233, 9 S.E. 839; *Sullings v. Shakespeare*, 46 Mich. 408, 9 N.W. 451; *Press Co. v. Stewart*, 119 Pa. 584, 14 Atl. 51; *Haynes v. Spokane Chronicle Publishing Co.*, 11 Wash. 503, 39 Pac. 969; etc.
37. *The People and the Press* (Los Angeles: Times Mirror, 1986), p. 35.
38. *Tavoulareas v. The Washington Post*, 567 F. Supp. 651 (1983) and 759 F. 2d. 90 (1985).
39. James Billington, *Fire in the Minds of Men* (New York: Basic Books, 1980), p. 33.
40. *Ibid.*, p. 35.
41. *Ibid.*, p. 33.
42. Bernard Fay, *The Two Franklins* (Boston: Little, Brown, 1933), is the best source for Bache material.
43. Early biographies of Paine were hostile to him. Twentieth-century biographies have tended to praise him. The most comprehensive biography is Moncure Conway, *The Life of Thomas Paine* (London: G. P. Putnam's Sons, 1892).
44. Boston *Recorder*, January 3, 1816, p. 1.
45. When kings are corrupt and a huge state public relations apparatus is cranking out false prophecies, those who follow God must speak up. In the Book of Jeremiah, state-subsidized prophets are predicting that all will be well; "No sword or famine will touch this land" (Jeremiah 14). They control major communications channels with their "visions from their own minds" (23:16). No one wants to listen to Jeremiah; yet his task is to tell the people of Judah, "Do not trust in deceptive words." He is obligated to tell them not to "steal and murder, commit adultery and perjury, burn incense to Baal and follow other gods. . . ." (Jeremiah 7:3, 9).

    Jeremiah does his task so well that state officials tell the king, "This man should be put to death. He is discouraging the soldiers who are left in this city, as well as all the people, by the things he is saying to them." Jeremiah is left to die in a cistern full of mud, but one of his supporters intervenes (38:4-13). Some journalists today want to deliver Jeremiads, but the test is whether what they are saying follows the Bible or their own oracle.

    In the Book of Ezekiel, false prophets and true prophets also are in conflict. God tells Ezekiel (13), "Woe to the foolish prophets who follow their own spirit and have seen nothing." Those individuals "prophesy out of their own imagination," God says: The false prophets "lead my people astray, saying, 'Peace,' when there is no peace." They build a flimsy wall and cover it with whitewash. Ezekiel's task (Ezekiel 3 and 33) is to be a watchman, warning the wicked and speaking out to dissuade them from their evil ways in order to save their lives. As a true prophet, Ezekiel cannot be savior: If he has warned the wicked and they do not repent, he is not accountable for their blood. But if he does not warn them, he is.
46. Henry, *loc. cit.*

47. Quoted in Goldstein, *The News at Any Cost*, *op. cit.*, p. 46.
48. Kurt Luedtke, speech before the American Newspaper Publishers Association, *ASNE Bulletin*, May/June 1982, reprinted in Rodman, *op. cit.*, p. 190.
49. Henry, *loc. cit.*
50. Rutherford, *op. cit.*
51. Ken Auletta, "Would You Lie, Steal or Cheat to Get a Story?" in *Hard Feelings: Reporting on the Pols, the Press, the People and the City* (New York: Random House, 1980), p. 244.
52. Tom Kelly, *The Imperial Post*, *op. cit.*, p. 158. Later, von Hoffman derided President Carter as "Jimmy Peanut . . . the gleamy-toothed, bushy-tailed anointed chipmunk of the Lord."
53. Kelly, p. 179; Dinesh D'Souza, "Mr. Donaldson Goes to Washington," *Policy Review*, Summer 1986, pp. 24-31.
54. S. Robert Lichter and Stanley Rothman, "Media and Business Elites," *Public Opinion*, October/November 1981, pp. 42-44; *Washington Journalism Review* (December 1982) also had a short Lichter-Rothman piece. Their critique was critiqued, but not very convincingly, by Herbert Gans in "Are U.S. Journalists Dangerously Liberal?," *Columbia Journalism Review*, November/December 1985, pp. 29-33.
55. Lichter and Rothman, *ibid.*
56. Henry, *loc. cit.*
57. *Ibid.* According to a Michigan State survey of press attitudes, such isolation has led to a "public-be-damned attitude" among some journalists and professors, complete with frequent speeches about the public's supposedly lackadaisical attitude toward press freedom. A survey for the American Society of Newspaper Editors found that many reporters thought thei readers did not appreciate the role of an independent press. Henry Kaufman of the Libel Defense Resource Center argued, "When a libel case gets to a jury, the First Amendment kind of drops to the wayside." University of Illinois professor Thomas Littlewood said, "Rarest of all in many sections of the country is the juror who has even the vaguest appreciation of what the First Amendment is" (*The Cost of Libel*, p. 12).

    The public may have more appreciation of the original meaning of the First Amendment than many members of the press.

CHAPTER EIGHT *Perceptive Media Watching*

1. Detroit *News*, June 5, 1986, p. 1; Detroit *Free Press*, June 5, p. 3.
2. *News*, June 6, 1986, p. 1; *Free Press*, June 6, p. 1.
3. *News*, June 2, 1986, p. 1; *Free Press*, June 2, p. 1.
4. See *Wall Street Journal*, July 27, 1982, p. 30.
5. See, for example, "A Reprise of Scopes," *Newsweek*, July 28, 1986, p. 19.
6. *Ibid.*
7. Lester A. Sobel, ed., *Media Controversies* (New York: Facts on File, 1981), p. 73.
8. See, for example, *Newsweek*, November 14, 1966, p. 92 and *Time*, September 17, 1965, p. 82.
9. Kathleen Jamieson and Karlyn Campbell, *The Interplay of Influence* (Belmont, CA: Wadsworth, 1983), p. 49.
10. Detroit *News*, June 3, 1986, p. 1; Detroit *Free Press*, June 4, p. 18A. The *Free Press* is a morning newspaper, the *News* technically an evening one.

The *News*, though, actually hits the streets at about noon, too early to include nonemergency coverage of the day's events. The *News*, like the *Free Press*, essentially deals with events of the previous day or before. None of the four Detroit stories referred to in this chapter appeared to be affected by the difference in timing.

11. Two books to read for information about the great case are Chambers' *Witness* (New York: Random House, 1952) and Allan Weinstein's *Perjury* (New York: Knopf, 1978). Alfred Kazin wrote in *Esquire* of Weinstein's work, "After this book, it is impossible to imagine anything new in this case except an admission by Alger Hiss that he had been lying for thirty years" (March 28, 1978, p. 21). Liberal historian Arthur Schlesinger, Jr., conservative columnist George Will, *Encounter* editor Melvin Lasky, and author Merle Miller all agreed that, in Will's words, "The myth of Hiss' innocence suffers the death of a thousand cuts, delicate destruction by a scholar's scalpel" *(Newsweek*, March 20, 1978, p. 96).
12. The *Post* did not listen to the words of prosecutor Thomas Murphy, who kept jurors' attention focused on the microfilm and the papers typed on Hiss' typewriter. "Always come back to the documents in applying reason to this case," he said, then asked, "If you caught a child in the kitchen with jam on his face and you asked him if he was in the kitchen and he said no—what does your normal, everyday intelligence tell you?"
13. Washington *Post*, November 24, 1949, p. 6; June 24, 1950, p. 1; June 25, p. 1.
14. Chicago *Tribune*, December 3, 1948, p. 1; June 16, 1949, p. 3; Washington *Post*, June 16, p. 1.
15. Washington *Post*, June 3, 1948, p. 1; Chicago *Tribune*, June 3, 1948, p. 1.
16. Washington *Post*, June 7, 1949, p. 1; Chicago *Tribune*, June 7, p. 2.
17. Washington *Post*, June 14, 1949, p. 1.
18. Chicago *Tribune*, June 14, p. 1.
19. Chicago *Tribune*, June 16, 1949, p. 3; Washington *Post*, June 16, p. 1.
20. *Saturday Evening Post*, November 15, 1952, p. 121. Those non-Christian journalists who are conservatives are valuable allies of Biblical Christians in many political and social battles because they often see clearly the material manifestations of disobedience to God, even if they refuse to admit the cause. Some, though, are like Hearst's long-time editor Arthur Brisbane, who "wrote approvingly of religion" because "he regarded it as a sort of merciful illusion which sustained people and comforted them when they might otherwise have had nothing on which to lean" (profile by Stanley Walker in *Post Biographies of Famous Journalists*, ed. John Drewry [Athens: University of Georgia Press, 1942], pp. 24, 25).

    Other non-Christian journalists who are politically involved may be similar to this description of Henry Luce, cofounder of *Time* magazine, by one of his editors, Ralph Ingersoll: Luce's "first faith had been in God," but in school "it had been challenged. And he had not met the challenge. He had seen that the boys who felt as he felt, truly, were not the 'in' group. . . . he was not drawn to Christ's defense, but to the company of His critics—the popular and the powerful. It was *their* challenge that he had felt the need to meet, to become one of them, to outdo them. He had given up his faith in God to meet it. He had learned what he really was—'a back-row Christian.' And something went out of him" (quoted in Roy Hoopes, *Ralph Ingersoll* [New York: Atheneum, 1985], pp. 160, 161).

21. In a continuation of this study, the Los Angeles *Times* (then a conservative newspaper) and the New York *Times* (a liberal newspaper, although closer to the center then than now) also were examined. Los Angeles *Times* coverage was similar to that of the *Tribune*. New York *Times* coverage was similar to that of the *Post* at first, but when overwhelming evidence against Hiss appeared, the *Times* bailed out and dropped its pro-Hiss stance. Presuppositions create presumptions as to the importance of particular facts or segments of testimony, but in some cases neither liberal nor conservative newspapers will *completely* disregard irrefutable evidence, as long as basic theological questions can be overlooked.
22. David Altheide, *Creating Reality* (Beverly Hills: Sage Publications, 1976), p. 73.
23. New York *Times*, July 26, 1962, p. 25.
24. *Ibid.*, July 27, 1962, p. 12.
25. New York *Journal-American*, August 5, 1962, p. 1; August 19, 1962, clipping from *Journal-American* archives, Humanities Research Center, University of Texas at Austin.
26. Los Angeles *Times*, July 31, 1962, p. 1.
27. Chicago *Tribune*, July 25, 1962, Part 3, p. 1.
28. New York *Times*, July 25, 1962, p. 22; July 27, 1962, p. 12; August 5, 1962, p. 12; Arizona *Republic*, July 27, 1962, p. 4.
29. New York *Journal-American*, August 18, 1962, clipping from *Journal-American* archives.
30. New York *Times*, August 19, 1962, p. 12.
31. Los Angeles *Times*, August 4, 1962, p. 15.
32. Chicago *Tribune*, July 27, 1962, p. 4.

CHAPTER NINE *Network News and Local Newspapers: The Coming Economic Judgment?*

1. For a basic discussion of the nature-grace issue, see Francis Schaeffer, *Escape from Reason* (Downers Grove, IL: InterVarsity Press, 1968), pp. 9-29.
2. New York *Times*, September 12, 1986, p. 1, "Behind the Revolt at CBS: An Erosion of Confidence."
3. See William J. Drummond, "Is Time Running out for Network News?," *Columbia Journalism Review*, May-June 1986, pp. 50-52. Also, the January 2-9, 1987 *TV Guide* noted that ABC-Cap Cities wanted to cut by 9 percent the amount (thought to be about $125 million annually) that ABC pays to local stations for carrying network programs. Upon receiving that news, the station managers were "not a bunch of happy campers," according to Jim Coppersmith, general manager of WCVB in Boston. The move, reportedly, "could cause a potentially dramatic schism in network-affiliate relationships."
4. See Desmond Smith, "You Can Go Home Again," *Washington Journalism Review*, June 1986, pp. 44-47. The power shift to local stations was symbolized late in 1986 by the decision of journalist Steve Bell to leave the ABC network in order to anchor a local news show in Philadelphia. Morton Dean of CBS already had gone to New York, Sylvia Chase of ABC to San Francisco, and Bill Curtis of CBS to Chicago, with Curtis saying, "I don't think the future is there anymore for the networks" (Smith, p. 44).

5. Dinesh D'Souza, "Mr. Donaldson Goes to Washington," *Policy Review*, Summer 1986, pp. 24-31.
6. Desmond Smith, "Is the Sun Setting on Network Nightly News?," *Washington Journalism Review*, January 1986, pp. 30-33.
7. *Ibid.*
8. *Ibid.* See also Barbara Matusow, "Learning to Do with Less: Lean Days Ahead for Network News," July 1986, pp. 23-25, and Gary Cummings, "Luring Ad Dollars From Network TV," *Washington Journalism Review*, October 1986, pp. 12, 31.
9. Before major advertising revenue came in, large bills had to be paid for the setting up of nine domestic and twelve international news bureaus as well as for everyday production costs. Negotiations with hundreds of domestic and international stations for news coverage exchange also were necessary.
10. "CBN News Tonight" ran from January 27 to March 28, 1986. Following the demise Earl Wierich, public relations director of CBN Cable, praised the program's staff but said that "at the end of the two months, the show was only 20 percent sold out to advertisers." The ratings—350,000 households, a 1.2 Nielsen by the end of the run—were not bad. CBN News executive director Jim Whelan told the *Washington Journalism Review* that his show had needed "years, not weeks to establish itself."
11. Technological change is increasing the variety of opportunities for both young journalists and viewers. For example, satellite dishes are likely to become smaller and cheaper (probably the size of a hand and the cost of a television set by the year 2000). More journalists will get the chance to cover national news stories, if they want it.
12. Former FCC Chairman Mark Fowler argued that electronic media should now be treated like print media. Throughout the 1980s Fowler pointed out that the "scarcity argument" based on physical limits of radio and television airwaves was the original reason for government regulation, but technological advances that have added many new radio and television outlets make that position obsolete. He noted correctly that the scarcer medium is the daily newspaper, not radio or television.
13. Satellite master-antenna television systems (SMATVs) have about one million subscribers now. SMATVs are used in big apartment buildings which typically have a satellite dish on top and wiring within. Tenants generally pay monthly subscription fees. Erected on private property, they are exempt from *all* FCC rules; unless they require a wire laid across public streets, they are also generally exempt from municipal regulation. Thus, there is more opportunity for flexibility.

    MDS (multipoint distribution service) is important in some urban areas. MDS uses an over-the-air, omnidirectional microwave signal which can transmit a huge variety of programs, video games, computer programs, videotext, etc. MDS signals travel an average of twenty-five miles in every direction to special rooftop antennas which are equipped with decoders that convert microwaves into television signals. There is one large shortcoming to this cheap way of sending television programs: The microwave signal can be disturbed by buildings, trees, or hills. MDS is really usable only when there is an unbroken line of sight between sending and receiving antennas.

    Other technological developments worth considering include LPTV and two-way cable. LPTV, low-power television, uses a weak signal that can be squeezed in between existing channels without causing interference. The availability of LPTV stations may be very helpful to minority groups, including Christians. In two-way cable, a second cable wire is used to send rudimentary electronic information entered when a viewer presses a small hand-held console akin to a calculator. Two-way cable has been highly touted, with fans talking about watching city council meetings and voting on issues, or shopping at home. It has been tried in Columbus, Ohio, and some other cities, but it is more expensive than ordinary cable and has created, so far, no huge demand.

The advent of VCRs is the technological development other than cable with the greatest impact so far. Audiotape cassettes have become a major means of communication among Christians; videocassettes may follow that path. VCRs are following the classic growth curve of innovative products in the U.S., with their first eight years of sales paralleling the 1959-1966 growth of color television almost unit for unit. But color television, for the most part, merely enhanced existing programs; VCRs, by allowing for the convenient home showing of independent products, and time shifting of broadcast and cable programs, will contribute to the development of a much more decentralized television communications system.

14. The development of public access channels through community cable companies could have an impact on local television news and information. In most cable cities it is easy for any group to have its own television show at very low cost. Of course, not many people may watch, but the opportunity is there, and successful programs are likely to emerge, with a resultant increase in diversity.
15. Smith, "Is the Sun Setting. . . ," *loc. cit.*
16. Information from various trade groups, market analysts and consultants, and the U.S. Department of Commerce. *Editor & Publisher* produces the most readily accessible circulation figures.
17. Jamieson and Campbell, p. 128.
18. Three-quarters of newspaper revenue typically come from advertising. The typical newspaper advertising mix is 50 percent localized retail ads, 30 percent classified ads, 10 percent inserts, 5 percent national ads, and 5 percent miscellaneous.
19. The American Newspaper Publishers Association (ANPA) provides information about average newspaper size, and some cost data as well.
20. The unproductive means frequently used to combat economic challenge is Washington lobbying. Newspaper trade groups have tried to slow down the advent of electronic competition and have pushed frequently for an increase in third class mail rates which would make direct mail more expensive.
21. Costs based on estimates by David Outten, a CBN University Institute of Journalism graduate.
22. Magazines and radio provide other opportunities for Christian journalists. Serious books often do not sell well in the United States, but Americans are a nation of magazine readers. One study showed 143 million adults, 90 percent of the nation's adult population, reading magazines regularly. Each of those 143 million Americans read an average of almost eight magazine copies a month and spent about one hour on each copy. From 1950 to 1980 circulation of American Bureau of Circulation-audited magazines

more than doubled, to over three hundred million, while the U.S. population in that same period grew by 55 percent. There is a great but hard-to-compute amount of unaudited circulation as well. In addition, the average copy of a magazine has at least four adult readers.

Some good magazines, though, die young, often because of a failure to obtain advertising. A typical magazine receives half its revenue from circulation and half from advertising. A few magazines get all their revenue from advertising, but opinion magazines such as *The New Republic* or *National Review* depend primarily on loyal subscribers and some well-heeled financial angels.

With adequate financial backing, non-Christian opinion magazines such as *Harper's* have displayed enormous journalistic influence over the years. *Christianity Today* and several other magazines have had a very positive influence, but we desperately need the Christian equivalent of *Harper*'s or *The Public Interest.*

The situation is much better in radio. Some Christian stations have sizable news and information segments. This parallels developments in some non-Christian stations; news, information and talk shows are the biggest audience-getters in New York, Los Angeles, and Chicago. Several news services, including UPI Christian Radio, provide news and commentaries.

23. Statistics available from the National Association of Broadcasters, the Magazine Publishers Association, the American Newspaper Publishers Association, and *Editor & Publisher.*
24. Many media companies *are* huge. NBC is now part of General Electric. Capital Cities Communications, which owns ABC, and CBS are both about $5 billion companies. At annual meetings during 1986 the Times Mirror Company, owner of the Los Angeles *Times* and many other media properties, announced annual revenues of $3 billion; the Knight-Ridder Company was at $1.7 billion, the New York Times Company at $1.3 billion. But faithfulness to God and diligent use of His gifts tends to bring Christians eventual success; mountains can be thrown into seas.
25. Christians should not press government to get involved for short-term gains, even if those could be procured. A system of private ownership and control of television and radio can be exasperating at times, but it is based on Biblical principles. Furthermore, a private enterprise system always escapes from stagnation, as new challenges arise. Such challenges must receive a response, or economic decline is certain. In countries with state-controlled media, though, stagnation dominates, unless a coup comes along.

CHAPTER TEN *Coverage of Sensation and Disaster: The Gaining and Keeping of Audiences*

1. *Outlook*, March 6, 1909, p. 510. See also *The Nation*, September 26, 1901, pp. 238, 239; *Collier's*, March 4, 1911, p. 18; *The Nation*, June 8, 1927, pp. 633, 634; *Saturday Review of Literature*, November 30, 1935, p. 18; *Discover*, September 1983; reprinted in Hiebert and Reuss, pp. 181, 182.
2. The gross kind of sensationalism Roosevelt despised was, during his lifetime, largely a Northern, big-city phenomenon. Turn-of-the-century

Southern newspaper editors also tended to criticize the way some of their Northern brethren were "raking the sewers of society high and low for material to fill their columns." One editor argued that New York newspapers were showing evil not to oppose it but to attract more to it: "The great Newspapers vie in an effort to present, in the most lurid style, every disgusting detail of evil-doing [and] to parade, with monster, glittering illustrations and with vivid narration every abnormal phase of life." A Houston editor hoped that the twentieth century would be saved from journalism that "is conscienceless, sensational, and disreputable, and to which nothing is sacred." (See papers by O. F. Dornblaser, in *Proceedings of the Texas Press Association*, 1893, p. 30; T. H. Napier, in TPA *Proceedings*, 1898, p. 35; W. A. Johnson, in *ibid.*, p. 25; E. W. Harris, in TPA *Proceedings*, 1899, pp. 19, 20; and M. E. Foster, in TPA *Proceedings*, 1901, p. 52.) Available at Barker Texas History Center, University of Texas at Austin.

3. Ephesians 5:11-13 are key verses on the question of how far to go in coverage of evil. "Have nothing to do with the fruitless deeds of darkness, but rather expose them," Paul wrote. "For it is shameful even to mention what the disobedient do in secret. But everything exposed by the light becomes visible." To some, the expression "shameful even to mention" has meant, "do not write about or talk about evil." That exegesis is hard to justify, though, in the context of the preceding and succeeding verses, and also in the light of Paul's own practice in other epistles (Romans 1:24-32; 1 Corinthians 6:9, 10; Galatians 5:19-21; 1 Timothy 1:9, 10).

   John Eadie, *Commentary on the Epistle to the Ephesians* (Edinburg: T. T. Clark, 1883; Zondervan reprint, 1955), p. 383, notes that scholars who have examined the original Greek have suggested several better translations: "Rebuke these sins, even though you should blush to mention them"; "It is a shame even to speak of their sins, yet that should not keep us from exposing and rebuking them"; "Rebuke these sins openly, for it is a shame to make mention of them in any other way than of reproof." Eadie recommends, "By all means reprove them, and there is the more need of it, for it is a shame even to speak of their secret sins."

4. Adultery and its aftermath were depicted in a *Courant* article the following month (April 29, p. 2): "On Sunday last the remains of the once prosperous, gay, beautiful, and almost incredibly engaging Miss TERESIA CONSTANTIA PHILLIPS, were interred in the Churchyard in this town." The *Courant* noted "that a catastrophe so striking and melancholy may prove an advantageous lesson to many of the surviving fair; and convince them, however flattering appearances may be, on their first deviation from the paths of rectitude and honour, that no admiration will be lasting, no happiness serene, which is not founded on the basis of rectitude."

   That article could be compared with an August 2, 1986, article from the Austin *American Statesman*. The front-page story contained a sympathetic interview with Priscilla Davis, whose lover and daughter had been shot by a masked intruder. An attorney probing the relationship of her adultery and the murder told her, "Priscilla, if you've done anything just pony up to it." Her response was, "Pony up to what? I mean if I had crawled in the sack with 50,000 people what did that have to do with" the case?

5. Boston *Recorder*, March 29, 1822, p. 1.

6. *Ibid.*
7. *Ibid.*
8. *Ibid.*
9. *Ibid.*
10. Dallas *Morning News*, January 1, 1890, p. 1.
11. Longview *Democrat*, March 6, 1885, p. 1. Headlines often noted that the adulteress had received her comeuppance also, as in this story of a wife who shot her husband's mistress: "Between the Eyes/Was the Place Ida Brown Got It and What She Got It For—The Penalty of Fooling with Another Woman's Husband. . . a tragedy that was the tragic outgrowth of marriage infidelity in high life" (Houston *Daily Post*, March 2, 1884, p. 3).
12. "Doran Done For," Houston *Daily Post*, August 21, 1880, p. 1.
13. Dallas *Morning News*, March 11, 1888, p. 6; Dallas *Daily Times Herald*, January 31, 1891, p. 2. Biblically, murderous thoughts are akin to murder itself; a *Daily Times Herald* reporter on January 31, 1891, showed the close connection of the two in his story of "The Deadly Fence": "John Black and James Goss, two highly respectable farmers . . . became involved in a quarrel today regarding a fence that stood on the dividing line between their farms. Black drew a revolver and began firing at his friend and neighbor. He shot three times, striking Goss in the abdomen. Goss cannot recover. Black escaped. Both are men of family."
14. Dallas *Morning News*, October 2, 1885, p. 3.
15. Dallas *Daily Times Herald*, January 28, 1891, p. 2.
16. E. W. Harris, in TPA *Proceedings*, 1889, p. 40; S. J. Thomas, in TPA *Procedings*, 1904, p. 34.
17. New York *Tribune*, February 17, 1877, p. 4.
18. *Ibid.*, p. 6.
19. Washington *Post*, November 12, 1894, p. 1.
20. New York *Tribune*, April 2, 1885, p. 1; September 22, 1894, p. 1.
21. Los Angeles *Times*, January 6, 1885, p. 1.
22. Chicago *Tribune*, November 3, 1888, p. 1.
23. New York *Times*, September 18, 1890, p. 5. See also New York *Journal*, January 1, 1896, and October 16, 1895.
24. New York *Tribune*, February 28, 1877, p. 8.
25. Dallas *Herald*, December 24, 1885, p. 4. See also Los Angeles *Times*, January 6, 1885, p. 1.
26. New York *Tribune*, January 15, 1895, p. 1.
27. New York *Times*, October 6, 1887, p. 1.
28. *Ibid.*, October 7, 1887, p. 9. Overall, it appears that suicide coverage indicated and strengthened the accepted values of the period. As Professor John Stevens observed, readers of sensational news are "participating, at least vicariously, in the redefinition of their own values." Sociologist Kai Erikson noted that "An enormous amount of modern 'news' is devoted to reports about deviant behavior and its punishment." News accounts, Erikson suggested, "constitute our main source of information about the normative contours of society" (*Journalism Quarterly*, Spring 1985, p. 53).

    There are greater concerns now about invasion of privacy than there were then. Compassion for the family is more evident now. Clearly, though, attitudes toward suicide itself have changed. Some questions need to be asked: Might the tendency in contemporary jounalism to cover suicides sympathetically be a factor in subsequent suicides? Might critically sensational coverage lead potentially suicidal individuals to think twice? Dostoyevski suggested that people who might otherwise commit suicide do not kill themselves because they fear physical pain and spiritual judgment; if he was right, newspaper's unwillingness to report pain and discuss the religious questions involved in suicide might actually increase the incidence of suicide. Christians are to act with compassion, but might compassion for those contemplating suicide require some harshness in coverage of those who have?

29. Jacob Riis, *The Making of an American* (New York: Macmillan, 1901), shows Riis' idealism about the power of journalism.
30. *Free Enquirer*, August 4, 1832, p. 1.
31. These are from the New York *Evening Graphic*, a newspaper that worshiped man and vigorously practiced non-Biblical sensationalism. The *Graphic* was founded by Bernard Macfadden with profits from his *True Story* and *Physical Culture* magazines. It editorialized for eugenics and offered rewards for "physically perfect" men and women to marry and produce offspring ($100 per baby). It crusaded against the wearing of hats by men.

    The *Graphic* was journalistically innovative, in its way. Crime reporter Jack Grey had done time for safe-cracking; he brought real expertise to the job. One *Graphic* gimmick, inspired by Macfadden's *True Story* magazine, was the use of first-person headlines; for instance, the story of a man who had killed his wife had the headline, "I Murdered My Wife Because She Cooked Fishballs for Dinner. I Told Her I Would Never Eat Them Again but She Defied Me to the End" (Emile Gauvreau, *My Last Million Readers* [New York: Arno, 1974]).
32. *The Nation*, July 30, 1908.
33. Biblically, the general penalties for disobeying God's rules are clear. In Jeremiah 16, after God commands a proclamation of bad news, Jeremiah is told that the Israelites will ask him, "Why has the Lord decreed such a great disaster against us? What wrong have we done?" Jeremiah is told to say, "Each of you is following the stubbornness of his evil heart instead of obeying [God]."
34. Lincoln Steffens, *Autobiography*, *op. cit.*, pp. 571-574.
35. Augustine, "Against Lying," quoted in *Treatises on Various Subjects*, Vol. 16, Chap. 2, ed. R. J. Deferrari, Fathers of the Church series (New York: Catholic University of American Press, 1952), quoted in Sissela Bok, *Lying* (New York: Random House, 1978).
36. Boston *Recorder*, *loc. cit.*
37. Luther, in his *Table Talk*, also noted, "No man ought to lay a cross upon himself . . . but if a cross or tribulation come upon him, then let him suffer it patiently, or know that it is good and profitable for him."
38. Circulation opportunities for newspapers practicing Christian sensationalism are tied to the economic questions discussed in the previous chapter. With newspapers selling about seventy-five copies per one hundred households now, compared to 124 copies for one hundred households in 1950, many people are not reading. Part of the decline may be due to television, but some nonsubscribers might be looking for a different kind of newspaper.

CHAPTER ELEVEN *Crusading on Social Issues: Personalization and Persistence*

1. Edwin and Michael Emery, *The Press and America*, 5th edition (Englewood Cliffs, NJ: Prentice-Hall, 1984), p. 311.
2. *Ibid.*, pp. 313, 316-318, 322.
3. The "Christian" justification for the original Crusades, of course, is somewhat dubious.
4. Jonathan Edwards' most famous sermon is included in Perry Miller, ed., *The Puritans* (New York: Harper and Row, 1963).
5. Readable histories of dueling in America include William Oliver Stevens, *Pistols at Ten Paces* (Boston: Houghton Mifflin, 1940) and Harnett Thomas Kane, *Gentlemen, Swords and Pistols* (New York: Morrow, 1951).
6. *Recorder* recommendations anticipated what Alexis de Tocqueville was to note in 1835: "Americans of all ages, all conditions, and all dispositions constantly form associations. . . . If it is proposed to inculcate some truth or to foster some feeling by the encouragement of a great example, they form a society . . . what political power could ever [do what Americans voluntarily] perform every day with the assistance of the principle of association?" (*Democracy in America*, Vol. 2, Book 2, Chap. 5, p. 116 in Vintage edition, New York, 1945).
7. Boston *Recorder*, June 22, 1822, p. 100: "The young man succeeded in concealing his intentions from his relatives until it was too late to interpose a check to the fatal meeting. He had a mother. She doted on him. From this mother he was most anxious to conceal his designs. She heard what her son was going to do, but not till it was too late. . . she saw her boy, only nineteen years of age, brought home, pale, bleeding, and just sinking in the cold embrace of death! It was too much for her. The dreadful shock hurled her reason from its throne, and she went mournfully about, pensively asking, 'where's my son—where's my son?' "
8. *Ibid.*, April 22, 1823, p. 57.
9. *Ibid.*, March 31, 1826, p. 52.
10. *Ibid.*, April 22, 1820, p. 57.
11. Some Southern editors who did not join the anti-dueling crusade were digging their own pits and eventually falling in; editors in Richmond, Vicksburg, and other cities died in duels with offended readers.
12. Such an advertising strategy would not have been possible shortly before. Advertising until the 1830s often was a moral as well as an economic exchange: Christian-based newspapers did not allow ads editors considered "objectionable." The New York *Journal of Commerce*, the *New England Palladium* of Boston, and many other newspapers would not accept advertisement of theaters, lotteries, or "business to be transacted on the Sabbath," let alone abortion.

    That sense of editorial responsibility changed as Christian newspapers declined in importance. Concerning the question of which advertisements to print, the Boston *Daily Times* comment in 1837 that it would not evaluate ads was typical of the new media: "It is sufficient for our purpose that the advertisements are paid for. . . . One man has as good a right as another to have his wares, his goods, his panaceas, his profession, published to the world in a newspaper, provided he pays for it."
13. The anti-abortion laws were rarely enforced for two reasons. First, there were no pregnancy tests; until "quickening" (generally the fifth month of

pregnancy, when fetal movement becomes evident) there was no invariably-accepted proof that a woman was pregnant.

Consequently, abortion before quickening was often termed merely "an attempt to remove female blockages," and prosecution was impossible. Nor was after-quickening prosecution likely either, since witnesses would be very hard to come by. (If the abortion was successful and the woman survived she would be unlikely to testify; if she died, pathologists at that time could not know for sure that an abortion had taken place.)

There also was some public unwillingness to attempt the enforcement of abortion statutes because there was widespread questioning of the pre-quickened infant's humanity, despite Biblical testimony. A common understanding from the 1830s through even the 1870s is indicated by a statement given to the Michigan State Board of Health: "There is very generally current among the people the notion that before . . . the fourth month of pregnancy, there is no real life in the fetus, or at least that it is not a 'living soul,' and to destroy it is no real crime" (James Mohr, *Abortion in America* [New York: Oxford University Press, 1978], p. 73).

14. New York *Sun*, March 3, 1846, p. 1.
15. *Ibid.*, December 11, 1839, p. 1. Also see New York *Herald*, March 6, 1840, p. 1; August 26, 1841, p. 3; September 22, 1843, p. 4; December 13, 1843, p. 4; January 25, 1844, p. 4; April 13, 1844, p. 4; August 2, 1844, p. 4; October 8, 1844, p. 4; November 21, 1844, p. 4; January 11, 1845, p. 4.
16. New York *Herald*, March 6, 1840, p. 4; January 15, 1845, p. 4.
17. *Ibid.*, October 25, 1841, p. 3; April 15, 1842, p. 4; December 13, 1843, p. 4; July 23, 1844, p. 4; January 29, 1845, p. 4.
18. *National Police Gazette*, November 15, 1845, p. 100.
19. *Ibid.* See also Gunning Bedford, "Madame Restell and Some of Her Dupes," *New York Medical and Surgical Reporter*, February 21, 1846, pp. 158-165.
20. Dan Schiller, *Objectivity and the News* (Philadelphia: University of Pennsylvania Press, 1981), has two chapters on the *Gazette*, but does not mention the anti-abortion crusade.
21. *National Police Gazette*, November 15, 1845, p. 100.
22. *Ibid.*, February 14, 1846, p. 205.
23. *Ibid.*, February 21, 1846, p. 218.
24. *Ibid.* The *Gazette* hit hard at the enormity of Madame Restell's crime: "We are not now demanding justice upon the perpetratess of a single crime, but upon one who might be drowned in the blood of her victims, did each but yield a drop, whose epitaph should be a curse, and whose tomb a pyramid of skulls. . . . We call again for action from the authorities in relation to this woman. She has been for nearly ten years involved in law, and her money has saved her, as yet, from the direct penalty of a single dereliction."
25. New York *Herald*, February 24, 1846, p. 1; New York *Tribune*, February 24, 1846, p. 2; New York *Morning News*, February 23, p. 1. Madame Restell, it seemed, had been warned and had gone to a friend's house. The crowd eventually dispersed. The *Morning News* concluded, "We trust that from the experience of yesterday, Madame Restell is now convinced of the necessity of immediately closing her unlawful business. . . ." So was the New York state legislature, which passed a new law making abortion of a quick child a felony except when the abortion was necessary to preserve

the mother's life. At this point the *Gazette* began a strong campaign for enforcement, complaining on April 25, 1846, of police "neglect of duty before the face of Heaven," and emphasizing once again that abortion is "murder . . . strangling the unborn."

26. Alan Keller, *Scandalous Lady* (New York: Atheneum, 1981), p. 38.
27. *Ibid.*, p. 68; New York *Tribune*, April 2, 1978, p. 1.
28. Quoted in Keller, p. 71.
29. New York *Times*, February 12, 1878, p. 8; Keller, *loc. cit.*
30. Mohr, pp. 86-118. No one knows for sure how many abortions were performed in the United States during the 1850s and 1860s. Statistics were not kept, but both pro- and anti-abortion physicians estimated or guessed that 20 percent of all pregnancies were ending in planned abortion. The New York *Times* noted that abortion during the 1860s was "very common." One doctor complained that both unmarried and married women frequently were having abortions because of unwillingness to undergo "the care, the expense, or the trouble of children, or some other motive equally trifling and degrading. . . ."

    Most ministers at that time did little to oppose the pro-abortion bandwagon. Missouri anti-abortion doctors in 1868 noted that "our clergy, with some very few exceptions, have thus far hesitated to enter an open crusade against . . . criminal abortions." An Illinois anti-abortion doctor contended that ministers "have been very derelict in handling this subject too delicately, and speaking of it too seldom."

    Some ministers were personally opposed to abortion but thought it impolitic to say so. One minister said that sermons on abortion would "turn the pulpit and church into a place that many people would not like to visit." A reporter noted that congregations were hearing "rose water balderdash, politico-religious harangues and cream-cheese platitudes ad nauseum" from ministers who were silent on abortion "lest the namby-pamby sensibilities of fashionable fops should be hurt."

    Those who believed abortion to be murder wanted to cut through that indifference. The ministers, for the most part, were not going to lead the way. Neither were the politicians. The American Medical Association was anti-abortion at that time, and doctors such as Gunning Bedford and Hugh Hodge had great persistence. (See Hodge, *Foeticide* [Philadelphia: University of Pennsylvania, 1869.]) For the most part, though, it was the newspapers during the late 1860s that began to, in the words of an Indiana minister, "sound the cry of MURDER!"
31. New York *Tribune*, August 30, 1871, p. 4.
32. *Ibid.*
33. Keller, p. 120. A description of the mansion's interior written by James McCabe in 1872 indicates the way Madame Restell lived: "On the first floor are the grand hall of tessellated marble, lined with mirrors; the three immense dining-rooms, furnished in bronze and gold, with yellow satin hangings, an enormous French mirror in mosaic gilding at every panel . . . more parlors and reception-rooms; butler's pantry, lined with solid silver services; dining room with all imported furniture. Other parlors on the floor above; a guest-chamber in blue brocade satin, with gold- and ebony-bedstead elegantly covered . . . [many bedrooms and lounges] . . . Fourth floor—servant's rooms in mahogany and Brussels carpet, and circular picture gallery; the fifth floor contains a magnificent billiards room, danc-

ing-hall, with pictures, piano, etc. . . . The whole house is filled with statuettes, paintings, rare bronzes, ornamental and valuable clocks, candelabras, silver globes and articles of many origins and rare worth."

34. New York *Times*, January 26, 1871, p. 3.
35. *Ibid.*, February 12, 1878, p. 8.
36. *Ibid.*, February 14, 1878, p. 8.
37. *Ibid.*, February 14, 1878, p. 4; February 24, p. 5; March 2, p. 1; April 2, p. 1.
38. *Ibid.*, April 2, 1878, p. 1. This denouement was announced at the top of page 1 by newspapers such as the *Times*: "End of a Criminal Life. Mme Restell Commits Suicide." The *Times* reported rumors that "Mme. Restell was murdered through the instigation of wealthy people who had patronized her in her criminal business, in order to prevent disclosures which they deemed inevitable at her trial." But this was never proven, and was termed "improbable" by reporters (*Times,* April 3, 1878, p. 1).
39. Nathanson, responsible by his own admission for thousands of abortions, became convinced of the humanity of unborn children and went on to make *The Silent Scream*.
40. New York *Times*, March 17, 1875, p. 7; March 19, p. 6; March 20, p. 12. Newspapers continued to report gruesome developments in the 1880s. The New York *Times* reported from Philadelphia that policemen, on a tip, dug in one downtown cellar and found "the bodies of 21 infants who had been killed before birth." The abortionist was sentenced to seven years hard labor after a trial in which jurors were shown a cigar box containing the bones of the murder victims: "Whenever the box was moved, they rattled like hard withered leaves. There were many bits of skulls among them, some almost complete." In Indianapolis, one story told of an abortion attempt in which a baby was expelled from the womb still alive. By the time a reporter arrived, he was able to witness only "the remains of a newly-born infant of the male gender, the umbilical cord showing the child to have been forcibly torn from its mother while yet alive, while upon its skull is the mark of a cruel blow, as if the helpless one had been swung by its heels against an unyielding surface, and its skull crushed until life was extinct."
41. New York *Times*, July 23, 1890, p. 8.
42. *Ibid.*, July 24, 1890, p. 2. McGonegal was sentenced to fourteen years. See also stories on July 25, p. 8; July 26, p. 2; July 27, p. 13; July 28, p. 8; July 29, p. 8; July 30, p. 8; July 31, p. 8; September 19, p. 8; September 23, p. 8; September 24, p. 9; September 25, p. 3; September 26, p. 2; September 27, p. 8; October 1, p. 8; October 2, p. 9; October 3, p. 3; October 4, p. 1; October 16, p. 9.
43. *Time*, March 16, 1936, pp. 52-54.
44. *Ibid.*, March 6, 1944, p. 60. My thanks to Rick Rutledge, a student at The University of Texas, for uncovering the *Time* stories.
45. For more details on the pro-abortion movement of the 1950s and early 1960s, see an article written by my wife and myself, "The Selling of Abortion," in *Eternity*, January 1986, pp. 20-24.
46. *Ibid.*
47. *National Right to Life News* is a biweekly published by the National Right to Life Committee and edited by Dave Andrusko (419 7th St. N.W., Suite 402, Washington, DC 20004).

48. *NRL News*, December 18, 1986, p. 9.
49. *Ibid.*, p. 4. Fetal surgery outside the mother's womb raises one more set of provocative questions for pro-abortionists: Does it make sense that a baby, once outside, could be put back inside and then legally aborted? Can an unborn baby still be referred to by the dehumanizing name "fetus" when he has had his own doctor, his own medical records, even his own medical bills?
50. *Ibid.*, pp. 2, 9.
51. *Ibid.*, p. 1.
52. *Ibid.*, p. 11. "It is something that is not natural," *NRL News* reported the other abortionist as testifying. "You have to convince yourself intellectually that what you are doing is necessary because some patients need it."

CHAPTER TWELVE *A Christian Journalism Revival?*

1. *A Manifesto for the Christian Church: Declaration and Covenant, July 4, 1986* (Mountain View, CA: Coalition on Revival, 1986).
2. *Twin Cities Christian*, July 3, 1986, p. 1. *TCC* is a biweekly edited by Doug Trouten (1619 Portland Avenue, Minneapolis, MN 55404). *World*, edited by Joel Belz, has this mailing address: Box 2330, Asheville, NC 28802.
3. *Ibid.*, February 15, 1983, p. 1.
4. *Ibid.*, April 12, 1984, p. 1.
5. *Ibid.*, April 24, 1986, p. 3.
6. *Twin Cities Christian* also has reported the more severe intrusions on religious liberty that prevail in other countries. One front-page story, "Christian Woman Interrogated by KGB at Moscow Airport," told of a woman who "will never forget Mother's Day 1985. On that day she was arrested at Moscow airport, interrogated for more than six hours, strip-searched and later expelled from the Soviet Union. Her crime? Wanting to give gifts to Russian Christians—Bibles, copies of the Sermon on the Mount, Christian music tapes, and clothing" (July 4, 1985, p. 1).
7. *Ibid.*, May 8, 1986, p. 1; August 29, 1985, p. 18
8. *Ibid.*, May 9, 1985, p. 18.
9. *Ibid.*
10. See Clay's autobiography, *The Life of Cassius Marcellus Clay* (Cincinnati: J. Fletcher Brennan and Co., 1886), and an essay he wrote in 1845: *Appeal of Cassius M. Clay to Kentucky and the World* (Boston: Macomber and Pratt, 1845). My thanks to the University of Kentucky library for allowing me access to several rare biographies.

APPENDIX *Public Relations, Theology and Practice*

1. Bureau of Labor Statistics figures quoted in Fraser P. Seitel, *The Practice of Public Relations*, 2nd edition (Columbus, OH: Charles Merrill, 1984), p. 65.
2. Bernays, "Manipulating Public Opinion: The Why and the How," *American Journal of Sociology*, May 1928, pp. 958-971; John T. Flynn, "Edward L. Bernays: The Science of Ballyhoo," *Atlantic Monthly*, May 1931, pp. 562-571.
3. Interview with Bernays, conducted at 7 Lowell Street, Cambridge, MA, August 10, 1984.

4. Edward Bernays, *Propaganda* (New York: Liveright, 1928), p. 28.
5. Interview.
6. Bernays, *Propaganda*, pp. 9, 10.
7. *Ibid.*, p. 28.
8. *Ibid.*, p. 37.
9. *Ibid.*, p. 25. Also see Bernays, "Molding Public Opinion," *The Annals of the American Academy of Political and Social Science*, May 1935, pp. 82-87.
10. *Ibid.*, p. 9.
11. *Ibid.*, p. 37.
12. For more information, see my book *Corporate Public Relations: A New Historical Perspective* (Hillsdale, NJ: Lawrence Erlbaum, 1987).
13. Matthew Henry, *A Commentary on the Whole Bible*, Vol. 5 (Old Tappan, NJ: Fleming H. Revell, n.d., orig. pub. in early 1700s), pp. 416, 417.
14. Some current public relations managers distinguish between "fact accuracy" and "impression accuracy," occasionally upholding the former as the cleverest way of sowing misimpressions, but the Bible makes no distinction between the two. "Do not lie," we are told in the Book of Leviticus, and immediately after that, "Do not deceive one another." Psalms condemns men who "take delight in lies, [for] with their mouths they bless, but in their hearts they curse," while Proverbs notes that things "detestable" to God include "haughty eyes, a lying tongue . . . a heart that devises wicked schemes" (Leviticus 19:11; Psalm 62:4; Proverbs 6:17, 18).
15. Code printed in Harold Nelson and Dwight Teeter, *Law of Mass Communications*, 5th edition (New York: The Foundation Press, 1986), pp. 756-758.
16. *Ibid.*, pp. 758-760.

SCRIPTURE INDEX

Genesis

3:17-19 177
4:23, 24 146
11:1-9 187
14:21 187
15:1 188
19 146

Exodus

15:1-21 31
20:16 220
21:22, 23 167
22:1-7 98
30:15 98

Leviticus

5:1 83
5:4 83
6:2-5 98
19:11 237

Numbers

5:5-7 99
13:31-33 143

Deuteronomy

19:15 81
21:19 81
22:15 81
22:13-19 98
25:7-9 81
28 146
29 180

Joshua

24:15-17 180

Judges

3:21, 22 146
4:22 146
5:26 146
8 31
9:5 146
19:25-30 146

Ruth

4:1, 11 81

1 Samuel

18 187

2 Kings

6:28, 29 146
9:33, 35 169
18 70

Ezra

4:5 187

Nehemiah

10:32 98

Esther

7:10 189

Psalms

7:15 149
9:15 149
15:4 83
19 35
62:4 237
78 180

Proverbs

6:17, 18 237
6:28 149
7:23 149
10:10, 19 80
11:12 80
13:3 80
16:28 80
17:27 80
18:6, 8 80
21:16 149
26:27 149

Isaiah

36 70
40:23 133

Jeremiah

7:3, 9 222
14:15 222
16:10-13 231
19:3 147
23:16 222
38:4-13 222

Ezekiel

3:13, 33 222
23:20, 21 147

Amos

7:7, 8 69

Matthew

5:37 83
6:11 179
7:1, 2 100
10:34 172
15:19 84
18 85
27 188

Mark

15:10, 15 188
15:34 188

Luke

6:41 39
13:2-7 39

Acts

7:2-53 180
17:23 177

Romans

1:18-32 40
1:20 35
1:27 147
3:23 169
8:6, 7 84
8:20-22 177

1 Corinthians

6:9, 10 229
7 203
8:2 85
10:5 177

Galatians

5:19-21 229

Ephesians

2:1, 4, 5 85
4:18 84
5:11-13 229

Colossians

1:17 180

1 Timothy

1:9, 10 229

James

5:12 83

1 John

1:8, 10 85

Revelation

19:21 172

(Scripture index prepared by Peter Olasky)

INDEX

Abbot, Lyman, 24
ABC, 42, 68, 87, 133, 135, 137
Abortion, coverage of, 20-22, 37-38, 68, 95, 116, 122, 128-129, 159-170, 176
Absence of malice, 93
Absolute privilege, 95
Adams, John, 113
Adams, Abigail, 113
Adversary journalism, 114
Advertising, 134, 138-141, 232
Ahab, 146, 169
AIDS, coverage of, 39-40, 210
Aleppo earthquake, 147, 148, 155
Altheide, David, 128
American Civil Liberties Union, 26
American Revolution, 113
American Society of Newspaper Editors, 79
Anderson v. Liberty Lobby, 94, 104
Andrews, "Shang," 48
Andrusko, David, 235
Angels in Stalin's Paradise, 57
AP (Associated Press), 59, 62, 134
Atheism, 29, 49
Augustine, 155
Austin *American-Statesman*, xiii

Baby Mitchell, 167
Bache, Benjamin Franklin, 113
Bakker, Jim, xii, xiii,
Balancing of subjectivities, 64
Baltimore *Chronicle*, 19
Barker, Benjamin, 147
Bastwick, John, 106
Batten, James K., 116
Bazell, Robert, 59
Bellah, Robert, 39
Belov, Fedor, 56
Belz, Joel, 235
Bernays, Edward, 183-189
Bieber, Owen, 121, 122
Billington, James, 112
Blackstone, Lord, 107
Bonneville, Nicholas, 112
Bonnie and Clyde, 151
Boston *Evening Post*, 107
Boston *Globe*, 78, 124
Boston *Recorder*, 17-19, 23, 60, 61, 69, 114, 147-148, 151, 155-159
Bovard, Oliver, 214
Bradford, William, 107, 110
Bradlee, Ben, 67
Branzburg v. Hayes, 219
Brennan, Justice William, 78, 79, 90, 98, 100, 104
Brisbane, Albert, 212
Brisbane, Arthur, 224
Brokaw, Tom, 43, 115
Brooklyn *Eagle*, 27
Bryan, William Jennings, 26, 28
Burger, Chief Justice Warren, 78, 79, 94
Burke, Edmund, 52
Burlington County (N.J.) *Times*, 77
Burton, Henry, 106

C-Span, 136
Cable News Network (CNN), 136, 137
Cable television, impact of, 134-137, 144
Calvin, John, 25, 106
Carey, Robert, 32, 33
Castro, Fidel, 55
Cater, Douglas, 65
CBS, 87, 94, 95, 124, 133, 134, 166
Censorship, 88
Central Christian Herald, 23
Chambers, Esther, 127
Chambers, Whittaker, 35-36, 126-128, 209, 224
Channing, William Ellery, 211
Chicago *Times*, 47-48
Chicago *Tribune*, 88, 126-129, 150
Christian Advocate, 17
Christian Broadcasting Network (CBN), 136, 137, 226
Christian newspapers, nineteenth-century, 19-25
Christian objectivity, 69, 70

Christian Union, 24
Christianity Today, 171
Citizen Kane, 54
Civil War, 24
Clapper, Raymond, 29-30
Clay, Cassius, 175
Coalition on Revival (COR), 171
Cocoa Today, 77
Codes of ethics, journalistic, 59, 80, 82
Common law, 90
Common Sense, 113
Communes, 46
Communism, 36, 55, 128
Communist Party, 35, 36, 65, 126
Commonwealth v. Clap, 110, 111
Compassion and ethics, 81, 85
Competition, 133-144
Computers, 140-141
Confidentiality, 83
Connecticut *Courant,* 147
Conus, 134, 135
Cooke, Janet, 75, 217
Corry, John, 41
Coughlin v. Westinghouse Broadcasting, 103
Creation, 27, 29, 41
Cronkite, Walter, 69
Crowl, James, 57
Crusade, definition of, 157
Crusading, journalistic, xiv, 45, 49, 157-170

Dallas *Herald,* 150
Dallas *Morning News,* 93
Damron, Leonard, 90, 98
Darrow, Clarence, 26, 29
Darwin, Charles, 24, 27
Davies, Marion, 54
Davis, Priscilla, 229
Decatur, Stephen, 19, 159
Defamatory falsehood see *Libel*
Depression, the, 56
Detroit *Free Press,* 120-125
Detroit *News,* 51, 120-125
De Young, Karen, 42, 115
Diabolis, definition, 96
Donaldson, Sam, 135
Dreiser, Theodore, 62
Dueling, 31, 158-159
Dumont, Etienne, 113
Duranty, Walter, 55-57, 213-214
Durham *Morning Herald,* 80

Eastern Argus, 18
Eastman, Max, 55
Editor and Publisher, 79
Edwards, Jonathan, 158
Ehud, 146
Elijah, 169
Ellerbee, Linda, 59
Elmer Gantry, xiii
Emerson, Ralph Waldo, 24
Epstein, Edward Jay, 65
Ethics, journalistic, 75, 79, 84, 86, 100
Ethiopia, 56
Evangelical Beacon, 32
Evangelism, 25
Evolution, 26-30, 41
Exposé, journalistic, 20, 21, 164

Fact, definition of, 60-63
Fairness, 88
False light, 93
False witness, 97
Falwell, Jerry, 87
Federal Communications Commission, 137-144
Fetus, significance of word, 129
Finkbine, Sherri, 37, 38, 128-129, 160, 167
Finney, Charles, 24
"Firing Line," 57
First Amendment, 78, 82, 90, 110
Fleet, Thomas, 107
Foreign correspondents, 55
Fowler, Mark, 226
Fox's Libel Act, 110
Frankel, Max, 115
Franklin, Benjamin, 113
Franklin, Marc, 93
Freeze frames, 124
French Revolution, 112, 114
Freud, Sigmund, 184
Freudianism, 24, 63
Fuller, Margaret, 46
Fundamentalists, depiction of, 17, 26, 27, 29, 41

Gallagher, Wes, 59
Gannett newspapers, 142
Garrett, Wyman, 168
Gatekeepers, 125
Goodwin, Gene, 81
Grayson, William, 46
Greeley, Arthur (Pickie), 46-47
Greeley, Horace, 45-47, 57, 164
Greeley, Mary, 46
Greider, William, 115
Grenada, 115
Gruson, Sydney, 59
Gulag, 56
Guttmacher, Alan, 166

Halberstam, David, 65, 114
Hamilton, Andrew, 105, 107
Hampton, John, 107
Hananiah, 96
Hand, Brevard, xiii
Hand, Judge Learned, 186
Harris, E. E., 149
Hart, Gary, xii
Harvard, 20, 24, 81
Headlines, 120-122
Hearst, William Randolph, 52, 53, 54, 142, 213
Heiskell, Andrew, 42
Henry VIII, 106
Henry, Matthew, 171, 187
Hepp v. Philadelphia Newspapers, 103
Herbert v. Lando, 94
Hersey, John, 75, 76
Hiss, Alger, 35, 36, 127, 128
Hitler, Adolf, 66
Holt, British Chief Justice, 105
Homosexual parades, coverage of, 40, 210
Hook, Sidney, 55
Houston *Post,* 43
How to Lie With Statistics, 124
Howe, E. W., 49, 212
Hughes, Charles Evan, 51
Humanism, xi
Hustler, 87
Hutchinson, Chief Justice, 110

Identification of sources, 95
Independent stations, 134
Interpretive reporting, 65
Invasion of privacy, 77
Investigative Reporters and Editors (IRE), 114
Investigative reporting, 103
Irvine, Reed, 208

Jael, 146
Jezebel, 169
"Jimmy's World," 75-76
Johnson, Nunnally, 27
Joram, 146
Journalism Quarterly, 89
Journalistic ethics, books about, 216
Junius Trials, 108
Jurors, 105-109, 111-112

Kant, Immanuel, 23
KCRA, 135
Kennedy, James, 171
Knight-Ridder newspapers, 116
Knox, John, 106
Kravchenko, Victor, 56
Ku Klux Klan, 56

LaHaye, Tim, 171
Lamech, 146
Lawrence, Alonzo, 91
Lawyer's fees, 87, 93, 94, 95, 100
Le Tribun du Peuple, 112
Lee, Chief Justice, 108
Lee, Ivy, 63
Leighton, Alexander, 106
Lenin, Vladimir, 52, 112
Levine, Irving R., 59
Lewis, Anthony, 92
Lex Rex, 115
Libel, 67, 87-117
Libel and gossip, 97
Libel as theft, 97
Libel Defense Resource Center, 8
Libel insurance, 88, 89, 101
Lichter, Linda, 116
Lichter, Robert, 116
Lindsell, Harold, 171
Lippmann, Walter, 63
Local news, 133-144
Los Angeles *Times,* 37, 89, 129, 150
Louis XIV, 107
Louisville *Courier-Journal,* 69
Luce, Henry, 63, 224

McCarthy, Joseph, 35, 65
Macfadden, Bernarr, 231
Machen, Gresham, 84
Makemie, Francis, 107
Malice, 90, 92, 94, 98, 100
Mann, Horace, 24
Mansfield, Lord Chief Justice, 108
Mao, 55
Marcos, Ferdinand, 31, 33
Markel, Lester, 33, 34
Marsden, George, 206
Marx, Karl, 112
Marxism, 24, 36, 55
Materialism, 23, 25, 34, 55, 62, 63, 64, 176
Maule, William, 107
Maynard, Robert, 81
MDS, 137
Meiklejohn, Alexander, 92
Mencken, H. L., 27, 207
Miami *Herald,* xii
Milton, John, 106
Monkey trial see *Scopes Trial*
Moody, Dwight, 24
Morse, Sidney, 18
Mother Jones, 115

Mott, Frank Luther, 203
Muckraking, 54
Muggeridge, Malcolm, 57

National Police Gazette, 161-165
National Right to Life News, 167-168
NBC, 43, 59, 133, 134
Network news, 133-137
New Deal, 54
New England Journal of Medicine, 161
New Jersey Supreme Court, 92
"New journalism," 59, 66, 76
New York *Daily News,* 76
New York *Herald,* 164
New York *Journal,* 38, 53, 54, 128
New York *Sun,* 160
New York *Times,* 20-22, 26-27, 32-34, 37-38, 41, 59, 65-66, 76, 115, 128-130, 150, 152, 160-173, 206, 207
New York Times v. Sullivan, 89-95, 103, 104
New York *Tribune,* 24, 45-46, 150, 164
New York *World,* 157
News analysis, 65, 67
News council, 88
News perspective, 128
Newsletters, 144
Newspaper chain, 51, 54
Newsweek, 40, 123, 124, 166
Newton, John, 35
"Nightline," 136
Nihilism, 64
Nixon, Richard, 38-39
North, Gary, 205
Northern Virginia Sun, 80
Northwestern Christian Advocate, 19

Oakland *Tribune,* 81, 114
Objectivity, xiv, 59-71, 75, 76, 179
Ogordinokov, Alexandr, xiii
Origin of Species, 27
Outlook, 24
Outten, David, 227
Owen, William, 108
Owen, Robert, 151
Oxford English Dictionary, 60, 145, 157

Paine, Thomas, 113
Pallavicino, Ferrante, 107
Panama Canal, 42
Pantheism, xi, 23, 24, 25
Parks, William, 108
Pate, Hilda, 76, 77
Paul, Apostle, 34, 39, 84
PBS, 57
Penny press, 62
Personalization and persistence, 164-171
Pharisees, 39
Philippines, 32-34
Pierce, Shangai, 86
Pilate, 187
Planned Parenthood, 167
Plumbline, 69
Political corruption, 20
Pope, James, 69
Portland Gazette, 19
Press bias, xiii
Privacy, invasion of, 81, 93, 218, 230
Private property, 46
Prodigal son, xi
Protecting sources, 82, 84
Protestant Reformation, 17
Prynne, William, 106
Public figure, 87-104
Public officials and libel, 87-104
Public opinion, 79-80, 84, 88-89, 93, 111, 112, 116, 135
Public relations, 63, 183-189
Public television, 143-144
Publick Occurrences Both Foreign and Domestic, 60
Pulitzer, Joseph, 49, 50, 51, 157, 160, 212
Pulitzer Prize, 51, 56, 57, 75
Purges, 55
Puritans, 106

Quarles, Norma, 67

Rahway (New Jersey) Taxpayers Association, 91
Rahway *News-Record,* 92
Rape, coverage of, 77-84, 177, 217
Rather, Dan, 43
Ratings, 135
Reality, definitions of, 31; 61, 62, 65, 70
Reason, 24
Reformational belief, 106
Rehnquist, Justice William, 92, 103
Restell, Madame, 160-168, 234, 235
Restitution, 97, 99, 100, 101
Reston, James, 65
Revivalism, 25
Rex v. Miller, 109
Rider, Dudley, 108
Riis, Jacob, 151
Ripley, George, 24
Risking the Future, 167
Rivera, Geraldo, 42, 114, 124
Rivers, William, 42
Rogers, Adrian, 171
Romanticism, 23

"Romper Room," 37
Roosevelt, Franklin, 66
Rothman, Stanley, 116
Rousseau, Jean-Jacques, 23
Rule, Elton, 135
Runaway juries, 93
Rushdoony, Rousas, 220
Rutherford, Samuel, 115
Rutledge, Rick, 235

Salisbury, Harrison, 66
San Francisco *Examiner,* 52, 87
Sandinistas, coverage of, 42, 55
Satellite news gathering, 134, 135, 137
Saturday Evening Post, 49
Scalia, Judge Antonin, 104
Schaeffer, Edith, 171
Schaeffer, Francis, 225
Scheer, Robert, 115
School prayer, 37
Scopes II, 4, 123
Scopes, John T., 26, 28
Scopes trial, 26, 27, 28, 29, 30, 41
Scripps, E. W., 51, 114, 157
Seditious libel, 109
Seib, Charles, 76
Sensation, definition of, 145
Sensationalism, xiv, 47, 49, 146-156, 171
Shield laws, 82, 83, 85
Siloam, 39
Simpson, James, 91
Singer, Isaac Bashevis, 17
Sisera, 146
Sixth Amendment, 82
"60 Minutes," 92, 136
Slander, 96
Slavery, 23, 35, 175
SMATV, 137
Socialism, 52
Society of Professional Journalists, Sigma Delta Chi, 64, 82
Solzhenitsyn, Alexander, 56, 209
Southern Christian Advocate, 25
Soviet collectivization, 57
Soviet Union, xiii, 55, 126, 135
Specific detail, importance of, 159, 170
Spiking the spiritual, 33, 35, 40-41, 43
Spirit of the Pilgrims, 23
Spiritual/material interface, 32, 33, 34, 63, 64, 176
St. Clair, Augustus, 20-22
Stalin, Josef, 55-57
Star Chamber, 106
State of mind in libel cases, 98
Steffens, Lincoln, 54, 55, 153-154, 157, 213
Stephens, J. F., 105
Stern, Larry, 114
Stevens, Justice John Paul, 103
Storey, Wilbur, 47, 48
Story setting, 121
Strategic ritual, 67, 68, 76
Strong, Augustus, 84
Subjectivism, 59, 61
Subjectivity, 67, 69, 71, 75
Subjectivity-balancing, 64-67, 76
Suicide, coverage of, 79, 150-152

Talese, Gay, 66
Taussig, Frederick, 166
Tavoulareas v. The Washington Post, 111, 216
Technological developments, 226-227
Television news, 43, 66, 77, 78, 111, 120, 121
Texas Press Association, 149
"The Defenders," 166
The Dial, 24
The Press in America, 17
The Public Interest, 66
Theological liberalism, 64
Thompson, Hunter, 66
Thomson, James C., 81
Time, 64, 87, 116, 123, 166
Tomas, S. J., 149
Transcendental Club, 24
Trouten, Doug, 174, 235
"Trunk murder," 21
Truth and journalism, 60, 64, 70, 76, 100, 105-112, 154-156
Twin Cities Christian, 173
Twyn, John, 106

Undercover reporting, 20
Unitarianism, 23, 24, 26
United Auto Workers, 121, 122
United Press International, 52
University of Iowa, 88, 89, 93
U.S. Circuit Court of Appeals, 80
U.S. Constitution, 28
U.S. News and World Report, 116
U.S. Senate, 42
U.S. Supreme Court, 36, 37, 51, 78, 89, 91-95, 97, 103-104, 126
USA Today, xiii, 142

Van Impe, Jack, 171
Van Til, Cornelius, 209, 215
VCRs, impact of, 227
Vietnam War, 115
Virginia *Gazette,* 108
Vitz, Paul, 17
Von Hoffman, Nicholas, 115

Wall Street Journal, The, 116
Warren, Joseph, 113
Washington, George, 113
Washington Journalism Review, 89
Washington *Post,* 36, 42, 67, 75, 76, 114-116, 126, 127
Washington *Times,* 139
Watergate, 38, 39, 76
Watterson, Henry, 50
Welles, Orson, 54
Westin, Av, 68, 136, 137
Westmoreland, Gen. William, 87
"Wheel of Fortune," 43
Wheel of fortune journalism, 43, 44, 53
White, Justice Byron, 82, 104
WHMA, 79
Wilkie, Franc B., 47
Willis, Nathaniel, 18, 19
Wolfe, Tom, 66
Woodward, Bob, 76
World, 173
World War II, 66

Yale University, 20
Yale Review, 75
Yellow journalism, 25, 47

Zenger, John Peter, 104-107